EXPERIENCE NAPA AND SONOMA

WHAT'S WHERE

1 Napa Valley. By far the best known of the California wine regions, Napa is home to many of the biggest names in wine. Densely populated with winery after winery, especially along Highway 29 and the Silverado Trail, it's also home to many luxury accommodations and some of the country's best restaurants.

2 Carneros District. Many visitors quickly pass through this compact region, which spans southern Napa and Sonoma counties, on their way north from San Francisco. Those who take the time to stop will discover wineries that specialize in Pinot Noir and Chardonnay. Both grapes thrive in its comparatively cool climate.

3 Sonoma Valley. Centered on the historic town of Sonoma, the Sonoma Valley is slightly less glitzy than Napa. Still, in addition to the hundreds of winery tasting rooms, there's no shortage of inns, bed-and-breakfasts, and fairly casual restaurants serving hearty California cuisine.

4 Northern Sonoma County. Ritzy, charming Healdsburg is a popular base for exploring three important grape-growing areas, the Russian River, Dry Creek, and Alexander valleys. In the county's western parts lie the Sonoma Coast wineries, just now coming into prominence for European-style wines from cool-climate grapes.

NAPA AND SONOMA PLANNER

About the Restaurants

Excellent meals can be found everywhere in the Wine Country, but the small town of Yountville has become a culinary crossroads under the influence of chef Thomas Keller, whose French Laundry is a perennial favorite of food critics. Such quality (and hype) often means high prices, but you can also find appealing, inexpensive eateries. With few exceptions (which are noted in individual restaurant listings), dress is informal.

About the Hotels

Upscale accommodations are concentrated in the Napa Valley towns of Yountville, Rutherford, St. Helena, and Calistoga; Sonoma County's poshest lodgings can be found in Healdsburg. The cities of Napa and Santa Rosa are the best bets for budget hotels and inns.

Getting Here and Around

San Francisco is the main gateway to the Wine Country, which lies due north of the city. Driving is the best way to explore this region. The easiest route to southern Napa and Sonoma counties is to head north across the Golden Gate Bridge on U.S. 101 and east on Highway 37 to Highway 121. Follow signs for the towns of Sonoma (45 miles from San Francisco) and Napa (about 52 miles). Remain on U.S. 101 if your destination is Santa Rosa (55 miles) or Healdsburg (70 miles).

By car. Well-maintained roads zip through the Napa and Sonoma, and scenic routes thread through the backcountry. Distances between towns are fairly short, and you can drive from one end to the other of either valley in less than an hour if there's no traffic. The Mayacamas Mountains divide Napa and Sonoma, though, and only a few winding roads traverse the middle sections, so the drive between valleys can be slow. The quicker connector is Highway 121, which runs east–west between southern Napa and Sonoma counties. The far-northern route—from Highway 128 just north of Calistoga, take Petrified Forest Road and Calistoga Road to Highway 12—has a few curves but also great vistas.

By public transportation. Visitors without cars can take van, bus, or limo tours from San Francisco. Taking public transit to hubs like Sonoma, Napa, Santa Rosa, and Healdsburg can be time-consuming, but once you arrive at your destination, you can take advantage of taxis and other options.

Planning Your Time

Many first-time visitors to the Wine Country pack as many wineries as possible into a short vacation. Besides being exhausting, this approach goes against the area's laid-back ethos. So you can experience the region without running yourself ragged, we've put together a few strategies for maximizing your wine-tasting fun.

Avoid driving during rush hour. From roughly 4 to 6 pm on weekdays the cars of tourists are joined by those of commuters, resulting in traffic jams. The worst bottlenecks occur on Highway 29 around St. Helena.

Get an early start. Tasting rooms are often deserted before 11 am. On the flip side, they're usually the busiest between 3:30 and closing.

Slip off the beaten track. When Napa Valley's tasting rooms along Highway 29 and the Silverado Trail are jammed, those just to the east in Coombsville and Chiles Valley might be nearly deserted. If you're based in Healdsburg, you might find the wineries in the Russian River Valley packed, whereas the ones in the Alexander Valley are comparatively quiet.

Think quality, not quantity. Spend most of your time at a few wineries each day, focusing on your interests. Perhaps you'd like to sample wines from a particular type of grape, or are curious about the different varietals offered by a certain vineyard. Wine-and-food seminars are also a good idea.

Visit on a weekday. From May through October, roads and wineries are less crowded on weekdays. Year-round, tasting rooms are usually the least busy on Tuesday and Wednesday.

Reservations

Book hotels well in advance. Hotel reservations, always advisable, are generally necessary from late spring through October and on many weekends. To be on the safe side, book smaller hotels and inns at least a month ahead.

Call restaurants ahead. Reserving a table, or asking your hotel to reserve one for you, can save you time waiting at the door.

Reserve at wineries, too. If you're keen to visit a specific winery, double-check hours and tour times and, if possible, make a reservation.

Visitor Resources

Napa Contacts
Napa Valley Vintners Association ⊕ www.napavintners.com. **Visit Napa Valley** ⊕ www.visitnapavalley.com.

Sonoma Contacts
Sonoma County Tourism Bureau ⊕ www.sonomacounty.com. **Sonoma County Vintners** ⊕ www.sonomawine.com.

TOP NAPA WINERIES

Artesa Vineyards & Winery

(A) The modern, minimalist layout of Artesa blends harmoniously with the surrounding landscape, yet this Napa winery makes a vivid impression with its outdoor sculptures and fountains. You can taste at your own pace here, savoring each wine—and the superb vineyard views—from the tasting bars, indoor seating areas, or outdoor terraces. Extend the pleasure with wine-and-food pairings that include tapas, cheeses, or chocolates.

Domaine Carneros

(B) You'll feel like the lord or lady of the manor at this winery in Napa, and with good reason: the main building was modeled after an 18th-century French château owned by the Champagne-making Taittinger family, which co-owns Domaine Carneros. On a sunny day, the experience of sipping a crisp sparkling wine on the outdoor terrace—with caviar on toast points, s'il vous plaît—is royal indeed.

Far Niente

(C) You can tour the 1885 stone winery and view the collection of gleaming classic cars before sitting down to taste Far Niente's famed Cabernet Sauvignon blend and Chardonnay. Although a visit to this Oakville winery costs more than most others in the Wine Country, the small size of the tour groups, the beauty of the grounds, and the quality of the wines make it worth a stop, especially if you're a fan of dessert wines. A sister property produces Dolce, one of the world's most highly regarded dessert wines.

Frog's Leap

(D) The rare winery that doesn't seem to take itself too seriously, Frog's Leap is known for its entertaining, lighthearted tours. While you learn about the Rutherford winery's history and get a glimpse of the organic gardens and deluxe chicken coop, the guides aren't afraid to crack a few jokes or describe all the whimsically named wines that have been produced over the years.

The Hess Collection

(E) Before heading to this Napa winery's tasting room to sip the excellent Cabernet Sauvignons and Chardonnays, take the time to wander through owner Donald Hess's personal art collection, full of large-scale canvases and other works by important 20th-century artists such as Robert Motherwell, Anselm Kiefer, Robert Rauschenberg, and Francis Bacon.

Joseph Phelps Vineyards

(F) In good weather, there are few more glorious tasting spots in the Napa Valley than the terrace at this St. Helena winery. The place is known for its delectable Cabernet Sauvignons and Insignia, a Bordeaux blend.

Schramsberg

(G) One of the most entertaining tours in the Napa Valley is at sparkling-wine producer Schramsberg, where the 19th-century cellars hold millions of bottles. After you learn how the bubblies at this Calistoga mainstay are made using the *méthode champenoise* process, and how the bottles are "riddled" (turned every few days) by hand, you can sip generous pours during a seated tasting.

TOP SONOMA WINERIES

Benziger Winery

(A) It's best to visit Benziger in fine weather so that you can enjoy a tram ride through the vineyards before tasting wines—most notably the Chardonnays, Cabernet Sauvignons, and Pinot Noirs—made from grapes grown using biodynamic farming methods. A great stop for a midday picnic, this winery in Glen Ellen is close to Jack London State Historic Park.

Copain Wines

(B) The emphasis at this hillside winery outside Healdsburg is on European-style Pinot Noirs whose grapes come from neither Napa nor Sonoma County, but rather from a series of vineyards to the north in Mendocino County. Winemaker Wells Guthrie, a master at crafting complex wines from cool-climate grapes, also makes Chardonnays and Syrahs, some from fruit grown about 100 miles south of San Francisco in the hilly Chalone appellation.

Merry Edwards Winery

(C) Serious lovers of Pinot Noir make pilgrimages to this winery in Sebastopol to experience wines that celebrate the singular characteristics of the Russian River Valley appellation. Tastings at Merry Edwards are offered several times a day—appointments are advised but walk-ins are welcome if there's space—and usually include several Pinots followed by a sultry Sauvignon Blanc that's lightly aged in oak.

Iron Horse Vineyards

(D) Proving that tasting sparkling wine doesn't have to be stuffy, Iron Horse pours its bubblies (and a few still wines) at an outdoor tast-

ing bar, where tremendous views over the vine-covered hills make the top-notch sparklers taste even better. Especially on fair days, it's well worth the drive down a winding one-lane road on the outskirts of Sebastopol.

Matanzas Creek Winery

(E) A sprawling field of lavender makes the grounds of Matanzas Creek especially beautiful in May and June, when the plants are in bloom. But the Santa Rosa winery's Asian-inspired aesthetic makes it delightful year-round, especially if you're a fan of Sauvignon Blanc, Chardonnay, or Merlot.

Ram's Gate Winery

(F) One of the flashiest tasting experiences in the entire Wine Country takes place a mere 30 miles northeast of the Golden Gate Bridge— you can leave San Francisco and be sipping in splendor in less than an hour if there's no traffic. The ultramodern yet rustic Ram's Gate, perched grandly on a windswept hill in southern Sonoma, specializes in Chardonnays, Pinot Noirs, and Syrahs made from grapes sourced from some of Napa and Sonoma's finest vineyards.

Ridge Vineyards

(G) Oenophiles will be familiar with Ridge, which produces some of the best Cabernet Sauvignon, Chardonnay, and Zinfandel in California. Although some of the Geyserville winery's most highly regarded wines are produced in the Santa Cruz Mountains, the tasting room in the Dry Creek Valley is a great place to sample these coastal wines, along with the Zinfandels and other vintages made from grapes grown nearby.

WHEN TO GO

Timing Your Trip

High season in the Wine Country extends from April to October. If you travel between July and September, expect the days to be hot and dry, the roads filled with cars, and tasting rooms mobbed with visitors.

In summer and early fall, it's often necessary to book smaller hotels a month or more in advance, and discounts are rare. November, except for Thanksgiving week, and December before Christmas are less busy, in part because the winter rains will have started.

Climate

The weather in Napa and Sonoma is pleasant nearly year-round, and even winter is comparatively mild. Daytime temperatures average from about 55°F during winter to the 80s in summer, when readings in the 90s and higher are common. April, May, and October are milder but still warm. Fall morning are cool but temperatures can rise quickly.

Festivals and Seasonal Events

The Wine Country celebrates the year's harvest with fairs and festivals. Here are a few high-profile events throughout the year.

Auction Napa Valley. Dozens of events culminate in the Napa Valley's glitziest night—an opulent dinner and auction of rare wines and other coveted items. It's held the first full weekend in June. ⊕ *www.auctionnapavalley.org.*

Flavor! Napa Valley. Several days of dinners, cooking demonstrations, and wine-and-food tastings take place the week before Thanksgiving. ⊕ *www.flavornapavalley.com.*

Napa Valley Festival del Sole. This acclaimed mid-July event attracts international opera, theater, dance, and musical performers to Castello di Amorosa and other venues. ⊕ *www.festivaldelsole.org.*

Pinot on the River. Pinot Noir fans flock to the Russian River Valley in late October for a grand weekend of tastings, seminars, and lively discourse. ⊕ *www.pinotfestival.com.*

Sonoma County Harvest Fair. Enjoy wine and olive-oil competitions, cooking demos, livestock shows, carnival rides, and the Harvest Dog Dash. ⊕ *www.harvestfair.org.*

Wine Road Barrel Tasting Weekends. In early March, more than 100 wineries open their cellars for tastings of wines right out of the barrels. ⊕ *www.wineroad.com.*

Winter Wineland. On Martin Luther King Jr. Day weekend, nearly all the northern Sonoma County wineries offer tastings, seminars, and entertainment. ⊕ *www.wineroad.com.*

GREAT ITINERARIES

First-Timer's Napa Tour

On this two-day tour, start your first morning browsing the food stands at Napa's Oxbow Public Market. Drive north on Highway 29 to Rutherford, where the tour of Inglenook provides a fascinating overview of Napa Valley wine making. Continue north on Highway 29 to St. Helena for lunch at Farmstead at Long Meadow Ranch, then visit Calistoga's over-the-top Castello di Amorosa, off Highway 29, or St. Helena's serene Joseph Phelps Vineyards, off the Silverado Trail.

Check into your lodgings—luxurious Meadowood Napa Valley or pleasantly downscale El Bonita Motel are two good options. Poke around St. Helena's shops until dinner, perhaps at Meadowood or Goose & Gander.

Begin day two enjoying coffee and a pastry at the Model Bakery, then drive south on Highway 29 and east on Rutherford Road to Frog's Leap. Make sure to book the winery's entertaining tour in advance. Return to Highway 29 and drive south, then turn west on Highway 121. Stop for lunch at Boon Fly Café, then continue west on Highway 121 to arts center di Rosa and tour its gardens and galleries. Cross Highway 121 to Domaine Carneros, where you can toast your trip with some sparkling wine.

Sonoma Back Roads Tour

Start your first day at Joseph Phelps Freestone Vineyards in western Sonoma, in Freestone, tasting cold-climate Chardonnays and Pinot Noirs. From Freestone, head north on Bohemian Highway. At Occidental, turn east on Graton Road to reach Willow Wood Market Cafe, where lunch awaits.

After lunch, drive north on Ross Road and west on Ross Station Road to visit Iron Horse Vineyards, known for its sparkling wines. Afterward, backtrack to Highway 116 and turn north. At Martinelli Road, hang a right to reach Forestville's Hartford Family Winery, producer of acclaimed Chards and Pinots. Splurge on a night's rest at the nearby Farmhouse Inn and dine at its stellar restaurant.

Start day two on Westside Road, tasting at Rochioli, then continue on Westside to West Dry Creek Road and turn north. Turn east at Lambert Bridge Road. Assemble a picnic at Dry Creek General Store, backtrack to West Dry Creek Road, and continue north to Preston of Dry Creek.

Head back on West Dry Creek, and turn east on Yoakim Bridge Road and south on Dry Creek Road. At Lytton Springs Road, make a left to reach Ridge Vineyards. End the day with a Cabernet.

THE JOYS OF EATING LOCAL

The concept "eat local, think global" may just be catching on elsewhere in the nation, but it's established doctrine in the Wine Country, home to many artisanal food producers, family farmers, and small ranchers. The catalyst for this culinary and agricultural revolution occurred in nearby Berkeley with the 1971 debut of Chez Panisse, run by food pioneer Alice Waters. Initially called California cuisine, her cooking style showcased local, seasonal ingredients in fresh preparations. It also introduced American chefs to international ingredients and techniques.

As the movement spread, it became known as New American cooking. In the early 1980s, John Ash began focusing on food's relationship to wine. His Santa Rosa restaurant helped set the standard for the variant later dubbed Wine Country cuisine. Ash credits Waters with inspiring him and other chefs to seek out "wholesome and unusual ingredients."

Today's appeals to reduce the nation's carbon footprint added another wrinkle to the culinary equation's "think global" component, prompting further emphasis on supporting local agriculture and food production. Much of the back-to-the-earth movement's R&D takes place at Napa and Sonoma's farms and enclaves of artisanal production.

Farmers' Markets

A good way to experience the Wine Country's agricultural bounty is to browse the same outdoor farmers' markets that local chefs do. The two biggest ones, both in Sonoma County, are the year-round market in the town of Sonoma and the Healdsburg market, held from May through November. Two popular Napa Valley markets, one in Crane Park in St. Helena on Friday morning, the other next to Napa's Oxbow Public Market on Tuesday and Saturday morning, operate from May through October. All of these markets are perfect places to assemble items for a picnic.

Fruit

The Wine Country's diverse climate makes it an ideal place to grow many types of fruit. Healdsburg's Dry Creek Peach & Produce, for instance, grows more than 30 varieties of white and yellow peaches, along with nectarines, plums, figs, persimmons, and other fruit. Rare-fruit varieties grown in Napa and Sonoma include prickly pears, loquats, and pluots, a plum-apricot hybrid. The pluot, a fairly recent creation, involved the reverse engineering of the plumcot, a hybrid developed in Sonoma County by horticulturist Luther Burbank.

Another fruit that fares well in these parts is the Meyer lemon.

Vegetables

Some chefs give top billing to their produce purveyors. One recent menu touted a salad containing heirloom tomatoes from Big Ranch Farms of Napa and Solano counties. Over in the Sonoma Valley, another restaurant described the main ingredients in a mushroom salad as all locally grown, in some cases in the wild. There's no equivalent of an appellation for vegetables, but that didn't stop a St. Helena restaurant from informing diners that its Swiss chard came from Mt. Veeder—what's good for Cabernet Sauvignon is apparently also good for leafy greens. Other local vegetables gracing Wine Country menus include artichokes, multi-hued beets and carrots, and heirloom varieties of butternut squash, beans, and even radishes.

Meat

Family-owned ranches and farms are prominent in the region, with many raising organic or "humane-certified" beef, pork, lamb, and poultry. Upscale restaurants are fervent about recognizing their high-quality protein producers. A well-known St. Helena restaurant, for example, credits Brandt Farms and Bryan Flannery for various beef cuts on its menu.

Seafood

Seafood from local waters abounds, from farm-raised scallops to line-caught California salmon. Around Thanksgiving, California's famous Dungeness crab begins appearing on menus, either steamed whole, in salads, or as a featured ingredient in cioppino, a tomato-based seafood stew that originated in San Francisco. Also look for Hog Island Oysters, whose namesake producer raises more than 3 million oysters a year just south of Sonoma County in Tomales Bay.

Cheese

Restaurant cheese plates, often served before—or in lieu of—dessert, are a great way to acquaint yourself with excellent local cheeses. You can also conduct your research by strolling through downtown Sonoma. Vella Cheese, just north of Sonoma Plaza on 2nd Street East, has been producing Dry Monterey Jack and other cheeses since 1931, the same year that the nearby Sonoma Cheese Factory, on Sonoma Plaza, got its start. To contemplate the future of Sonoma cheese making, drop by the Epicurean Connection, a few steps from Sonoma Plaza on West Napa Street. Owner Sheana Davis's rich and creamy Delice de la Vallee cheese, a blend of triple-cream cow and goat milk, recently earned a top prize from the American Cheese Society.

KIDS AND FAMILIES

By its very nature, the Wine Country isn't a particularly child-friendly destination. Don't expect to see many children or to find tons of activities organized with them in mind. That said, you'll find plenty of playgrounds (there's one in Sonoma Plaza, for instance), as well as the occasional kid-friendly attraction, most notably the Charles M. Schulz Museum and Safari West, both in Santa Rosa.

Choosing a Place to Stay

If you're traveling with kids, always mention it when making your reservations. Most of the smaller, more romantic inns and B&Bs discourage or prohibit children, and those places that do allow them may prefer to put such families in a particular cottage or room so that any noise is less disruptive to other guests. Larger hotels are a mixed bag. Some actively discourage children, whereas others are more welcoming. Of the large, luxurious hotels, Meadowood tends to be the most child-friendly.

Eating Out

Unless your kid is a budding Thomas Keller, it's best to call ahead to see if a restaurant can accommodate those under 12 with a special menu. You will find inexpensive cafés in almost every town, and places like Gott's Roadside, a retro burger stand in St. Helena, are big hits with kids.

At the Wineries

Children are few and far between at most wineries, but well-behaved children will generally be greeted with a smile. Some wineries offer a small treat—grape juice or another beverage or sometimes coloring books or another distraction.

When booking a tour, ask if kids are allowed (for insurance reasons, wineries sometimes prohibit children under a certain age), how long it lasts, and whether there's another tour option that would be more suitable.

A few particularly kid-friendly wineries include Calistoga's Castello di Amorosa (what's not to like about a 107-room medieval castle, complete with a dungeon?) and Sterling Vineyards, where a short aerial tram ride whisks you from the parking lot to the tasting room. In Sonoma County, Benziger conducts vineyard tours in a tractor-pulled tram. The picnic grounds are kid-friendly, as are the ones at Sonoma's Bartholomew Park Winery, which also has hiking trails.

You'll find plenty of kids poolside at the Francis Ford Coppola Winery in Geyserville, and Honig Vineyard & Winery in Rutherford prides itself on making sure kids enjoy a visit as much as their parents do.

BEST BOOKS AND FILMS

Books

Cookbooks *Bottega: Bold Italian Flavors from the Heart of California's Wine Country* (2010), by Michael Chiarello. The Food Network star's book takes its name and inspiration from his southern Italian–style Yountville restaurant.

Bouchon Bakery (2012), by Thomas Keller and Sebastien Rouxel. The legendary Keller and his executive pastry chef share recipes that made Yountville's Bouchon Bakery an instant hit.

The Cakebread Cellars American Harvest Cookbook: Celebrating Wine, Food, and Friends in the Napa Valley (2011), by Dolores and Jack Cakebread. This book collects 25 years' worth of recipes from the authors' annual cooking workshops.

The Essential Thomas Keller: The French Laundry Cookbook & Ad Hoc at Home (2010), by Thomas Keller. Recipes inspired by Keller's upscale and down-home Yountville establishments show the chef's great range.

Plats du Jour: the girl & the fig's Journey Through the Seasons in Wine Country (2011), by Sondra Bernstein. The chef behind Sonoma County's two "fig" restaurants reveals her cooking secrets and adapts some of her signature dishes.

Mustards Grill Napa Valley Cookbook (2001), by Cindy Pawlcyn and Brigid Callinan. Pawlcyn describes her iconic eatery as "a cross between a roadside rib joint and a French country restaurant." She shares recipes and expounds on her culinary philosophy.

Fiction *Murder Uncorked* (2005), *Murder by the Glass: A Wine-Lover's Mystery* (2006), and *Silenced by Syrah* (2007), by Michele Scott. Vineyard manager Nikki Sands is the protagonist of this light and humorous mystery series that unfolds in the Napa Valley.

Nose: A Novel (2013), by James Conaway. A fictitious Northern California wine-making region (couldn't be Napa or Sonoma, could it?) is the setting for a mystery.

Nonfiction *The Emperor of Wine: The Rise of Robert M. Parker, Jr. and the Reign of American Taste* (2005), by Elin McCoy. Examination of the American critic's enormous influence considers the sources and worldwide impact of his wine rating system's dominance.

The Far Side of Eden: The Ongoing Saga of Napa Valley (2002), by James Conaway. Conaway's second book on the Wine Country picks up where the first (*Napa, 1992)* left off.

The Finest Wines of California: A Regional Guide to the Best Producers and Their Wines (2011), by Stephen Brook. Part of the World's Finest Wines series, this book profiles 90 top producers.

Harvests of Joy: How the Good Life Became Great Business (1999), by Robert Mondavi and Paul Chutkow. Wine tycoon Robert Mondavi tells his story.

The House of Mondavi: The Rise and Fall of an American Wine Dynasty (2007), by Julia Flynn Siler. The author ruffled a lot of feathers in Napa when she published this tell-all book.

Judgment of Paris: California vs. France and the Historic 1976 Paris Tasting That Revolutionized Wine (2005), by George M. Taber. The journalist who originally broke the story of the pivotal event analyzes its history and repercussions.

Matt Kramer's New California Wine: Making Sense of Napa Valley, Sonoma, Central Coast & Beyond (2004), by Matt Kramer. The *Wine Spectator* columnist on the development of California wine and the wine industry.

Napa Valley: The Land, the Wine, the People (2001), by Charles O'Rear. A former *National Geographic* photographer portrays the valley in this lush book.

The New Connoisseurs' Guidebook to California Wine and Wineries (2010), by Charles E. Olken and Joseph Furstenthal. An excellent survey of the state's main wine regions.

Sniff, Swirl & Slurp (2002), by Max Allen. This compact handbook provides guidelines on maximizing the wine-drinking experience.

When the Rivers Ran Red: An Amazing Story of Courage and Triumph in America's Wine Country (2009), by Vivienne Sosnowski. The author chronicles the devastating effect of Prohibition on Northern California winemakers.

Zinfandel: A History of a Grape and Its Wine (2003), by Charles Sullivan. The story of America's unique varietal is the story of California wine country.

Movies

Bottle Shock (2008). Filmed primarily in the Napa and Sonoma valleys, this lighthearted, fictionalized feature about the 1976 Paris tasting focuses on Calistoga's Chateau Montelena.

Mondovino (2005). Documentary filmmaker Jonathan Nossiter probes the rocky relationship between the wine industries of California and Europe.

VISITING THE WINERIES

LIFE IS LIVED WELL in the California Wine Country, where eating and, above all, drinking are cultivated as high arts. And if all those magazines, epicurean memoirs, and gorgeously shot movies saturated with lush, romantic images of the area have made you pine for a visit, the good news is that you likely won't be disappointed when you get here. The meandering back roads, vineyard-blanketed hills, and ivy-draped wineries—not to mention the luxurious restaurants, hotels, and spas—really *are* that beautiful.

Whether you're a serious wine collector making your annual pilgrimage to the Napa Valley or a wine newbie who doesn't know the difference between a Merlot and Mourvèdre but is eager to learn, you can have a great time touring California. Your gateway to the wine world is the tasting room, where the staff (and occasionally even the actual winemaker) are almost always happy to chat with curious guests. Tasting rooms range from the grand to the humble, offering everything from a few sips of wine to in-depth tours of the winemaking facilities and vineyards. The one constant, however, is a deep, shared pleasure in the experience of wine tasting.

To prepare you for your visit, we've covered the basics: tasting rooms and what to expect, how to save money on tasting fees, and the types of tours typically offered by wineries. A list of common tasting terms will help you interpret what your mouth is experiencing as you sip. We've also provided a description of the major grape varietals, as well as the specific techniques employed to craft white, red, sparkling, and rosé wines. Because great wines begin in the vineyards, we've included a section on soils, climates, and organic and biodynamic farming methods. A handy Wine-Lover's Glossary of terms, from *acidity* to *yeast,* covers what you may come across in the tasting room or on a tour.

WINE TASTING 101

Don't be intimidated by sommeliers who toss around esoteric adjectives as they swirl their glasses. At its core, wine tasting is simply about determining which wines you like best. However, knowing a few basic tasting steps and a few key quality guidelines can make your winery visit much more enjoyable and help you remember which wines you liked, and why, long after you return home. ■ TIP→ Above all, follow your instincts at the tasting bar: there is no right or wrong way to describe wine.

Before tasting, wine should be clear and free of sediment.

If you watch the pros, you'll probably notice that they take time to inspect, swirl, and sniff the wine before they get around to sipping it. Follow their lead and take your time, going through each of the following steps for each wine. Starting with the pop of the cork and the splashing of wine into a glass, all of your senses play a part in wine tasting.

USE YOUR EYES

Before you taste it, take a good look at the wine in your glass. Holding the glass by the stem, raise it to the light. Whether it's white, rosé, or red, your wine should be clear, without cloudiness or sediments, when you drink it. Some unfiltered wines may seem cloudy at first, but they will clear as the sediments settle.

In the natural light, place the glass in front of a white background such as a blank sheet of paper or a tablecloth. **Check the color.** Is it right for the wine? A California white should be golden: straw, medium, or deep, depending on the type. Rich, sweet, dessert wine will have more intense color, but Chardonnay and Sauvignon Blanc will be paler. A Rosé should be a clear pink, from pale to deep, without too much red or any orange. Reds may lean toward ruby or garnet coloring; some have a purple tinge. They shouldn't be pale (the exception is Pinot Noir, which can be quite pale yet still have character). In any color of wine, a brownish tinge is a flaw that indicates the wine is too old, has been incorrectly stored, or has gone bad. If you see brown, try another bottle.

BREATHE DEEP

You might notice that experienced wine tasters spend more time sniffing the wine than drinking it. This is because this step is where the magic happens: aroma plays a huge role in wine's flavor. After you have looked at the wine's color, **sniff the wine once or twice** to see if you can identify any aromas. Then gently move your glass in a circular motion to swirl the wine around. Aerating the wine this way releases more of its aromas. (It's called "volatilizing the esters," if you're trying to impress someone.) Stick your nose into the glass and take another long sniff.

Wine should smell good to you. You might pick up the scent of apricots, peaches, ripe melon, honey, and wildflowers in a white wine; black pepper, cherry, violets, and cedar in a red. Rosés (which are made from red-wine grapes) smell something like red wine, but in a scaled-back way, with hints of raspberry, strawberry, and sometimes a touch of rose petal. You might encounter surprising smells, such as tar—which some people actually appreciate in certain (generally expensive, red) wines.

For the most part, a wine's aroma should be clean and pleasing to you, not "off." If you find a wine's odor odd or unpleasant, there's probably something wrong. Watch out for hints of wet dog or skunk, or for moldy, horsey, mousy, or sweaty smells. Sniff for chemical faults such as sulfur, or excessive vanilla scents (picked up from oak barrels) that overwhelm the other aromas. A vinegar smell indicates that the wine has started to spoil. A rotten wood or soggy cardboard smell usually means that the cork has gone bad, ruining the wine. It's extremely rare to find these faults in wines poured in the tasting rooms, however, because staffers usually taste each bottle before pouring from it.

JUST A SIP

Once you've checked its appearance and aroma, **take a sip**—not a swig or a gulp—of the wine. As you sip a wine, **gently swish it around in your mouth**—this releases more aromas for your nose to explore. Do the aroma and the flavor complement each other, improve each other? While moving the wine around in your mouth, also think about the way it feels: silky or crisp? Does it coat your tongue or is it thinner? Does it seem to fill your mouth with flavor or is it weak? This combination of weight and intensity is referred to as *body*: a good wine may be light-, medium-, or full-bodied.

DID YOU KNOW?

Before tasting a wine, you should always smell it. The odors of fruit, flowers, and spices are not uncommon.

Do you like it? If not, don't drink it. Even if there is nothing actually wrong with a wine, what's the point of drinking it if you don't like it? A wine can be technically perfect but nevertheless taste strange, unpleasant, or just boring to you. It's possible to learn to appreciate wine that doesn't appeal to your tastes, but unless you like a wine right off the bat, it probably won't become a favorite. In the tasting room, dump what you don't like and move on to the next sample.

The more complex a wine, the more flavors you will detect in the course of tasting. You might experience different things when you first take a sip (*up front*), when you swish (*in the middle* or *at mid-palate*), and just before you swallow (*at the end* or *on the back-palate*). A good table wine should be neither too sweet nor too tart, and never bitter. Fruitiness, a subtle near-sweetness, should be balanced by acidity, but not to the point that the wine tastes sour or makes your mouth pucker. An astringent or drying quality is the mark of tannins, a somewhat mysterious wine element that comes from grape skins and oak barrels. In young reds this can taste almost bitter—but not quite. All these qualities, together with the wine's aroma, blend to evoke the flavors—not only of fruit but also of unlikely things such as leather, tobacco, or almonds.

SPIT OR SWALLOW?

You may choose to spit out the wine (into the dump bucket or a plastic cup) or swallow it. The pros typically spit, because they want to preserve their palates (and sobriety!) for the wines to come, but you'll find that swallowers far outnumber spitters in the winery tasting rooms. Either way, **pay attention to what happens after the wine leaves your mouth**—this is the finish, and it can be spectacular. What sensations stay behind or appear? Does the flavor fade away quickly or linger pleasantly? A long finish is a sign of quality; wine with no perceptible finish is inferior.

TASTING ROOMS AND WINERY TOURS

Some wineries in Napa and Sonoma have opulent faux châteaus with vast gift shops; others welcome guests with rough converted barns where you might have to step over the vintner's dog in the doorway. But it doesn't matter if you're visiting an elaborate tasting room complete with art gallery and upscale restaurant, or you're squeezed into the corner of a cinder-block warehouse amid stacked boxes and idle equipment: either way, tasting rooms are designed to introduce newcomers to the pleasures of wine and to inform visitors about the wines made at that winery. So don't worry if you're new to tasting. Relax, grab a glass, and join in for a good time.

At most wineries, you'll have to pay for the privilege of tasting—from $5 to $25 for a standard tasting of some or all of a winery's current releases and from $15 to $35 (and up at truly high-end wineries) to taste reserve, estate, or library wines. To experience wine making at its highest level, consider splurging for a special tasting at one winery at least.

In general, you'll find the fees slightly higher in Napa than in Sonoma, though there are plenty of exceptions to this rule. No matter which region you're in, you'll still find the occasional freebie—though it's likely to be at a spot that's off the major tourist thoroughfares and on some little-traveled back road.

In tasting rooms, tipping is very much the exception rather than the rule. Most frequent visitors to the Wine Country never tip those pouring the wines in the tasting rooms, though if a server has gone out of his or her way to be helpful—by pouring special wines not on the list, for example—leaving $5 or so would be a nice gesture.

Many wineries are open to the public, usually daily from around 10 or 11 am to 5 pm. They may close as early as 4 or 4:30, especially in winter, so it's best to get a reasonably early start if you want to fit in more than a few spots. ■TIP➔ Most wineries stop serving new visitors 15 to 30 minutes before the posted closing time, so don't expect to skate in at the last moment. Some wineries require reservations, and still others are closed to the public entirely. When in doubt, call in advance.

Though you might have the tasting room all to yourself if you visit midweek in winter, in summer, during crush (harvest season), and on weekends it's likely you'll be bumping elbows with other tasters and vying for the attention of the server behind the bar. If you prefer smaller crowds, look for wineries off the main drags of Highway 29 in Napa and Highway 12 in Sonoma. Look for wineries that are open by appointment only; they tend to schedule visitors carefully to avoid big crowds. Keep in mind that many wineries require appointments not to be snooty or exclusive, but because zoning requirements or occupancy limits mean they have to limit the number of guests.

Wineries tend to have fewer tasters early in the morning and get busiest between 3 pm and closing. On weekends, do what the locals do—visit on Sunday rather than Saturday. As many veteran tasting-room pourers will attest, Sunday is generally mellower. Saturday crowds include more people in weekend party mode and on bus and limo tours.

Finally, remember that those little sips add up, so pace yourself. If you plan to visit several wineries, try just a few wines at each so you don't hit sensory overload, when your mouth can no longer distinguish subtleties. (This is called palate fatigue.) ■TIP➔ Choose a designated driver for the day: roads are often narrow and curvy. You may be sharing your lane with bicyclists and wildlife as well. Although wineries rarely advertise it, many will provide a free nonalcoholic drink for the designated driver; it never hurts to ask.

IN THE TASTING ROOM

In most tasting rooms, a list of the wines available that day will be on the bar or offered by the server. The wines will be listed in a suggested tasting order, starting with the lightest-bodied whites and progressing to the most intense reds. Dessert wines will come at the end.

You'll usually find an assortment of wines from the winery's most recent vintages. There might also be a list of reserve vintages (special wines that have aged longer) that you can taste for a separate fee. To create a more cohesive experience, tasting rooms sometimes offer "flights" consisting of three or more particular wines selected to complement or contrast with one another. These might be vertical (several vintages of one wine), horizontal (several different varietals from one season), or more intuitively assembled.

Don't feel the need to try all the wines you're offered. In fact, many wineries indicate at the bottom of the list that you're limited to four or five. (In reality, however, servers rarely hold you to this limit if the tasting room isn't too crowded and you're showing a sincere interest in the wines.) If you can't decide which wines to choose, tell the server what types of wines you usually like and ask for a recommendation.

Barrel sampling at DeLoach Winery in Sonoma's Russian River Valley

The server will pour you an ounce or so of each wine you select. As you taste it, feel free to take notes or ask questions. ■TIP→ If you use the list of the wines for your note taking, you'll have a handy record of your impressions at the end of your trip. There might be a plate of crackers on the bar; nibble them when you want to clear your palate before tasting the next selection.

If you don't like a wine, or you've simply tasted enough, feel free to pour the rest into one of the dump buckets on the bar (if you don't see one, just ask).

TAKING A TOUR

Even if you're not a devoted wine drinker, seeing how grapes become wine can be fascinating. Tours tend to be most exciting (and most crowded) in September and October, when the harvest and crushing are under way. In harvest season you'll likely see workers picking in the vineyards and hauling bins and barrels around with forklifts. At other times of the year, the work consists of monitoring wine, "racking" it (eliminating sediment by transferring it from one tank or barrel to another), and bottling the finished wine.

Depending on the size of the winery, tours range from a few people to large groups and typically last 30 minutes to an hour. The guide explains what happens at each stage of the wine-making process, usually emphasizing the winery's

Money-Saving Tips

Those $20 tasting fees can add up awfully quickly if you're not careful, so consider the following tips for whittling down your wine-tasting budget.

■ Many hotels, bed-and-breakfasts, and visitor centers distribute coupons for free or discounted tastings—don't forget to ask. Also check winery websites for similar coupons you can print or send to your smartphone.

■ If you and your travel partner don't mind sharing a glass, servers are happy to let you split a tasting. (This is also a good way to pace yourself to keep from becoming tipsy.)

■ Get off the beaten track. Wineries along heavily traveled routes in Napa and Sonoma typically charge the most. Smaller spots along the back roads often charge less—or sometimes nothing at all.

■ Some wineries refund the tasting fee if you buy a bottle. Usually one fee is waived per bottle, though high-end wineries may require you to buy two or three. If the tasting list doesn't indicate that the fee is waived with a purchase, make sure to ask.

---

particular approach to growing and wine making. Feel free to ask questions at any point in the tour. If it's harvest or bottling time, you might see and hear the facility at work. Otherwise, the scene is likely to be quiet, with just a few workers tending the tanks and barrels.

Some winery tours are free, in which case you usually pay a separate fee to taste the wine. If you've paid for the tour— often $10 to $30—your wine tasting is usually included in the price. ■ TIP→ Wear comfortable shoes, because you might be walking on wet floors or stepping over hoses or other equipment. Dress in layers, since many tours take you to facilities where temperatures may be hot or cold.

At large wineries, introductory tours are typically offered several times daily. Less frequent are specialized tours and seminars focusing on such subjects as growing techniques, sensory evaluation, wine blending, and food-and-wine pairing. Prices for these events typically range from $20 to $50, sometimes a bit more if lunch is included. If you're spending a few days in the Wine Country, it's worth making a reservation for at least one of these in-depth experiences.

WORD OF MOUTH. "Save money wine-tasting at wineries with free wine-tasting coupons. You can find and print them online before you leave home. Do an online web search for free wine-tasting coupons." —Howfortunate

TOP CALIFORNIA GRAPE VARIETALS

Several dozen grape varietals are grown in the Wine Country, from favorites like Chardonnay and Cabernet Sauvignon to less familiar types like Albariño and Tempranillo. Although you don't need to be on a first-name basis with them all, you'll likely come across many of the following varietals as you visit the wineries.

WHITE

Albariño. One of the most popular wine grapes in Spain (it's also a staple of Portuguese wine making), this cool-climate grape creates light, citrusy wines, often with overtones of mango or kiwi. Some wineries in the Carneros region are experimenting with Albariño.

Chardonnay. California Chardonnays spent many years chasing big, buttery flavor, but the current trend is toward more restrained wines that let the grapes shine through. Because of Napa and Sonoma's warmer, longer growing seasons, Chardonnays from those regions will always be bolder than their counterparts in Burgundy.

Chenin Blanc. This Loire Valley native can produce a smooth, pleasingly acidic California wine. It gets short shrift with a lot of wine reviewers because of its relative simplicity and light body, but many drinkers appreciate the style.

Gewürztraminer. Cooler California climes such as the Russian River Valley are great for growing this German-Alsatian grape, which is turned into a boldly perfumed, fruity wine.

Marsanne. A white-wine grape of France's northern Rhône Valley, Marsanne can produce an overly heavy wine unless handled with care. It's becoming more popular in California in these Rhône-blend-crazy times.

Pinot Gris. Known in Italy as Pinot Grigio, this varietal yields a more deeply colored wine in California. It's not highly acidic and has a medium to full body.

Buying and Shipping Wine

Don't feel obliged to buy a bottle of wine just because the winery has given you a taste, especially if you have paid a tasting fee. Still, many visitors like to buy a bottle or two from small wineries as a courtesy, especially when they have taken more than a few minutes of the staff's time.

If you discover a bottle you particularly like, ask where it's available. Some wines, especially those from bigger operations, are widely distributed, but many are available only at the wineries themselves, and perhaps at a handful of restaurants or shops in the area. You might want to stock up if you won't be able to get a desired wine at home.

If several of a winery's offerings appeal to you and you live in a state that allows you to order wines directly from wineries (most staffers have this information at the ready), consider joining its wine club. You'll receive offers for members-only releases, invitations to winery events, and a discount on all of your purchases.

Ask about the winery's direct-shipment program. Most wineries are happy to ship your wine, as long as you live in a state where it's permitted. Wineries offer the full range of shipping options, and they'll sell you Styrofoam chests or wheeled, padded cases you can use on your flight home. For up-to-date information about whether your state allows shipping, check out the website run by the Wine Institute, ⊕ *www.wineinstitute. org/programs/shipwine.*

Riesling. Also called White Riesling, this cool-climate German grape has a sweet reputation in America. When made in a dry style, though, it can be crisply refreshing, with lush aromas.

Roussanne. This grape from the Rhône Valley makes an especially fragrant wine that can achieve a lovely balance of fruitiness and acidity.

Sauvignon Blanc. Hailing from Bordeaux and France's Loire Valley, this white grape does very well almost anywhere in California. Wines made from this grape display a wide range of personalities, from herbaceous to tropical-fruity.

Viognier. Until the early 1990s, Viognier was rarely planted outside France's Rhône Valley, but today it's one of California's hottest white-wine varietals. Usually made in a dry style, the best Viogniers have an intense fruity or floral bouquet.

RED

Barbera. Prevalent in California thanks to 19th-century Italian immigrants, Barbera yields easy-drinking, low-tannin wines with big fruit and high acid.

Cabernet Franc. Most often used in blends, often to add complexity to Cabernet Sauvignon, this French grape can produce aromatic, soft, and subtle wines. An often earthy, or even stinky, aroma repels some drinkers and makes avid fans of others.

Cabernet Sauvignon. The king of California reds, this Bordeaux grape is at home in well-drained soils. At its best, the California version is dark, bold, and tannic, with black currant notes. On its own it can require a long aging period, so it's often softened with Cabernet Franc, Merlot, and other red varieties for earlier drinking.

Gamay. Also called Gamay Beaujolais, this vigorous French grape variety is widely planted in California. It produces pleasant reds and rosés that should be drunk young.

Grenache. This Spanish grape, which makes some of the southern Rhône Valley's most distinguished wines, ripens best in hot, dry conditions. Done right, Grenache is dark and concentrated, improved with age.

Merlot. This blue-black Bordeaux varietal makes soft, full-bodied wine when grown in California. It's often fruity, and can be complex even when young. Merlot's rep was tarnished by the movie *Sideways* (and by the introduction of cheap, too-sweet versions), but aficionados of the Napa Valley's high-quality representatives have never lost faith.

Mourvèdre. This red-wine grape makes wine that is deeply colored, very dense, high in alcohol, and at first harsh, but it mellows with several years of aging. It's a native of France's Rhône Valley and is increasingly popular in California.

Nebbiolo. The great red-wine grape of Italy's Piedmont region is now widely planted in California. It produces sturdy, full-bodied wines that are fairly high in alcohol and age splendidly.

Petite Sirah. Unrelated to the Rhône grape Syrah, Petite Sirah may be a hybrid created in the mid-19th-century California vineyard—no one is sure. It produces a hearty wine that is often used in blends.

DID YOU KNOW?

Tasting rooms sometimes offer "flights" consisting of three or more wines selected to complement or contrast with one another.

Pinot Noir. The darling of grape growers in cooler parts of Napa and Sonoma, including the Carneros region and the Russian River Valley, Pinot Noir is also called the "heartbreak grape" because it's hard to cultivate. At its best it has a subtle but addictive earthy quality.

Sangiovese. This red grape dominates the Chianti region and much of central Italy. Depending on how it's grown and vinified, it can be made into vibrant, light- to medium-bodied wines, as well as into long-lived, very complex reds.

Syrah. Another big California red, this grape originated in the Rhône Valley. With good tannins it can become a full-bodied, almost smoky beauty (without them it can be flabby and forgettable). California plantings increased rapidly after the mid-1990s, thanks to the soaring reputation of Rhône-style wines and the popularity of Syrah from Australia, where it is called Shiraz.

Tempranillo. The major varietal in Spain's Rioja region, sturdy Tempranillo makes inky purple wines with a beautifully rich texture. Wines made from this grape are great on their own but excel when paired with red-meat and game dishes.

Zinfandel. Celebrated as California's own (though it has distant old-world origins), Zinfandel is rich and spicy. Its tannins can make it complex and well suited for aging, but too often it is made in an overly jammy, almost syrupy, style. Typically grown to extreme ripeness, the grape can produce wines with high alcohol levels.

HOW WINE IS MADE

THE CRUSH

The process of turning grapes into wine generally starts at the **crush pad,** where the grapes are brought in from the vineyards. Good winemakers carefully monitor their grapes throughout the year, but their presence is especially critical at harvest, when ripeness determines the proper day for picking. Once that day arrives, the crush begins.

Wineries pick their grapes by machine or by hand, depending on the terrain and on the type of grape. Some varietals are harvested at night with the help of powerful floodlights. Why at night? In addition to it being easier on the workers (daytime temperatures often reach 90°F [32°C] or more in September), the fruit-acid content in the pulp and juice of the grapes peaks in the cool night air. The acids—an essential component during fermentation and aging, and an important part of wine's flavor—plummet in the heat of the day.

Grapes must be handled with care so that none of the juice is lost. They arrive at the crush pad in large containers called gondolas and are dropped gently onto a conveyor belt that deposits them into a **stemmer-crusher.** A drum equipped with steel fingers knocks the grapes off their stems (stems and leaves are recycled as natural fertilizer) and pierces their skins so that the juice can flow freely. The grapes and juice fall through a grate and are carried via stainless-steel pipes to a press or vat. After this step, the production process goes one of four ways, depending on whether you're making a white, red, rosé, or sparkling wine.

WHITE WINES

The juice of white-wine grapes first goes to **settling tanks,** where the skins and solids sink to the bottom, separating from the free-run juice on top. The material in the settling tanks still contains a lot of juice, so after the free-run juice is pumped off, the rest goes into a **press.** A modern press consists of a perforated drum containing a Teflon-coated bag. As this bag is inflated like a balloon, it slowly pushes the grapes against the outside wall and the liquids are gently squeezed from the solids. Like the free-run juice, the press juice is pumped into a stainless-steel **fermenter.**

Press juice and free-run juice are fermented separately, but a little of the press juice may be added to the free-run juice for complexity. Because press juice tends to be strongly flavored and may contain undesirable flavor components, winemakers are careful not to add too much. Most white wines are fermented at 59°F to 68°F (15°C to 20°C). Cooler temperatures, which develop delicacy and fruit aromas, are especially important for Sauvignon Blanc and Riesling.

During fermentation, yeast feeds on the sugar in grape juice and converts it to alcohol and carbon dioxide. Wine yeast dies and fermentation naturally stops in two to four weeks, when the alcohol level reaches 15% (or sometimes more). If there's not enough sugar in the grapes to reach the desired alcohol level, the winemaker can add extra sugar before or during fermentation in a process called **chaptalization.**

To prevent oxidation that damages wine's color and flavor and kills wild yeast and bacteria that produces off fla-

DID YOU KNOW?

After the grapes have been crushed and fermentation begins, the solids that rise to the top are "punched down" into the liquid to keep them moist and to enhance the fermentation process.

vors, winemakers almost always add sulfur dioxide, in the form of sulfites, before fermenting. A winemaker may also encourage **malolactic fermentation** (or simply malo) to soften a wine's acidity or deepen its flavor and complexity. This is done either by inoculating the wine with lactic bacteria soon after fermentation begins or right after it ends, or by transferring the new wine to wooden vats that harbor the bacteria. Malo, which can also happen by accident, is undesirable in lighter-bodied wines because it overpowers the flavor from the grapes.

For richer results, free-run juice from Chardonnay grapes, as well as some from Sauvignon Blanc grapes, might be fermented in oak barrels. **Barrel fermentation** creates more depth and complexity, as the wine picks up vanilla flavors and other harmonious traits from the wood. The barrels used by California winemakers may be made in America or imported from France or Eastern Europe. They are very expensive and can be used for only a few years.

When the wine has finished fermenting, whether in a tank or a barrel, it is generally **racked**—moved into a clean tank or barrel to separate it from any remaining grape solids. Sometimes Chardonnay and special batches of Sauvignon Blanc are left "on the lees" for extended periods of time before being racked to pick up extra complexity. Wine may be racked several times as the sediment continues to settle out.

After the first racking, the wine may be **filtered** to take out solid particles that can cloud the wine and any stray yeast or bacteria that can spoil it. This is especially common for whites, which may be filtered several times before bottling. This is a common practice among commercial producers, but many fine-wine makers resist filtering, as they believe it leads to less complex wines that don't age as well.

White wine may also be **fined** by mixing in a fine clay called bentonite or albumen from egg whites. As they settle out, they absorb undesirable substances that can cloud the wine. As with filtering, the process is more common with ordinary table wines than with fine wines.

Winemakers typically blend several batches of wine together to balance flavor. Careful **blending** gives them an extra chance to create a perfect single-varietal wine or to combine several varietals that complement each other in a blend. Premium vintners also make unblended wines that highlight the attributes of grapes from a single vineyard.

New wine is stored in stainless-steel or oak containers to rest and develop before bottling. This stage, called **maturation** or **aging,** may last anywhere from a few months to more than a year. Barrel rooms are kept dark to protect the wine from both light and heat, either of which can be damaging. Some wineries keep their wines in air-conditioned rooms or warehouses; others use long, tunnel-like caves bored into hillsides, where the wine remains at a constant temperature.

If wine is aged for any length of time before bottling, it will be racked and perhaps filtered several times. Once it is bottled, the wine is stored for **bottle aging.** This is done in a cool, dark space to prevent the corks from drying out; a shrunken cork allows oxygen to enter the bottle and spoil the wine. In a few months, most white wines will be ready for release.

RED WINES

Red-wine production differs slightly from that of white wine. Red-wine grapes are crushed in the same way, but the juice is not separated from the grape skins and pulp before fermentation. This is what gives red wine its color. After crushing, the red-wine **must**—the thick slurry of juice, pulp, and skins—is fermented in vats. The juice is "left on the skins" for varying amounts of time, from a few days to a few weeks, depending on the type of grape and on how much color and flavor the winemaker wants to extract.

Fermentation also extracts chemical compounds such as **tannins** from the skins and seeds, making red wines more robust than whites. In a red designed for drinking soon after bottling, tannin levels are kept down; they should have a greater presence in wine meant for aging. In a young red not ready for drinking, tannins feel dry or coarse in your mouth, but they soften over time. A wine with well-balanced tannin will maintain its fruitiness and backbone as its flavor develops. Without adequate tannins, a wine will not age well.

Creating the **oak barrels** that age the wine is a craft in its own right. At Demptos Napa Cooperage, a French-owned company that employs French barrel-making techniques, the process involves several elaborate production phases. The staves of oak are formed into the shape of a barrel using metal bands, and then the rough edges of the bound planks are smoothed. Finally, the barrels are literally toasted to give the oak its characteristic flavor, which will in turn be imparted to the wine.

A winemaker checks on a vintage being aged in barrels.

Red-wine fermentation occurs at a higher temperature than that for whites—about 70°F to 90°F (21°C to 32°C). As the grape sugars are converted into alcohol, large amounts of carbon dioxide are generated. Carbon dioxide is lighter than wine but heavier than air, and it forms an **"aerobic cover"** that protects the wine from oxidation. As the wine ferments, grape skins rise to the top and are periodically mixed back in so the wine can extract the maximum amount of color and flavor. This is done either in the traditional fashion by punching them down with a large handheld tool or by pumping the wine from the bottom of the vat and pouring it back in at the top.

At the end of fermentation, the free-run wine is drained off. The grape skins and pulp are sent to a press, where the remaining liquid is extracted. As with white wines, the winemaker may blend a little of the press wine into the free-run wine to add complexity. Otherwise, the press juice goes into bulk wine—the lower-quality, less expensive stuff. The better wine is racked and then perhaps fined; some reds are left unfined for extra depth.

Next up is **oak-barrel aging,** which takes from a half year to a year or longer. Oak, like grapes, contains natural tannins, and the wine extracts these tannins from the barrels. The wood also has countless tiny pores through which water slowly evaporates, making the wine more concentrated. To

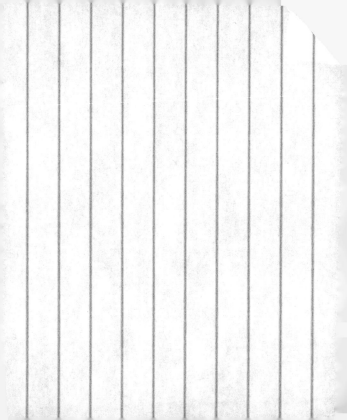

It's All on the Label

If you look beyond the photograph of a weathered château or the quirky drawing of a cartoon creature, a wine's label will tell you a lot about what's inside. If you want to decode the details, look for the following information:

■ **Alcohol content:** In most cases, U.S. law requires bottles to list the alcohol content, which typically hovers around 13% or 14%, but big red wines from California, especially Zinfandel, can soar to 16% or more.

■ **Appellation:** At least 85% of the grapes must have come from the AVA (American Viticultural Area) listed on the bottle. A bottle that says "Mt. Veeder," for example, contains mostly grapes that are grown in the compact Mt. Veeder appellation, but if the label simply says "California," the grapes could have come from anywhere in the state.

■ **Estate or Estate Grown:** Wines with this label must be made entirely of grapes grown on land owned or farmed by the winery.

■ **Reserve:** An inexact term

meaning "special" (and therefore usually costing more), reserve can refer to how or where the grapes were grown, how the wine was made, or even how long it was aged.

■ **Varietal:** If a type of grape is listed on the label, it means that at least 75% of the grapes in this wine are of that varietal. If there's none listed, it's almost certainly a blend of various types of grapes.

■ **Vineyard name:** If the label lists a vineyard, then at least 95% of the grapes used must have been harvested there. A vineyard name is more commonly, though not exclusively, found on higher-end bottles.

■ **Vintage:** If a year appears on the label, it means that at least 95% of the grapes were harvested in that year (85% if the wine is not designated with an AVA). If no vintage is listed, the grapes may come from more than one year's harvest.

■ **Wine name:** Many wineries will give their wines a catchy name, to help consumers pick it out in a crowd.

make sure the aging wine does not oxidize, the barrels have to be regularly **topped off** with wine from the same vintage.

New, or virgin, oak barrels impart the most tannins to a wine. With each successive use the tannins are diminished, until the barrel is said to be "neutral." Depending on the varietal, winemakers might blend juice aged in virgin oak barrels with juice aged in neutral barrels. In the tasting room you may hear, for instance, that a Pinot Noir was

aged in 30% new oak and 70% two-year-old oak, meaning that the bulk of the wine was aged in oak used for two
previous agings.

The only way even the best winemaker can tell if a wine is
finished is by tasting it. A winemaker constantly tastes wines
during fermentation, while they are aging in barrels, and,
less often, while they age in bottles. The wine is released for
sale when the winemaker's palate and nose say it's ready.

SPARKLING WINES

Despite the mystique surrounding them, sparkling wines are
nothing more or less than wines in which carbon dioxide
is suspended, making them bubbly. Good sparkling wine
will always be fairly expensive because a great deal of work
goes into making it.

White sparkling wines can be made from either white or
black grapes. In France, Champagne is traditionally made
from Pinot Noir or Chardonnay grapes, whereas in California sparkling wine might be made with Pinot Blanc, Riesling, or sometimes other white grapes. If black grapes are
used, they must be picked very carefully to avoid crushing
them. The goal is to minimize contact between the inner
fruit (which is usually white) and the skins, where the
purplish-red color pigments reside. The grapes are rushed
to the winery and crushed very gently, preventing the juice
from coming in contact with the pigments and turning red.
Even so, some sparklers have more of a pink tinge to them
than the winemaker intends.

The freshly pressed juice and pulp, or must, is **fermented
with special yeasts** that preserve the characteristic fruit flavor of the grape variety used. Before bottling, this finished
"still" wine (wine without bubbles) is mixed with a *liqueur
de tirage,* a blend of wine, sugar, and yeast. This mixture
causes the wine to ferment again—in the bottle, where
it stays for up to 12 weeks. **Carbon dioxide,** a by-product
of fermentation, is produced and trapped in the bottle,
where it dissolves into the wine (instead of escaping into
the air, as happens during fermentation in barrel, vat, or
tank). This captive carbon dioxide transforms a still wine
into a sparkler.

New bottles of sparkling wine are stored on their sides in
deep cellars. The wine now ages *sur lie,* or "on the lees" (the
dead yeast cells and other deposits trapped in the bottle).

This aging process enriches the wine's texture and increases the complexity of its bouquet. The amount of time spent *sur lie* has a direct relation to its quality: the longer the aging, the more complex the wine.

The lees must be removed from the bottle before a sparkling wine can be enjoyed. This is achieved in a process whose first step is called **riddling.** In the past, each bottle, head tilted slightly downward, was placed in a riddling rack, an A-frame with many holes of bottleneck size. Riddlers gave each bottle a slight shake and a downward turn—every day, if possible. This continued for six weeks, until each bottle rested upside down in the hole and the sediment had collected in the neck, next to the cork. Simple as it sounds, this process is actually very difficult. Hand-riddling is a fine art perfected after much training. Today most sparkling wines are riddled in ingeniously designed machines called gyro palettes, which can handle 500 or more bottles at a time, though at a few wineries, such as Schramsberg, the work is still done by hand.

After riddling, the bottles are **disgorged.** The upside-down bottles are placed in a very cold solution, which freezes the sediments in a block that attaches itself to the crown cap that seals the bottle. The cap and frozen plug are removed, and the bottle is topped off with a wine-and-sugar mixture called **dosage** and recorked with the traditional Champagne cork. The dosage ultimately determines the sparkler's sweetness.

Sparkling wines with 1.5% sugar or less are labeled **brut,** those with 1.2% to 2% sugar are called **extra dry,** those with 1.7% to 3.5% are called **sec** (French for "dry"), and those with 3.5% to 5% are **demi-sec** (half dry). Sparkling wines labeled **doux** (sweet) have more than 5% sugar. Most sparkling-wine drinkers refuse to admit that they like their bubbly on the sweet side, and this labeling convention allows them to drink sweet while pretending to drink dry. It's a marketing ploy invented in Champagne at least a century ago. A sparkling wine to which no dosage has been added will be bone dry (and taste sour to some) and may be called natural or **extra-brut.**

Most sparkling wines are not vintage dated but are *assembled* (the term sparkling-wine makers use instead of *blended*) to create a **cuvée,** a mix of different wines and sometimes different vintages consistent with the house style. However, sparkling wines may be vintage dated in particularly great years.

Sparkling wine may also be made by time- and cost-saving bulk methods. In the **Charmat process,** invented by Eugene Charmat early in the 20th century, the secondary fermentation takes place in large tanks rather than individual bottles. Basically, each tank is treated as one huge bottle. After the bubbles have developed, the sediments are filtered out and the wine is bottled. This comes at a price: although the sparkling wine may be ready in as little as a month, it has neither the complexity nor the bubble quality of traditional sparklers. In the United States, sparkling wine made in this way must be labeled "Bulk Process" or "Charmat Process." Sparkling wines made in the traditional, time-consuming fashion may be labeled "Méthode Champenoise" or "Wine Fermented in This Bottle."

ROSÉ WINES

Rosé or blush wines are made from red-wine grapes, but the juicy pulp is left on the skins for a matter of hours—typically 12 to 36—rather than days. When the winemaker decides that the juice has reached the desired color, it is drained off and filtered. Yeast is added, and the juice is left to ferment. Because the must stays on the skins for a shorter time, fewer tannins are leached from the skins, and the resulting wine is not as full flavored as a red. You might say that rosé is a lighter, fruitier version of red wine, not a pink version of white.

Rosé has gotten a bad rap in recent years, perhaps because it's sometimes confused with inexpensive, sickly sweet white Zinfandels that are a similar hue, but the French have been making excellent dry rosés for decades. Many California vintners have jumped on the rosé bandwagon, and it seems like almost every tasting room features at least one of these refreshing wines.

GRAPE GROWING: THE BASICS

Most kinds of wine grapes are touchy. If the weather is too hot, they can produce too much sugar and not enough acid, resulting in overly alcoholic wines. Too cool and they won't ripen properly, and some will develop an unpleasant vegetal taste. And rain at the wrong time of year can wreak havoc on vineyards, causing grapes to rot on the vine. What's more, the wrong type of soil can leave vines with "wet feet," which can seriously hamper their growth. These and many other conditions must be just right to coax the best out of

CLOSE UP

The French Connection

Sparkling wines were perfected in Champagne, France's northernmost wine district, where wines tend to be a bit acidic because grapes do not always fully ripen. That's why sparkling wines have traditionally been naturally tart, even austere. Because of their progenitor's birthplace, many sparkling wines are called "Champagne." However, this term designates a specific region, so it shouldn't be used for American wines. That's not to say that Napa and Sonoma County sparkling wines are in any way inferior to French ones. The French Champagne houses are fully aware of the excellence of the California product and have been quick to cash in on the laurels gathered by such pioneers as Hanns Kornell, Schramsberg, and Iron Horse by establishing sparkling-wine cellars in Sonoma and Napa with American partners.

persnickety wine grapes, and Napa and Sonoma have that magical combination of sun, rain, fog, slope, and soil that allows many varieties of wine grape to thrive.

LOCATION, LOCATION, LOCATION

California growers and winemakers generally agree that no matter what high-tech wine-making techniques might be used after the grapes are picked, in fact the wine is really made in the vineyard. This emphasis on *terroir* (a French term that encompasses a region's soil, microclimate, and overall growing conditions) reflects a belief that the quality of a wine is determined by what happens before the grapes are crushed. Even a small winery can produce spectacular wines if it has the right location and grows the grapes best suited to its soil and microclimate.

In the United States, the Alcohol and Tobacco Tax and Trade Bureau can designate a unique wine-growing region as an American Viticultural Area (AVA), more commonly called an **appellation.** An appellation refers to the source of a wine's grapes, not to where it was made. Wineries can indicate the appellation on a bottle's label only if 85% of the grapes were grown in that appellation. Many wineries buy grapes from outside their AVA, so they might label different wines with the names of different regions.

What makes things a little confusing is that appellations often overlap, allowing for increased levels of specificity.

The Russian River Valley, where Pinot Noir and Chardonnay are widely grown

California is an appellation, for example, but so is the Napa Valley. Napa and Sonoma counties are each county appellations, but they, too, are divided into even smaller subappellations. Different appellations—there are more than 100 AVAs in California, with 16 in the county of Napa alone—are renowned for different wines.

When it is to their advantage, winemakers make sure to mention prestigious appellations, and even specific vineyards, on their labels. If the grapes have come from multiple AVAs within a given region—say, the North Coast—the wine can be labeled with the name of the whole region. Wines simply labeled "California," then, are usually made of grapes from more than one region.

GEOLOGY 101

Wherever grapes are grown, geology matters. Grapevines are among the few plants that give their best fruit when grown in poor, rocky soil. On the other hand, grapes just don't like wet feet. The ideal vineyard soil is easily permeable by water. Until the 1990s, California growers were more interested in climate than geology when deciding where to plant vineyards and how to manage them. As demand for premium wine exploded, though, winemakers began paying much more attention to the soil part of the terroir equation. Geologists now do a brisk business advising growers.

Different grape varieties thrive in different types of soil. For instance, Cabernet Sauvignon does best in well-drained, gravelly soil. If it's too wet or contains too much heavy clay or organic matter, the soil will give the wine an obnoxious vegetative quality that even the best wine-making techniques cannot remove. Merlot, however, can grow in soil with more clay and still be made into a delicious, rich wine. Sauvignon Blanc does quite well in heavy clay soils, but the winegrower has to limit irrigation and use some viticultural muscle to keep the grapes from developing unacceptable flavors. Chardonnay likes well-drained vineyards but will also take heavy soil.

The soils below Napa Valley's crags and in the valleys of Sonoma County are dizzyingly diverse, which helps account for the unusually wide variety of grapes grown in such a small area. Some of the soils are composed of dense, heavy, sedimentary clays washed from the mountains; others are very rocky clays, loams, or silts of alluvial fans. These fertile, well-drained soils cover much of the valleys' floors. Other areas have soil based on serpentine, a rock that rarely appears aboveground. In all, there are about 60 soil types in the Napa and Sonoma valleys.

In Wine Country you'll hear a lot about limestone, a nutrient-rich rock in which grapevines thrive. Some California winemakers claim to be growing in limestone when in fact they are not. In fact, only small patches of California's Wine Country have significant amounts of limestone. The term is often used to describe the streak of light-color, almost white soil that runs across the Napa Valley from the Palisades to St. Helena and through Sonoma County from the western flanks of the Mayacamas Mountains to Windsor. The band is actually made of volcanic material that has no limestone content.

DOWN ON THE FARM

Much like a fruit or nut orchard, a vineyard can produce excellent grapes for decades—even a century—if it's given the proper attention. The growing cycle starts in winter, when the vines are bare and dormant. While the plants rest, the grower works to enrich the soil and repair the trellising system (if there is one) that holds up the vines. This is when **pruning** takes place to regulate the vine's growth and the upcoming season's crop size.

DID YOU KNOW?

Beltane Ranch is a B&B on a real working ranch near Glen Ellen that grows olives, grapes, and cattle; the ranch was originally a turkey farm.

2

In spring, the soil is aerated by plowing, and new vines go in. The grower trains established vines so they grow, with or without trellising, in the shape most beneficial for the grapes. **Bud break** occurs when the first bits of green emerge from the vines, and a pale green veil appears over the winter's gray-black vineyards. A late frost can be devastating at this time of year. Summer brings the flowering of the vines, when clusters of tiny green blossoms appear, and **fruit set,** when the grapes form from the blossoms. As the vineyards turn luxuriant and leafy, more pruning, along with leaf pulling, keeps foliage in check so the vine directs nutrients to the grapes, and so the sun can reach the fruit. As summer advances, the grower will **thin the fruit,** cutting off (or "dropping") some bunches so the remaining grapes intensify in flavor. A look at the vineyards reveals heavy clusters of green or purple grapes, some pea-size, others marble-size, depending on the variety.

Fall is the busiest season in the vineyard. Growers and winemakers carefully monitor the ripeness of the grapes, sometimes with equipment that tests sugar and acid levels and sometimes simply by tasting them. As soon as the grapes are ripe, **harvest** begins amid the lush foliage. In California this generally happens in September and October, but sometimes a bit earlier or later, depending on the type of grape and the climatic conditions. Picking must be done as quickly as possible, within just a day or two, to keep the grapes from passing their peak. Most California grapes are harvested mechanically, but some are picked by hand. After harvest, the vines start to regenerate for the next year.

Sometimes by preference and sometimes by necessity, winemakers don't grow all the grapes they need. Small wineries with only a few acres of grapes are limited in the varietals and quantities they can grow. (The smallest producers don't even have their own wineries, so they pay to use the equipment and storage space at custom crush facilities.) Midsize wineries may aim to get bigger. If it doesn't buy more acreage, a winery that wants to expand production has to buy grapes from independent growers.

Many winemakers purchase at least some of their grapes. Some have negotiated long-term contracts with top growers, buying grapes from the same supplier year after year. This way, the winemaker can control the consistency and quality of the fruit, just as if it came from the winery's own vineyard. Other wineries buy from several growers, and many growers sell to more than one winery.

Winemakers who buy from growers face a paradoxical problem: it's possible to make a wine that's too good and too popular. As the demand for a wine—and its price—rises, so will the price of the grapes used to make it. Other wineries sometimes bid up the price of the grapes, meaning that a winemaker can no longer afford the grapes that made a wine famous. This competitiveness among winemakers for specific batches of grapes underscores the faith put in the importance of growers.

ORGANIC AND BIODYNAMIC

If, as many grape growers insist, a wine is only as good as the vineyard it comes from, those who have adopted organic and biodynamic agricultural methods may be on to something. But when using terms like *organic* and *biodynamic,* what do vintners mean? Although organic viticulture is governmentally recognized and regulated, it is vaguely defined and its value is hotly debated—just like the rest of organic farming. It boils down to a rejection of chemical fertilizers, pesticides, and fungicides. Biodynamic farmers also reject these artificial agents, and their vineyard maintenance involves metaphysical principles as well.

Partly because it's difficult and expensive to qualify for official certification, partly because organic vineyards have smaller yields, and partly because it's hard to grow grapes organically except in warm, dry climates, organic viticulture remains the exception rather than the rule, although more vineyards are being certified organic every year.

Even rarer than wines produced from organically grown grapes are completely organic wines. For a wine to be certified as organic, not only do the grapes have to come from organic vineyards, but the processing must use a minimum of chemical additives. Some winemakers argue that it is impossible to make truly fine wine without using additives like sulfur dioxide, an antioxidant that protects the wine's color, aroma, flavor, and longevity.

Many wineries that might qualify as partially organic resist the label, wary of its effect on their reputation. Still, the movement is gaining momentum. Many major players, even if they are not certified organic, have taken steps to reduce their use of pesticides or implement other eco-friendly policies. Others grow some or all of their grapes organically. Very few producers make completely organic wine.

Benziger tram tours take to the fields to show biodynamic farming techniques in action.

If demand for organic products continues to grow, supply will no doubt follow suit. In the meantime, if you want organic wine, read the label carefully. To be called organic, a wine must contain certified organic grapes and have no added sulfites. Remember that some wines made from certified organic grapes still contain sulfites.

Their interest in organic farming has led some winery owners and vineyard managers to adopt biodynamic farming methods. The principles of biodynamic agriculture were conceived in the 1920s by the Austrian scholar and mystic Rudolf Steiner and refined in the 1930s by Ehrenfried Pfeiffer, a German scientist and specialist in soil management.

Biodynamic farmers view the land as a living, self-sustaining organism requiring a healthy, unified ecosystem to thrive. To nurture the soil, for instance, vineyard workers spray specially formulated herbal "teas" (the ingredients include yarrow, dandelion, valerian, and stinging nettle flowers) onto compost spread in the fields. Grazing animals such as sheep or goats maintain the ground cover between the vines (the animals' manure provides natural fertilizer), and natural predators, among them insect-eating bats, control pests that might damage the crop. Steiner and his successors believed that the movements of the sun and the moon influence plant development, so astronomical calendars play a role in the timing of many vineyard activities.

At its most elevated level, the biodynamic philosophy recognizes a farm as a metaphysical entity that requires its human inhabitants not merely to tend it but to form a spiritual bond with it, a notion that other organic farmers share in theory even if their methods sometimes diverge. Among wineries whose practices have been certified organic are Hall in the Napa Valley, and Preston of Dry Creek in Northern Sonoma County. The Napa Valley's Robert Sinskey Vineyards is certified both organic and biodynamic, as is the Sonoma Valley's Benziger Family Winery.

WINE-LOVER'S GLOSSARY

Like most activities, wine making and tasting require specialized vocabularies. Some words are merely show-off jargon, but some are specific and helpful.

Acidity. The tartness of a wine, derived from the fruit acids of the grape. Acids stabilize a wine (i.e., preserve its character), balance its sweetness, and bring out its flavors. Too little or too much acid spoils a wine's taste. Tartaric acid is the major acid in wine, but malic, lactic, and citric acids also occur.

Aging. The process by which some wines improve over time, becoming smoother and more complex and developing a pleasing bouquet. Wine is most commonly aged in oak vats or barrels, slowly interacting with the air through the pores in the wood. Sometimes wine is cellared for bottle aging. Today many wines are not made for aging and are drunk relatively young, as soon as a few months after bottling. Age can diminish a wine's fruitiness and also dull its color: whites turn brownish, rosés orange, reds brown.

Alcohol. Ethyl alcohol is a colorless, volatile, pungent spirit that not only gives wine its stimulating effect and some of its flavor but also acts as a preservative, stabilizing the wine and allowing it to age. A wine's alcohol content must be stated on the label, expressed as a percentage of volume, except when a wine is designated table wine.

American Viticultural Area (AVA). More commonly termed an *appellation*. A region with unique soil, climate, and other grape-growing conditions can be designated an AVA by the Alcohol and Tobacco Tax and Trade Bureau. When a label lists an appellation—Napa Valley or Mt. Veeder, for example—at least 85% of the grapes used to make the wine must come from that AVA.

Appellation. *See American Viticultural Area.*

Aroma. The scent of young wine derived directly from the fresh fruit. It diminishes with fermentation and is replaced by a more complex bouquet as the wine ages. The term may also be used to describe special fruity odors in a wine, such as black cherry, green olive, ripe raspberry, or apple.

Astringency. The puckery sensation produced in the mouth by the tannins in wine.

AVA. *See American Viticultural Area.*

Balance. A quality of wine in which all desirable elements (fruit, acid, tannin) are present in the proper proportion. Well-balanced wine has a pleasing nose, flavor, and mouth feel.

Barrel fermenting. The fermenting of wine in small oak barrels instead of large tanks or vats. This method allows the winemaker to keep grape lots separate before blending the wine. The cost of oak barrels makes this method expensive.

Barrique. An oak barrel used for aging wines.

Biodynamic. An approach to agriculture that focuses on regarding the land as a living thing; it generally incorporates organic farming techniques and the use of the astronomical calendar in hopes of cultivating a healthy balance in the vineyard ecosystem.

Blanc de blancs. Sparkling or still white wine made solely from white grapes.

Blanc de noirs. White wine made with red grapes by removing the skins during crush. Some sparkling whites, for example, are made with red Pinot Noir grapes.

Blending. The mixing of several wines to create one of greater complexity or appeal, as when a heavy wine is blended with a lighter one to make a more approachable medium-bodied wine.

Body. The wine's heft or density as experienced by the palate. A full body makes the mouth literally feel full. It is considered an advantage in the case of some reds, a disadvantage in many lighter whites. *See also Mouth feel.*

Bordeaux blend. A red wine blended from varietals native to France's Bordeaux region—Cabernet Sauvignon, Cabernet Franc, Malbec, Merlot, and Petit Verdot.

Botrytis. *Botrytis cinerea,* a beneficial fungus that can perforate a ripe grape's skin. This dehydrates the grape and concentrates the remaining juice while preserving its acids. Botrytis grapes make a sweet but not cloying wine, often with complex flavors of honey or apricot.

Bouquet. The odors a mature wine gives off when opened. They should be pleasantly complex and should give an indication of the wine's grape variety, origin, age, and quality.

Brix. A method of telling whether grapes are ready for picking by measuring their sugars. Multiplying a grape's Brix number by .55 approximates the potential alcohol content of the wine.

Brut. French term for the driest category of sparkling wine. *See also Demi-sec, Sec.*

Case. A carton of 12 750-ml bottles of wine. A magnum case contains six 1.5-liter magnum bottles. Most wineries will offer a discount if you purchase wine by the case (or sometimes a half case).

Cask. A synonym for *barrel.* More generally, any size or shape wine container made from wood staves.

Cellaring. Storage of wine in bottles for aging. The bottles are laid on their sides to keep the corks moist and prevent air leakage that would spoil the wine.

Champagne. The northernmost wine district of France, where the world's only genuine Champagne is made. The term is often used loosely in America to denote sparkling wines in general.

Cloudiness. The presence of particles that do not settle out of a wine, causing it to look and taste dusty or even muddy. If settling and decanting do not correct cloudiness, the wine has been badly made or is spoiled.

Complexity. The qualities of good wine that provide a multilayered sensory experience to the drinker. Balanced flavors, harmonious aromas or bouquet, and a long finish are components of complexity.

Corked. Describes wine that is flawed by the musty, wet-cardboard flavor imparted by cork mold, technically known as TCA, or 2,4,6-Trichloroanisole.

Crush. American term for the harvest season, or vintage. Also refers to the year's crop of grapes crushed for wine.

Cuvée. Generally a sparkling wine, but sometimes a still wine, that is a blend of different wines and sometimes different vintages. Most sparkling wines are cuvées.

Decant. To pour a wine from its bottle into another container either to expose it to air or to eliminate sediment. Decanting for sediment pours out the clear wine and leaves the residue behind in the original bottle.

Demi-sec. French term that translates as "half-dry." It is applied to sweet wines that contain 3.5%–5% sugar.

Dessert wines. Sweet wines that are big in flavor and aroma. Some are quite low in alcohol; others, such as port-style wines, are fortified with brandy or another spirit and may be 17%–21% alcohol.

Dry. Having very little sweetness or residual sugar. Most wines are dry, although some whites, such as Rieslings, are made to be "off-dry," meaning on the sweet side.

Estate bottled. A wine entirely made by one winery at a single facility. The grapes must come from the winery's own vineyards or vineyards farmed by the winery within the same appellation (which must be printed on the label).

Fermentation. The biochemical process by which grape juice becomes wine. Enzymes generated by yeast cells convert grape sugars into alcohol and carbon dioxide. Fermentation stops when either the sugar is depleted and the yeast starves or when high alcohol levels kill the yeast.

Fermenter. Any vessel (such as a barrel, tank, or vat) in which wine is fermented.

Filtering, Filtration. A purification process in which wine is pumped through filters to rid it of suspended particles.

Fining. A method of clarifying wine by adding egg whites, bentonite (a type of clay), or other natural substances to a barrel. As these solids settle to the bottom, they take various dissolved compounds with them. Most wine meant for everyday drinking is fined; however, better wines are fined less often.

Finish. Also known as *aftertaste*. The flavors that remain in the mouth after swallowing wine. A good wine has a long finish with complex flavor and aroma.

Flight. A few wines—usually from three to five—specially selected for tasting together.

Fortification. A process by which brandy or another spirit is added to a wine to stop fermentation and to increase its level of alcohol, as in the case of port-style dessert wines.

Fruity. Having aromatic nuances of fresh fruit, such as fig, raspberry, or apple. Fruitiness, a sign of quality in young wines, is replaced by bouquet in aged wines.

Fumé Blanc. A nonspecific term for wine made with Sauvignon Blanc. Robert Mondavi originally coined the term to describe his dry, crisp, oak-aged Sauvignon Blanc.

Green. Said of a wine made from unripe grapes, with a pronounced leafy flavor and a raw edge.

Horizontal tasting. A tasting of several different wines of the same vintage.

Late harvest. Wine made from grapes harvested later in the fall than the main lot, and thus higher in sugar levels. Many dessert wines are late harvest.

Lees. The spent yeast, grape solids, and tartrates that drop to the bottom of the barrel or tank as wine ages. Wine, particularly white wine, gains complexity when it is left on the lees for a time.

Library wine. An older vintage that the winery has put aside to sell at a later date.

Malolactic fermentation. A secondary fermentation in the tank or barrel that changes harsh malic acid into softer lactic acid and carbon dioxide. Wine is sometimes inoculated with lactic bacteria or placed in wood containers that harbor the bacteria to enhance this process. Often referred to as *ML* or *malo*. Too much malo can make a wine too heavy.

Meritage. A trademarked name for American (mostly California) Bordeaux blends that meet certain wine-making and marketing requirements and are made by member wineries of the Meritage Association.

Méthode champenoise. The traditional, time-consuming method of making sparkling wines by fermenting them in individual bottles.

Mouth feel. Literally, the way wine feels in the mouth. Mouth feel, such as smoothness or astringency, is detected by the sense of touch rather than of smell or taste.

Must. The slushy mix of crushed grapes—juice, pulp, skin, seeds, and bits of stem—produced by the stemmer-crusher at the beginning of the wine-making process.

Neutral oak. The wood of older barrels or vats that no longer pass much flavor or tannin to the wine stored within.

New oak. The wood of a fresh barrel or vat that has not previously been used to ferment or age wine. It can impart desirable flavors and enhance a wine's complexity, but if used to excess it can overpower a wine's true character.

Noble rot. *See Botrytis.*

Nonvintage. A blend of wines from different years. Nonvintage wines have no date on their label. Wine may be blended from different vintages to showcase strong points that complement each other, or to make a certain wine taste the same from one year to the next.

Nose. The overall fragrance (aroma or bouquet) given off by a wine; the better part of its flavor.

Oaky. A vanilla-woody flavor that develops when wine is aged in oak barrels. Leave a wine too long in a new oak barrel and that oaky taste overpowers the other flavors.

Organic viticulture. The technique of growing grapes without the use of chemical fertilizers, pesticides, or fungicides.

Oxidation. Undesirable flavor and color changes to juice or wine caused by too much contact with the air, either during processing or because of a leaky barrel or cork. Most often occurs with white wine, especially if it's over the hill.

pH. Technical term for a measure of acidity. It is a reverse measure: the lower the pH level, the higher the acidity. Most wines range in pH from 2.9 to 4.2, with the most desirable level between 3.2 and 3.5. Higher pHs make wine flabby and dull, whereas lower pHs make it tart.

Phylloxera. A disease caused by the root louse *Phylloxera vastatrix,* which attacks and ultimately destroys the roots. The pest is native to the United States; it traveled to France with American grape vines in the 19th century and devastated nonresistant vineyards.

Pomace. Spent grape skins and solids left over after the juice has been pressed, commonly returned to the fields as fertilizer.

Unsurprisingly, wine bars are very popular in Napa and Sonoma.

Racking. Moving wine from one tank or barrel to another to leave unwanted deposits behind; the wine may or may not be fined or filtered in the process.

Reserve wine. Inexact term applied by vintners to indicate that a wine is better in some way (through aging, source of the grapes, and so on) than others from their winery.

Residual sugar. The natural sugar left in a wine after fermentation, which converts sugar into alcohol. If the fermentation was interrupted or if the must has very high sugar levels, some residual sugar will remain, making a sweeter wine.

Rhône blend. A wine made from grapes hailing from France's Rhône Valley, such as Marsanne, Roussanne, Syrah, Cinsault, Mourvèdre, or Viognier.

Rosé. Pink wine, usually made from red-wine grapes (of any variety). The juice is left on the skins only long enough to give it a tinge of color.

Rounded. Said of a well-balanced wine in which fruity flavor is nicely offset by acidity—a good wine, though not necessarily a distinctive or great one.

Sec. French for "dry." The term is generally applied within the sparkling or sweet categories, indicating the wine has 1.7%–3.5% residual sugar. Sec is drier than demi-sec but not as dry as brut.

Sediment. Dissolved or suspended solids that drop out of most red wines as they age in the bottle, thus clarifying their appearance, flavors, and aromas. Sediment is not a defect in an old wine or in a new wine that has been bottled unfiltered.

Sparkling wines. Wines in which carbon dioxide is dissolved, making them bubbly. Examples are French Champagne, Italian prosecco, and Spanish cava.

Sugar. Source of grapes' natural sweetness. When yeast feeds on sugar, it produces alcohol and carbon dioxide. The higher the sugar content of the grape, the higher the potential alcohol level or sweetness of the wine.

Sulfites. Compounds of sulfur dioxide that are almost always added before fermentation to prevent oxidation and to kill bacteria and wild yeasts that can cause off flavors. Sulfites are sometimes blamed as the culprit in headaches caused by red wine, but the connection has not been proven.

Sustainable viticulture. A viticultural method that aims to bring the vineyard into harmony with the environment. Organic and other techniques are used to minimize agricultural impact and to promote biodiversity.

Table wine. Any wine that has at least 7% but not more than 14% alcohol by volume. The term doesn't necessarily imply anything about the wine's quality or price—both super-premium and jug wines can be labeled as table wine.

Tannins. You can tell when they're there, but their origins are still a mystery. These natural grape compounds produce a sensation of drying or astringency in the mouth and throat. Tannins settle out as wine ages; they're a big player in many red wines.

Tartaric acid, Tartrates. The principal acid of wine. Crystalline tartrates form on the insides of vats or barrels and sometimes in the bottle or on the cork. They look like tiny shards of glass but are not harmful.

Terroir. French for "soil." Typically used to describe the soil and climate conditions that influence the quality and characteristics of grapes and wine.

Varietal. A wine that takes its name from the grape variety from which it is predominantly made. California wines that qualify are almost always labeled with the variety of the source grape. According to U.S. law, at least 75% of a wine must come from a particular grape to be labeled with its variety name.

Vat. A large container of stainless steel, wood, or concrete, often open at the top, in which wine is fermented or blended. Sometimes used interchangeably with *tank*.

Vertical tasting. A tasting of several vintages of the same wine.

Vinification. Wine making, the process by which grapes are made into wine.

Vintage. The grape harvest of a given year, and the year in which the grapes are harvested. A vintage date on a bottle indicates the year in which the grapes were harvested rather than the year in which the wine was bottled.

Viticulture. The cultivation of grapes.

Woody. Describes excessively musty wood aromas and flavors picked up by wine stored in a wood barrel or cask for too long. The term woody is always a negative.

Yeast. A minute, single-celled fungus that germinates and multiplies rapidly as it feeds on sugar with the help of enzymes, creating alcohol and releasing carbon dioxide in the process of fermentation.

3

NAPA VALLEY

WHEN IT COMES TO WINE PRODUCTION in the United States, Napa Valley rules the roost with hundreds of wineries and many of the biggest brands in the business. Vastly diverse soils and microclimates give Napa winemakers the chance to make a tremendous variety of wines. But what's the area like beyond the glossy advertising and boldface names?

For every blockbuster winery whose name you'll recognize from the shelves of wine stores and the pages of *Wine Spectator*—Robert Mondavi, Charles Krug, Beringer, and Stag's Leap Wine Cellars, to name a very few—you'll also find low-frills wineries that will warmly welcome you into their modest tasting rooms. At the other end of the spectrum are Napa's "cult" cabernet producers—Screaming Eagle, Harlan Estate, Dalla Valle, and Dominus Estate among them—whose doors are closed tight to visitors.

The handful of small towns strung along Highway 29 are where wine industry workers live, and they're also where you'll find most of the area lodgings. The up-and-coming city of Napa—the valley's largest community—is the best place to find (relatively) reasonably priced accommodations. A few miles farther north, compact Yountville is a culinary boomtown, densely packed with top-notch restaurants and hotels, including a few luxury properties. Continuing north, St. Helena is teeming with high-style boutiques and eateries. Mellow Calistoga, known for spas and hot springs, feels a bit like an Old West frontier town, and has a more casual attitude than many others in Wine Country.

Because the Napa Valley attracts everyone from hard-core wine collectors to bachelorette partyers, it's not necessarily the best place to get away from it all. But there's a reason why it's California's number one Wine Country destination. The local viticulture has inspired a robust passion for food, and several outstanding chefs have sealed Napa's reputation as one of the country's best restaurant destinations. You will also get a glimpse of California's history, from the wine cellars dating back to the late 1800s to the flurry of Steamboat Gothic architecture dressing up Calistoga. Binding all these temptations together is the sheer scenic beauty of the place. Much of Napa Valley's landscape unspools in orderly, densely planted rows of vines. Even the climate cooperates, as the warm summer days and refreshingly cool evenings that are so favorable for grape growing also make perfect weather for traveling.

DID YOU KNOW?

Sterling Vineyards is perched on a hilltop south of Calistoga. Instead of driving to the winery, you board an aerial tram for the scenic trip up to the tasting room.

GETTING AROUND THE NAPA VALLEY

From San Francisco there are two main routes into the Napa Valley, both getting you there in a little less than an hour in normal traffic. You can head north across the Golden Gate Bridge and U.S. 101, east on Highway 37 and then Highway 121, and north on Highway 29; or east across the San Francisco–Oakland Bay Bridge and north on Interstate 80, west on Highway 37, and north on Highway 29.

Highway 29, the Napa Valley Highway, heads north from Vallejo first as a busy four-lane highway, then narrows to a two-lane road at Yountville. Beyond Yountville, expect Highway 29 to be congested, especially on summer weekends. Traveling through St. Helena can be particularly slow during morning and afternoon rush hours. You'll probably find slightly less traffic on the Silverado Trail, which roughly parallels Highway 29 all the way from Napa to Calistoga. Cross streets connect the two like rungs on a ladder every few miles, making it easy to cross from one to the other.

NAPA VALLEY APPELLATIONS

Nearly all of Napa County, which stretches from the Mayacamas Mountains in the west to Lake Berryessa in the east, makes up the Napa Valley American Viticultural Area (AVA). This large region is divided into many smaller AVAs, or subappellations, each with its own unique characteristics.

Four of these subappellations—Oak Knoll, Oakville, Rutherford, and St. Helena—stretch clear across the valley floor. Chilled by coastal fog, the **Oak Knoll District of Napa Valley AVA** has some of the coolest temperatures. The **Oakville AVA,** just north of Yountville, is studded by both big-name wineries (such as Robert Mondavi and Opus One) and awe-inspiring boutique labels (such as the super-exclusive Screaming Eagle). Oakville's gravelly, well-drained soil is especially good for Cabernet Sauvignon.

A sunny climate and well-drained soil make **Rutherford AVA** one of the best locations for Cabernet Sauvignon in California, if not the world. North of Rutherford, the **St. Helena AVA** is one of Napa's toastiest, as the slopes surrounding the narrow valley reflect the sun's heat. Bordeaux varietals are the most popular grapes grown here—particularly Cabernet Sauvignon but also Merlot. Just north, at the foot of Mt. St. Helena is the **Calistoga AVA;** Cabernet Sauvignon does well here, but also Zinfandel, Syrah, and Petite Sirah.

The design of the Opus One winery combines space-age and Mayan elements.

Stags Leap District AVA, a small district on the eastern side of the valley, is marked by dramatic volcanic palisades. As with the neighboring **Yountville AVA,** Cabernet Sauvignon and Merlot are by far the favored grapes. In both subappellations, cool evening breezes encourage a long growing season and intense fruit flavors. Some describe the resulting wines as "rock soft" or an "iron fist in a velvet glove." Also on the valley's eastern edge is a recent addition, the **Coombsville AVA.** Cabernet Sauvignon grows on the western-facing slopes of the Vaca Mountains, with Merlot, Chardonnay, Syrah, and Pinot Noir more prevalent in the cooler lower elevations.

The **Mt. Veeder** and **Spring Mountain AVAs** each encompass parts of the mountains that give them their names. Both demonstrate how stressing out grapevines can yield outstanding results; the big winner is Cabernet Sauvignon. Growing grapes on these slopes takes a certain recklessness—or foolhardiness, depending on your point of view—since many of the vineyards are so steep that they have to be tilled and harvested by hand.

The great variety of the climates and soils of the remaining subappellations—the **Atlas Peak, Chiles Valley, Diamond Mountain District,** and **Howell Mountain AVAs,** along with the part of **Los Carneros** that pokes into the southern Napa Valley—explains why vintners here can make so many different wines, and make them so well, in what in the end is a relatively compact region.

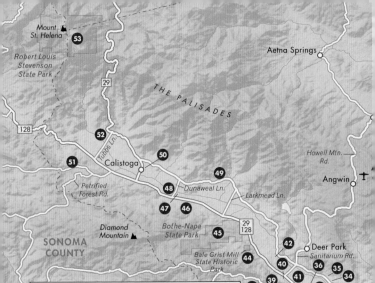

Bale Grist Mill State Historic Park, **44**

Beaulieu Vineyard, **22**

Beringer Vineyards, **41**

Cakebread Cellars, **19**

Castello di Amorosa, **46**

Caymus Vineyards, **26**

Charles Krug Winery, **36**

Chateau Montelena, **52**

Chimney Rock Winery, **9**

Clos du Val, **8**

Clos Pegase, **48**

Culinary Institute of America, **38**

Darioush, **6**

Domaine Chandon, **13**

Domaine Charbay Winery and Distillery, **39**

Duckhorn Vineyards, **42**

Dutch Henry Winery, **49**

Far Niente, **15**

Franciscan Estate, **30**

Frog's Leap, **24**

Hall, **32**

The Hess Collection, **1**

Honig Vineyard and Winery, **18**

Inglenook, **20**

Joseph Phelps Vineyards, **34**

Ma(i)sonry Napa Valley, **5**

Merryvale Vineyards, **33**

Mumm Napa, **25**

Napa Valley Museum, **14**

Napa Valley Wine Train, **3**

Nichelini Family Winery, **35**

Opus One, **17**

Oxbow Public Market, **2**

PlumpJack, **27**

Raymond Vineyards, **31**

Robert Louis Stevenson Museum, **37**

Robert Louis Stevenson State Park, **53**

Robert Mondavi, **16**

Robert Sinskey Vineyards, **11**

Round Pond Estate, **23**

RustRidge Winery, **28**

Rutherford Hill Winery, **29**

St. Clement Vineyards, **40**

St. Supéry Estate, **21**

Schramsberg, **45**

Sharpsteen Museum, **50**

Sodaro Estate Winery, **4**

Spring Mountain Vineyard, **43**

Stag's Leap Wine Cellars, **10**

Sterling Vineyards, **47**

Storybook Mountain Vineyards, **51**

Trefethen Family Vineyards, **7**

V Marketplace, **12**

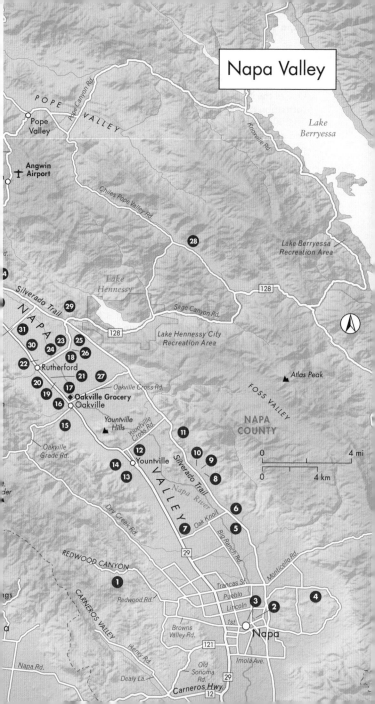

Napa Valley

NAPA

46 miles northeast of San Francisco.

One of the Napa Valley's recent success stories is the transformation of Napa, its largest and oldest city (population 78,000), into a spry, hip destination with cool nightspots and affordable lodgings. Although it's definitely a work in progress—you'll still find empty storefronts amid the wine bars, bookstores, and restaurants—Napa attracts more visitors every year.

Napa was founded in 1848 in a strategic location on the Napa River, where the Sonoma-Benicia Road (Highways 12 and 29) crossed at a ford. The first wood-frame building was a saloon, and the downtown area still projects an old-river-town vibe. Many Victorian houses have survived, and in the original business district a few older buildings have been preserved, including the turn-of-the-20th-century courthouse and several riverfront warehouses. A walkway follows the river through town, making it more pedestrian-friendly, and new restaurants and hotels keep popping up. If you base yourself here, you'll undoubtedly want to spend some time exploring the beautiful countryside, but don't miss seeing what the Napa Valley's least pretentious town has to offer.

GETTING HERE AND AROUND

To get to downtown Napa from Highway 29, take the 1st Street exit and follow the signs for Central Napa. In less than a mile you'll reach the corner of 2nd Street and Main Street. Most of the town's sights and many of its restaurants are clustered in an easily walkable area near this intersection (you'll find street parking and garages nearby). Most of the wineries with city of Napa addresses are on or just off Highway 29 or the parallel Silverado Trail.

EXPLORING

TOP ATTRACTIONS

Darioush. The lavish visitor center at this winery is unlike any other in the valley: 16 freestanding, sand-color columns loom in front of a travertine building that looks like a cross between the Parthenon and a sultan's palace. You'll sense the pride that proprietor Darioush Khaledi feels for his Persian heritage throughout your visit, most notably in the warmth of the hospitality here. Although walk-in parties of six or fewer can taste at the bar, call in advance or book online to

CLOSE UP

Best Bets for Napa Valley Wineries

WINE TASTING

Hall, Rutherford or St. Helena. Two choices: a quiet brick-lined cave at a hillside retreat or (after its opening in late 2013) a flashy glass-walled visitor center amid the vineyards.

Joseph Phelps Vineyards, St. Helena. Tastings at Phelps unfold like everything else here, with class, grace, and precision—an apt description of the wines themselves.

Ma(i)sonry Napa Valley, Yountville. No ordinary tasting facility, this art and design gallery pours vintages from limited-production wineries.

WINERY TOURING

Beringer Vineyards, St. Helena. Of the three Napa wineries that provide the best overview of California wine-making (Beaulieu and Mondavi being the other two), Beringer occupies the prettiest site.

Frog's Leap, Rutherford. A lighthearted tone and well-informed tour guides make for entertaining education at Frog's Leap. By tour's end you'll be able to pronounce Trockenbeerenauslese, the name of the winery's splendid dessert wine.

The Hess Collection, Napa. The guided tour of the facilities at Hess is enlightening, but the real revelations come on the self-guided tours of the owner's modern-art holdings.

Schramsberg, Calistoga. Deep inside 19th-century caves created by Chinese laborers, you'll learn all about crafting *méthode champenoise* sparkling wines. Back aboveground, you'll taste the fruits of the winemaker's labors.

SETTING

Castello di Amorosa, Calistoga. You have to admire a guy who dreams of building a 107-room replica of a medieval castle—and then makes it happen. Crazy. Eccentric. Worth a peek.

Far Niente, Oakville. Something's always abloom in Far Niente's landscaped gardens. Splurge on the tasting and tour and bask for a moment in the sublime sophistication that is the Napa Valley.

Rutherford Hill Winery, Rutherford. Few publicly accessible perches in the valley outshine this one for panoramic views.

FOOD-WINE PAIRING

Robert Sinskey Vineyards, Napa. "Eat seasonally, drink good wine, and live a long and prosperous life," advises culinary director and cookbook author Maria Helm Sinskey.

Round Pond Estate, Rutherford. Excellent morsels accompany the sips and samples at both the high-tech olive mill and the country-chic winery.

3

sit at a table. In either case, the wines—often a Chardonnay, a Viognier, a Merlot, a Cabernet Sauvignon, a Shiraz, and Duel, a Cabernet-Shiraz blend—are the same. The Cabernet, the blend, and the Shiraz garner deserved praise. The Chardonnay, daringly buttery for this day and age, is the best of the whites. ✉ *4240 Silverado Trail, near Shady Oaks Dr.* ☎ *707/257–2345* ⊕ *www.darioush.com* ☜ *Tastings $40–$300* ⊙ *Daily 10:30–5; tour by appointment.*

★ Fodor'sChoice **The Hess Collection.** About 9 miles northwest of Napa, up a winding road ascending Mt. Veeder, this winery is a delightful discovery. The simple limestone structure, rustic from the outside but modern and airy within, contains Swiss owner Donald Hess's personal art collection, including mostly large-scale works by contemporary artists such as Robert Motherwell, Anselm Kiefer, Robert Rauschenberg, and Francis Bacon. Cabernet Sauvignon is a major strength, and the Mount Veeder 19 Block Mountain Cuvée—available only at the winery and through the Hess wine club—shows off the Malbec and other estate varietals. ■TIP→ Several food and wine pairings are available, including one with chocolates that go ever so well with the robust Mount Veeder Cabernet. ✉ *4411 Redwood Rd., west off Hwy. 29 at Trancas St./Redwood Rd. exit* ☎ *707/255–1144* ⊕ *www.hesscollection.com* ☜ *Art gallery free, tastings $10–$75* ⊙ *Daily 10–5:30; guided tours daily 10:30–3:30.*

★ Fodor'sChoice **Oxbow Public Market.** This market's two dozen shops, wine bars, and artisanal food producers provide an introduction to Napa Valley's wealth of foods and wines. Swoon over decadent charcuterie at the Fatted Calf, slurp down bivalves at Hog Island Oyster Company, chow down on tacos with homemade tortillas at C Casa, or get a whiff of hard-to-find seasonings at Whole Spice Company before sitting down to a glass of wine at the Oxbow Wine Merchant & Wine Bar. The retro fast-food joint Gott's Roadside tempts those who prefer hamburgers (or egg-and-cheese breakfast sandwiches) to duck-liver mousse. ■TIP→ Locals line up at Model Bakery around 3 pm for hot-from-the-oven "late bake" bread. ✉ *610 and 644 1st St., at McKinstry St.* ⊕ *www.oxbowpublicmarket.com* ☜ *Free* ⊙ *Weekdays 9–9, weekends 10–9; hrs of some merchants vary.*

Trefethen Family Vineyards. This winery makes superb Chardonnay, Cabernet Sauvignon, and Pinot Noir—if you'd like to find out for yourself how well they age, pay for the reserve tasting, which includes pours of limited-release

Both the art and the wine inspire at The Hess Collection.

wines and one or two of the older vintages. The big terra-cotta-color building where tastings take place is a remnant of the old Eshcol Winery, built in 1886. It's the only three-story gravity-flow winery built from wood remaining in Napa (others are made from stone, which has weathered the last century much better). There's a cork tree planted in the garden outside the tasting room—so *that's* what the stuff looks like before it ends up on the sharp end of the corkscrew. ⊠ *1160 Oak Knoll Ave., off Hwy. 29* ☎ *866/895–7696* ⊕ *www.trefethen.com* 🍷 *Tastings $15–$25, tour $25* ⊙ *Daily 10–4:30; tour daily at 10:30 by appointment.*

WORTH NOTING

Napa Valley Wine Train. Leave driving to someone else—a train engineer. The Napa Valley Wine Train runs a scenic route between Napa and St. Helena with several restored 1915–17 Pullman railroad cars. The ride often includes a meal, such as brunch or dinner. Although it's no bargain and can feel a bit hokey, the train gives you a chance to enjoy the vineyard views without any driving worries. ⊠ *1275 McKinstry St., off 1st St.* ☎ *707/253–2111, 800/427–4124* ⊕ *www.winetrain.com* 🍷 *Lunch and dinner $114* ⊙ *Lunch: Mar.–Nov., daily 11:30; Dec.–Feb., Fri.–Sun. 11:30. Dinner: Jan.–Mar., Sat. 6:30; Apr., Nov., and Dec., Fri. and Sat. 6:30; May, Fri.–Sun. 6:30; June–Sept., Thurs. and Fri. 6:30; Oct., Thurs.–Sun. 6:30.*

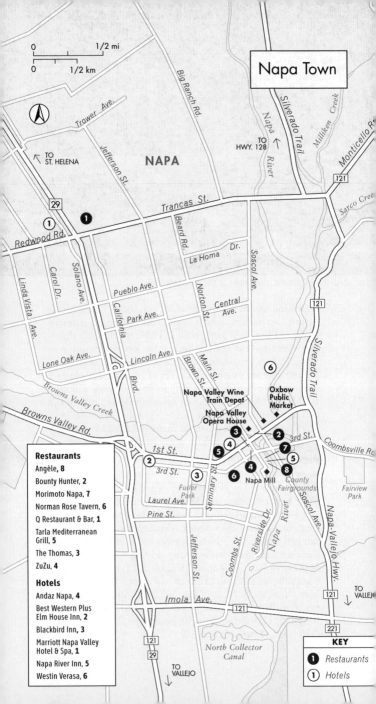

Napa Town

Scale
0 — 1/2 mi
0 — 1/2 km

TO
ST. HELENA →

Trower Ave.

Big Ranch Rd.

Jefferson St.

Silverado Trail

Milliken Creek

Napa River

NAPA

TO
HWY. 128 ↑

Monticello Rd.

121

Sarco Creek

Trancas St.

Beard Rd.

29

① Redwood Rd.

❶

La Homa Dr.

Solano Ave.

Carol Dr.

Pueblo Ave.

California

Park Ave.

Norton St.

Soscol Ave.

Central Ave.

121

Linda Vista Ave.

Lone Oak Ave.

Lincoln Ave.

Blvd.

Browns Valley Creek

Main St.

Brown St.

Napa Valley Wine Train Depot

Napa Valley Opera House

Oxbow Public Market

❻

Silverado Trail

Browns Valley Rd.

1st St.

❸

❹

❺

② ②

3rd St.

③

Fuller Park

Laurel Ave.

Pine St.

Seminary St.

❻

❷

❼

❺

❽

③rd St.

Coombsville Rd.

Napa Mill

County Fairgrounds

Fairview Park

Soscol Ave.

Napa-Vallejo Hwy.

Restaurants
Angèle, **8**
Bounty Hunter, **2**
Morimoto Napa, **7**
Norman Rose Tavern, **6**
Q Restaurant & Bar, **1**
Tarla Mediterranean Grill, **5**
The Thomas, **3**
ZuZu, **4**

Hotels
Andaz Napa, **4**
Best Western Plus Elm House Inn, **2**
Blackbird Inn, **3**
Marriott Napa Valley Hotel & Spa, **1**
Napa River Inn, **5**
Westin Verasa, **6**

Jefferson St.

Coombs St.

Riverside Dr.

Napa River

Imola Ave.

121

121

221

29

TO
VALLEJO ↓

North Collector Canal

TO
VALLEJO

TO
VALLEJO

KEY	
❶	Restaurants
①	Hotels

Sodaro Estate Winery. Upscale-yet-modest Sodaro is a great introduction to the Coombsville AVA. Tours start on a crush pad with a view of rolling vineyards, then head inside the wine cave for a seated tasting of the signature wines: a Cabernet Sauvignon and a Bordeaux-style blend. You might also taste a special limited release, perhaps a Malbec. All wines are paired with local cheeses and breadsticks. The tour concludes with a walk through the wine cave itself. It's no surprise that the vibe here is so luxurious: owners Don and Deedee Sodaro also own several area hotels. ✉ *24 Blue Oak La., east of Silverado Trail (take Hagen Rd. east to 3rd Ave. south)* ☎ *707/251–8216* 🌐 *www.sodarowines.com* 🎟 *Tour and tasting $30* 🕒 *By appointment only.*

WHERE TO EAT

$$$ 🍴 **Angèle.** *French.* An 1890s boathouse with a vaulted wood-beam ceiling sets the scene for romance at this cozy French bistro. Though the style is casual—tables are close together, and warm, crusty bread is plunked down on paper-top tables—the food is always well executed. Look for classic French dishes like rabbit confit salad or braised lamb shank in Jura wine. Banana gratin (ask for the salty caramel ice cream instead of vanilla) stands out among several super homemade desserts. In fair weather, dine at one of the charming outdoor tables. [$] *Average main: $28* ✉ *540 Main St., at 5th St.* ☎ *707/252–8115* 🌐 *www.angelerestaurant.com.*

$$$ FAMILY 🍴 **Bistro Don Giovanni.** *Italian.* Co-owner Giovanni Scala might be around to warmly welcome you to this lively bistro, where you can peek past the copper pots hanging in the open kitchen to see the 750-degree wood-burning oven. The Cal-Italian food is simultaneously inventive and comforting: an excellent fritto misto usually composed of onions, fennel, calamari, and plump rock shrimp; pizza with wild mushrooms, roasted garlic, and smoked mozzarella; and whole roasted fish. Children are welcome here, catered to with paper-topped tables and crayons and such tempting offerings as pizza topped with cheese, french fries, and "no green stuff." Fodors.com users suggest angling for a table on the covered patio for a "more intimate and quiet" experience. [$] *Average main: $27* ✉ *4110 Howard La., off Hwy. 29* ☎ *707/224–3300* 🌐 *www.bistrodongiovanni.com.*

★ Fodor'sChoice $$$ 🍴 **Bounty Hunter.** *American.* A triple threat, Bounty Hunter is a wine store, wine bar, and restaurant in one. You can stop by for just a glass—about 40 choices are available in both 2- and 5-ounce pours—or a bottle,

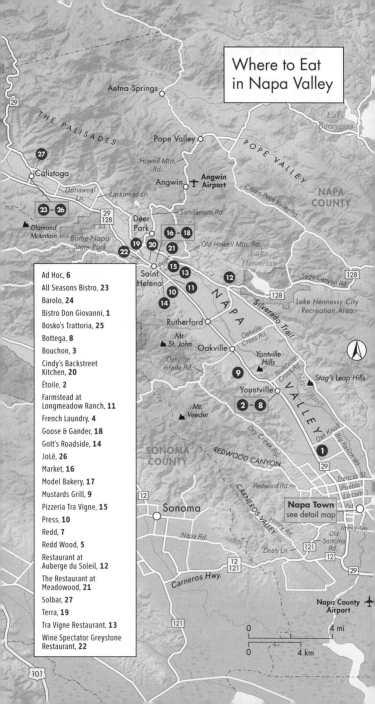

Where to Eat in Napa Valley

Ad Hoc, **6**
All Seasons Bistro, **23**
Barolo, **24**
Bistro Don Giovanni, **1**
Bosko's Trattoria, **25**
Bottega, **8**
Bouchon, **3**
Cindy's Backstreet Kitchen, **20**
Étoile, **2**
Farmstead at Longmeadow Ranch, **11**
French Laundry, **4**
Goose & Gander, **18**
Gott's Roadside, **14**
Jolē, **26**
Market, **16**
Model Bakery, **17**
Mustards Grill, **9**
Pizzeria Tra Vigne, **15**
Press, **10**
Redd, **7**
Redd Wood, **5**
Restaurant at Auberge du Soleil, **12**
The Restaurant at Meadowood, **21**
Solbar, **27**
Terra, **19**
Tra Vigne Restaurant, **13**
Wine Spectator Greystone Restaurant, **22**

but it's best to come with an appetite. A minuscule kitchen means the menu is also small, but every dish is a standout, including the pulled-pork and beef brisket sandwiches served with three types of barbecue sauce, the signature beer-can chicken, and meltingly tender St. Louis–style ribs. The space is whimsically rustic, with stuffed game trophies mounted on the wall and leather saddles standing in for seats at a couple of tables. ■TIP→ The restaurant remains open until midnight on Friday and Saturday, making it popular for late-night bites. [$] *Average main: $24* ✉ *975 1st St., at Main St.* ☎ *707/226–3976* 🌐 *www.bountyhunterwinebar.com* ✍ *Reservations not accepted.*

$$$$ 🍴 **Morimoto Napa.** *Japanese. Iron Chef* star Masuharu Morimoto, owner of eponymous restaurants around the world, is the big name behind this hot spot in downtown Napa. Organic materials like twisting grapevines above the bar and rough-hewn wooden tables seem simultaneously earthy and modern, which seems a fitting setting for the gorgeously plated Japanese fare, from super-fresh sashimi served with grated fresh wasabi to elaborate concoctions like sea-urchin carbonara, made with udon noodles. For the full experience, consider leaving the choice up to the chef with the *omakase* menu ($120 and up). If no tables are available, you can order many dishes in the lounge, where a young and lively crowd drinks specialty cocktails along with quirky fare like the pork skins, peanut butter, and wasabi-powder appetizer. [$] *Average main: $44* ✉ *610 Main St., at 5th St.* ☎ *707/252–1600* 🌐 *www.morimotonapa.com.*

$$ 🍴 **Norman Rose Tavern.** *American.* If downtown Napa had its own version of the bar in *Cheers*, it would be the Norman Rose Tavern. Casual and family-friendly, "The Rose" serves such classic American fare as hamburgers, sandwiches, and fish-and-chips, and proudly pours local wines and regional beers until 9 or 10 pm. Happy hour, held weekdays from 3 to 6 pm, is particularly rollicking, with specials on hot wings (by the pound) and sliders. On warm days, arrive early for a spot on the open-air patio. [$] *Average main: $17* ✉ *1401 1st St., at Franklin St.* ☎ *707/258–1516* 🌐 *www.normanrosenapa.com.*

$$ 🍴 **The Q Restaurant & Bar.** *Southern.* Hardly a ramshackle barbecue shack, this spot inside a local shopping center has a clean, modern aesthetic, with black-and-white photos on the wall and brushed-aluminum chairs. Chef Randy Lewis has revitalized the menu while retaining such favorites as the half or full rack of cherrywood-smoked baby back ribs and the beef brisket. The fried-chicken sandwich, made

with supremely juicy free-range chicken, is also popular. If you can save any room, the root-beer float or the chocolate bourbon pecan pie is a fitting end to a homey meal. [$] *Average main: $18* ✉ *3900D Bel Aire Plaza, off Trancas St.* ☎ *707/224–6600* 🌐 *www.barbersq.com.*

★ $$ Fodor's Choice ✕ **Tarla Mediterranean Grill.** *Mediterranean.* Celebrating his Greek roots, hip chef Michael Benjamin Powell challenges the Napa Valley's notoriously Italo-centric diners to venture deeper into the Mediterranean. You might be tempted to build a meal by combining such traditional mezes (tapas) as stuffed grape leaves with fresh *tzatziki* (a thick yogurt sauce with cucumber, dill, and mint) and spanakopita (phyllo dough stuffed with spinach and feta cheese) with contemporary ones like the roasted bone marrow paired with a lemon-zesty gremolata sauce and served on grilled ciabatta bread. With his entrées, Powell proves himself equally comfortable updating moussaka and other Greek and Turkish standbys or going fancifully modern, as he does with beef short ribs, braising them with a pomegranate-wine sauce and accompanying them with pumpkin-sage risotto, pickled sweet peppers, and fried shallot petals. Locals have really bonded with this place. [$] *Average main: $17* ✉ *1480 1st St., at School St.* ☎ *707/255–5599* 🌐 *www.tarlagrill.com* ✍ *Reservations essential.*

$$$ ✕ **The Thomas.** *Modern American.* Chef Brad Farmerie, formerly at New York's famed Public, tickles the palates of locals, visitors, and his peers with earthy-yet-lofty preparations—served inside an iconic downtown building that was closed for decades, shrouded in murder and mystery. There's no mystery to Farmerie's winning approach, though. Appetizers like chicken-fried sweetbreads with yam waffles and Asian pear salad with Point Reyes blue cheese contain subtle surprises, setting up diners for the in-your-face delights of such main dishes as roasted saddle of monkfish with chorizo, clams, eggplant, and tomato-caper stew; Moroccan braised lamb shank with cheesy grits; and a killer burger made of Angus and Kobe beef and served with bacon-onion jam. The on-site Fagiani's Bar at the Thomas serves mod cocktails to a youngish crowd. ■ **TIP→** In good weather head up to the rooftop deck for its perfect views. [$] *Average main: $26* ✉ *813 Main St., at 3rd St.* ☎ *707/226–7821* 🌐 *www.thethomas-napa.com* ⊗ *No lunch weekdays.*

★ $$$ Fodor's Choice ✕ **ZuZu.** *Spanish.* A recent seismic retrofitting changed the look of ZuZu but not the festive vibe or the sharp focus on Spanish favorites like tapas and paella. Diners down *cava* (Spanish sparkling wine) or sangria with such dishes as white anchovies with boiled egg and remoulade on grilled bread. Locals revere the paella, made with Spanish Bomba rice. Latin jazz on the stereo helps make this place a popular spot for get-togethers. ■TIP→ Reservations aren't accepted, so expect a wait on weekends, when local young adults flood the zone. [$] *Average main: $29* ✉ *829 Main St., near 3rd St.* ☎ *707/224–8555* 🌐 *www.zuzunapa.com* ✍ *Reservations not accepted* ⊗ *No lunch weekends.*

3

WHERE TO STAY

★ Fodor'sChoice 🏨 **Andaz Napa.** *Hotel.* Hands down, this bou-
$ tique hotel is the hippest place to stay in Napa; the rooms, most of them suites, are modern, but welcomingly so. **Pros:** proximity to downtown restaurants, theaters, and tasting rooms; modern fitness center. **Cons:** parking can be a challenge on weekends; though generally good, service can be inconsistent. [$] *Rooms from: $169* ✉ *1450 1st St.* ☎ *707/224–3900* 🌐 *www.napa.andaz.hyatt.com* 🛏 *50 rooms, 91 suites.*

★ Fodor'sChoice 🏨 **Best Western Plus Elm House Inn.** *Hotel.* In a
$ region known for over-the-top architecture and amenities and prices to match, this inn delivers style and even a touch of grace at remarkably affordable prices. **Pros:** smart, gracious service; generous continental breakfasts; complimentary freshly baked cookies in lobby. **Cons:** hot tub but no pool; not walking distance to downtown; some road noise in streetside rooms. [$] *Rooms from: $185* ✉ *800 California Blvd.* ☎ *855/799–6858, 707/255–1831* 🌐 *www.bestwestern.com* 🛏 *22 rooms* 🍴 *Breakfast.*

$$ 🏨 **Blackbird Inn.** *B&B/Inn.* Arts and Crafts style infuses this home from the turn of the last century, from the lobby's enormous fieldstone fireplace to the lamps that cast a warm glow over the impressive wooden staircase. **Pros:** gorgeous architecture and period furnishings; convenient to downtown Napa; free afternoon wine service. **Cons:** must be booked well in advance; some rooms are on the small side. [$] *Rooms from: $225* ✉ *1755 1st St.* ☎ *707/226–2450, 888/567–9811* 🌐 *www.blackbirdinnnapa.com* 🛏 *8 rooms.*

$$ 🏨 **Marriott Napa Valley Hotel & Spa.** *Hotel.* Ignore the Marriott's drab front—the outside doesn't do justice to the polished elegance that awaits within: Italian tile in the foyer, fire pits on the patio, and luxurious spa treatments like the truly sweet honey body wrap with essential oils. **Pros:** food grown on-site; relaxing pool; extensive spa. **Cons:** rooms facing the parking lot have disappointing views;

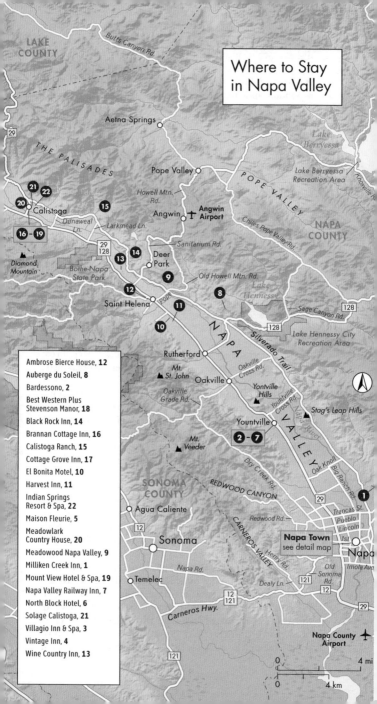

Where to Stay in Napa Valley

LAKE COUNTY

Butts Canyon Rd.

THE PALISADES

Aetna Springs

Pope Valley

POPE VALLEY

Lake Berryessa

Lake Berryessa Recreation Area

NAPA COUNTY

Howell Mtn. Rd.

Angwin

Angwin Airport

Chiles Pope Valley Rd.

21 22

20 Calistoga

15

16 – 19

Dunaweal Ln. Larkmead Ln.

Diamond Mountain

29 128

13 14

Deer Park

9

Old Howell Mtn. Rd.

8

Lake Hennessy

Sage Canyon Rd.

128

Bothe-Napa State Park

12

Saint Helena

11

10

Pope

NAPA

128

Silverado Trail

Lake Hennessy City Recreation Area

Rutherford

Mt. St. John

Oakville

Oakville Cross Rd.

Yontville Hills

Stag's Leap Hills

Oakville Grade Rd.

Mt. Veeder

Yontville

2 – 7

Yontville Cross Rd.

Napa River

Oak Knoll

Big Ranch Rd.

SONOMA COUNTY

Agua Caliente

REDWOOD CANYON

Dry Creek Rd.

12

29

1

Trancas St.

Pueblo

Lincoln

1st

Sonoma

Napa Town
see detail map

Napa

Redwood Rd.

CARNEROS VALLEY

Henry Rd.

Napa Rd.

Temelec

Dealy Ln.

Old Sonoma Rd.

Imola Ave.

12

121

Carneros Hwy.

12 121

121

Napa County Airport

0   4 mi
0   4 km

Ambrose Bierce House, **12**

Auberge du Soleil, **8**

Bardessono, **2**

Best Western Plus Stevenson Manor, **18**

Black Rock Inn, **14**

Brannan Cottage Inn, **16**

Calistoga Ranch, **15**

Cottage Grove Inn, **17**

El Bonita Motel, **10**

Harvest Inn, **11**

Indian Springs Resort & Spa, **22**

Maison Fleurie, **5**

Meadowlark Country House, **20**

Meadowood Napa Valley, **9**

Milliken Creek Inn, **1**

Mount View Hotel & Spa, **19**

Napa Valley Railway Inn, **7**

North Block Hotel, **6**

Solage Calistoga, **21**

Villagio Inn & Spa, **3**

Vintage Inn, **4**

Wine Country Inn, **13**

hallways are endless; a 10-minute drive to downtown Napa. [$] *Rooms from: $219* ✉ *3425 Solano Ave.* ☎ *707/253–8600* 🌐 *www.napavalleymarriott.com* ⇨ *275 rooms, 5 suites.*

$$$ 🏨 **Milliken Creek Inn.** *B&B/Inn.* Wine-and-cheese receptions at sunset set a romantic mood in this hotel's intimate lobby, with its terrace overlooking a lush lawn and the Napa River. **Pros:** soft-as-clouds beds; serene spa; breakfast delivered to your room (or wherever you'd like to eat on the grounds). **Cons:** expensive; road noise can be heard from the admittedly beautiful outdoor areas. [$] *Rooms from: $379* ✉ *1815 Silverado Trail* ☎ *707/255–1197, 800/835–6112* 🌐 *www.millikencreekinn.com* ⇨ *12 rooms.*

$$ 🏨 **Napa River Inn.** *B&B/Inn.* Almost everything's close here: this waterfront inn is part of a complex of restaurants, shops, a nightclub, and a spa, all within easy walking distance of downtown Napa. **Pros:** a pedestrian walkway connects the hotel to downtown Napa; unusual pet-friendly policy; wide range of room sizes and prices. **Cons:** river views could be more scenic; some rooms get noise from nearby restaurants. [$] *Rooms from: $248* ✉ *500 Main St.* ☎ *707/251–8500, 877/251–8500* 🌐 *www.napariverinn.com* ⇨ *65 rooms, 1 suite.*

$$$ 🏨 **Westin Verasa Napa.** *Hotel.* Across the street from the Napa Valley Wine Train depot and adjacent to the Oxbow Public Market, this spacious resort is sophisticated and soothing, with pristine white bedding, and furniture in warm earth tones. **Pros:** pool is heated year-round; most rooms have well-equipped kitchenettes; spacious double-headed showers. **Cons:** "amenities fee" added to room rate. [$] *Rooms from: $350* ✉ *1314 McKinstry St.* ☎ *707/257–1800, 800/937–8461* 🌐 *www.westinnapa.com* ⇨ *160 suites, 20 rooms.*

3

NIGHTLIFE AND THE ARTS

The bars at popular restaurants and hotels constitute much of the nightlife action in Napa, but because of its size the city does attract big-name performers to a few venues downtown. The wine bars draw a younger and sportier crowd than elsewhere in the Napa Valley.

NIGHTLIFE

1313 Main. This sexy lounge increased Napa's cool exponentially, at least among the youngish set that has flocked here since day one. They drink in the hip vibe along with flights of fancy, well-selected sparkling and still wines. The bar menu includes cheeses, charcuterie, breads, and sweets. ✉ *1313 Main St., at Clinton St.* ☎ *707/258–1313* 🌐 *www.1313main.com.*

Hot-air balloon rides typically take off at the crack of dawn.

Carpe Diem Wine Bar. A convivial mood prevails at this sophisticated spot specializing in wines by small producers from California and beyond. It's also a great spot for a light meal—the harissa-spiced fries are ever so addictive. ✉ *1001 2nd St., at Brown St.* ☎ *707/224–0800* ⊕ *www.carpediemwinebar.com.*

Silo's. At this club inside the Historic Napa Mill, locals sip wine and listen to excellent live music—mostly jazz, but also rock, blues, and other styles. The cover varies, but it's generally $10 to $25. ✉ *530 Main St., near 5th St.* ☎ *707/251–5833* ⊕ *www.silosjazzclub.com.*

THE ARTS
Napa Valley Opera House. The interior of the Italianate Victorian Napa Valley Opera House, which opened its doors in 1880, isn't quite as majestic as the facade, but the intimate 500-seat venue is still an excellent place to see all sorts of performances, from comedian Paul Reiser to the Vienna Boys Choir to the Napa Valley Film Festival. There's even the occasional opera. ✉ *1030 Main St., at 1st St.* ☎ *707/226–7372* ⊕ *www.nvoh.org.*

Uptown Theatre. Dating from 1937, this Napa icon opened as a movie house and now serves as a top-notch live-music venue that attracts performers like Bootsy Collins, Clint Black, and Los Lobos. ✉ *1350 3rd St., at Franklin St.* ☎ *707/259–0123* ⊕ *www.uptowntheatrenapa.com.*

Wine Country Balloon Rides

CLOSE UP

Thought those vineyards were beautiful from the highway? Try viewing them from an altitude of about a thousand feet, serenely drifting along with the wind, the only sound the occasional roar of the burners overhead.

Many companies organize hot-air-ballooning trips over Napa and Sonoma, offering rides that usually cost between $200 and $250 per person for a one-hour flight, which typically includes brunch or lunch afterward. If you were hoping for the ulti-

mate in romance—a flight with no one else but your sweetie (and an FAA-approved pilot) on board—be prepared to shell out two to four times as much.

Flights typically take off at the crack of dawn, when winds are the lightest, so be prepared to make an early start and dress in layers. Flights are dependent on weather, and if there's rain or too much fog, expect to be grounded. Hotels can hook you up with nearby companies, some of which will pick you up at your lodgings.

3

SPORTS AND THE OUTDOORS

BALLOONING

Balloons Above the Valley. Few experiences in the world are more exhilarating—and yet marvelously serene—than an early-morning balloon ride above the vineyards. This company's personable and professional pilots make its outings among the valley's best. Flights depart from the Napa Valley Marriott, in the city of Napa. ☎707/253–2222, 800/464–6824 ⊕ www.balloonrides.com ☒$209.

KAYAKING

Napa Valley Adventure Tours. This outfitter offers several half- and full-day outdoor trips, including kayaking along the Napa River. You can also rent bikes and book bike tours here. ✉1147 1st St., at Coombs St. ☎707/224–9080, 707/259–1833 ⊕ www.napavalleyadventuretours.com.

SHOPPING

Napa's most interesting shops and boutiques can be found downtown west of the Napa River, along Pearl and 1st through 5th streets between Main and about Franklin streets. East of the river at the Oxbow Public Market (⇨ *Exploring*), you'll also find stands worth visiting.

Bounty Hunter Rare Wine & Provisions. Near the Napa Valley Opera House, Bounty Hunter stocks Napa cult Cabernets and other hard-to-find wines. The store shares space with a charming wine bar with exposed-brick walls and a stamped-tin ceiling. ⊠ *975 1st St., near Main St.* ☎ *707/255–0622* ⊕ *www.bountyhunterwine.com.*

Napa Premium Outlets. Even travelers zipping through Napa sometimes yield to temptation and take a detour to this mall where such national chains as Kenneth Cole, J. Crew, Barneys New York, and Coach sell their wares at discounted prices. ⊠ *629 Factory Stores Dr., off Hwy. 29 at 1st St. exit* ☎ *707/226–9876* ⊕ *www.premiumoutlets.com/napa.*

Shackford's Kitchen Store. The gracious Mr. Shackford's shop looks more like a hardware store than the low-key celebration of the art of cooking that it is, but if you need it—kitchenware, accessories, hard-to-find replacement items—he's probably got it. ⊠ *1350 Main St., at Caymus St.* ☎ *707/226–2132.*

YOUNTVILLE

9 miles north of downtown Napa; 9 miles south of St. Helena.

★ **Fodor's**Choice These days Yountville is something like Disneyland for food lovers. It all started with Thomas Keller's French Laundry, one of the best restaurants in the United States. Now Keller is also behind two more casual restaurants a few blocks from his mother ship—and that's only the tip of the iceberg. You could stay here for a week and not exhaust all the options in this tiny town with a big culinary reputation.

Yountville is full of small inns and luxurious hotels catering to those who prefer to be able to stagger a short distance home after a decadent dinner. But it's also well located for excursions to big-name Napa wineries. Near Yountville, along the Silverado Trail, the Stags Leap District helped put Napa on the wine-making map with its big, bold Cabernet Sauvignons. Volcanic soil predominates on the eastern slopes of Stags Leap, apparent from the towering volcanic palisades and crags hovering over the vineyards.

On the other side of Highway 29 rises the Mayacamas Range. Unlike on the valley floor, where wineries stand cheek-by-jowl along Highway 29 and the Silverado Trail, the vineyards here are fewer and farther between, hidden among stands of oaks, madrones, and redwoods. Even though the Mt. Veeder AVA gets more rain than the Napa Valley (as witnessed by those redwoods), the soils are poor and rocky and the water runs off quickly, forcing grapevines to grow deep roots. Vines thus stressed produce grapes that are smaller, with a higher ratio of grape surface to liquid volume, resulting in intensely flavored wines. This comes at a price: the vines on the steep slopes of the 2,677-foot volcanic peak of Mt. Veeder must be laboriously picked by hand. Merlot and Syrah thrive in these conditions, but the big winner is Cabernet.

Though many visitors use Yountville as a home base, touring wineries by day and returning to town for dinner, you could easily while away a few hours in town, picking up picnic fixings at a bakery or deli.

WORD OF MOUTH. "We stayed in Yountville, which I would highly recommend; good location, fabulous restaurants (think Michelin stars), and easy access to the wine trails."—jbass

GETTING HERE AND AROUND

If you're traveling north on Highway 29, take the Yountville exit, stay east of the highway, and take the first left onto Washington Street. Traveling south on Highway 29, turn left onto Madison Street and right onto Washington Street. Nearly all of Yountville's businesses and restaurants are clustered along a half-mile stretch of Washington Street. Yountville Cross Road connects downtown Yountville to the Silverado Trail, where you'll find many of the area's best wineries. A note about addresses: the city of Napa surrounds Yountville, so many places north of Yountville, and closely associated with the town, are in fact in Napa.

EXPLORING

TOP ATTRACTIONS

Domaine Chandon. On a knoll shaded by ancient oak trees, this French-owned winery west of downtown claims one of Yountville's prime pieces of real estate. Basic tours of the sleek, modern facilities ($15) don't include a tasting, but other tours ($36–$42) focusing on topics ranging from food-and-wine pairing to sparkling-wine production end with a seated tasting. The top-quality sparklers are made using the laborious *méthode champenoise*. For the complete experience, order hors d'oeuvres to accompany the wines in the tasting room. Although Chandon is best known for its bub-

Domaine Chandon claims a prime piece of real estate.

blies, the Cabernet Sauvignon, Chardonnay, Pinot Noir, and Pinot Meunier still wines are also worth a try. The tasting lounge is restricted to those 21 years or older, but guests with children are welcome on the outdoor terrace. ⊠ *1 California Dr., at Solano Ave., west of Hwy. 29* ☎ *707/204–7530, 888/242–6366* ⊕ *www.chandon.com* ☑ *Tastings $18–$25* ☉ *Daily 10–5; tours daily at 10:30, 1, and 3.*

★ **Fodor's Choice Ma(i)sonry Napa Valley.** An art-and-design gallery that also pours the wines of 19 limited-production wineries, Ma(i)sonry occupies an atmospheric stone manor house constructed in 1904. Tasting flights can be sampled in fair weather in the beautiful garden, in a private nook, or at the communal redwood table, and in any weather indoors among the contemporary artworks and some well-chosen *objets*—which might include 17th-century furnishings, industrial lamps, or slabs of petrified wood. ■TIP→ Walk-ins are welcome if space permits, but during summer, at harvest-time, and on weekends and holidays it's best to book in advance. ⊠ *6711 Washington St., at Pedroni St.* ☎ *707/944–0889* ⊕ *www.maisonry.com* ☑ *Tastings $10–$35* ☉ *Mid-Nov.– May, daily 10–7; June–mid-Nov., Sun.–Thurs. 10–7 and Fri. and Sat. 10–9.*

★ **Fodor's Choice Robert Sinskey Vineyards.** Although the winery produces a well-regarded Stags Leap Cabernet Sauvignon, two supple red blends called Marcien and POV, and white wines, it's best known for intense, brambly Pinot Noirs

A Great Southern Napa Drive

Traffic permitting, you could easily traverse the entire Napa Valley in about 45 minutes, passing scores of wineries along Highway 29. Many visitors do this, but a better strategy would be to tour just the southern Napa Valley at a more leisurely pace.

Have coffee at the Model Bakery in Napa's **Oxbow Public Market,** then drive north on Highway 29 to the Trancas Street/Redwood Road exit. At the top of the exit ramp, turn west (left) onto Trancas Street. After you cross over Highway 29, the name of the road changes to Redwood. Follow Redwood Road west, bearing left at the fork that appears when the road narrows from four lanes to two. After this point, two signs on Redwood Road will direct you to **The Hess Collection.** Allow an hour or so to browse the excellent modern art collection before or after tasting the wines.

After your visit, backtrack on Redwood Road about 1¼ miles to Mt. Veeder Road and turn left. After a little more than 8 miles, turn right (east) onto Dry Creek Road. After ½ mile the road becomes signed as the Oakville Grade. From here, twist your way back downhill to Highway 29 and turn north. (If you're prone to car sickness, take Redwood Road all the

way back to Highway 29 and turn north.) On Highway 29 a bit north of the Oakville Grade you'll see the driveway to **Robert Mondavi** on your left. The introductory tour here is good for wine newbies. If sporty and casual suits you better, sit and sip at nearby **PlumpJack** instead.

After visiting Mondavi or PlumpJack, repair to the **Oakville Grocery** and put together a picnic you can enjoy right out back. For a serious, no-frills wine-tasting experience, head to **Stag's Leap Wine Cellars** to taste the descendants of the 1973 Cabernet Sauvignon that scored so well in the famous Paris tasting of 1976. Or head over to **Trefethen,** whose first-place Chardonnay at a 1979 tasting in the City of Light also helped secure the Napa Valley's reputation.

Your trip down memory lane complete, head to **Yountville,** where bakeries and boutiques tempt body and bank account. Stroll Washington Street and enjoy the scenery and the parade of well-heeled visitors. If you find yourself yearning for more tasting, slip into **Ma(i)sonry Napa Valley** to sample wines from small-lot producers. As evening approaches, remain in Yountville for dinner or return to Napa.

grown in the cooler Carneros District. All the grapes are grown in organic, certified biodynamic vineyards. The influence of Robert's wife, Maria Helm Sinskey—a chef and cookbook author and the winery's culinary director— is evident during the tastings, accompanied by a few bites of food with each wine. Reserve a spot on the culinary tour ($75), which takes you through the winery's gardens and ends with a seated pairing of food and wine. ⊠ *6320 Silverado Trail, at Yountville Cross Rd., Napa* ☎ *707/944– 9090* ⊕ *www.robertsinskey.com* ☜ *Tasting $25, tour $75* ☉ *Daily 10–4:30; tours daily at 11 by appointment.*

Stag's Leap Wine Cellars. The 1973 Cabernet Sauvignon produced here put the winery—and the Napa Valley—on the map by placing first in the famous Paris tasting of 1976. Today, a visit to the winery is a no-frills affair. Visitors in the tasting room are clearly serious about tasting wine, and aren't interested in distractions like a gift shop. It costs $30 to taste the top-of-the-line wines, including the limited-production estate-grown Cabernets, a few of which sell for well over $100. If you're interested in more-modestly priced wines, try the $15 tasting, which usually includes a Sauvignon Blanc, Chardonnay, Merlot, and Cabernet. (Note: Don't confuse this winery with Stags' Leap Winery; that's a different operation entirely.) ⊠ *5766 Silverado Trail, at Wappo Hill Rd., Napa* ☎ *707/944–2020, 866/422–7523* ⊕ *www.cask23.com* ☜ *Tastings $15–$30, tour $40* ☉ *Daily 10–4:30; tours by appointment.*

V Marketplace. This vine-covered market, which once housed a winery, a livery stable, and a brandy distillery, contains a smattering of clothing boutiques, art galleries, and gift stores. NapaStyle, a large deli and wine bar, sells cookbooks, luxury food items, and kitchenware, as well as an assortment of prepared foods perfect for picnics. The complex's signature restaurant, Bottega, features the food of celebrity chef Michael Chiarello. ⊠ *6525 Washington St., near Mulberry St.* ☎ *707/944–2451* ⊕ *www.vmarketplace.com.*

QUICK BITES. ★ Fodor's Choice **Bouchon Bakery.** To satisfy that craving you didn't know you had—but soon will—for macarons (meringue cookies), stock up on hazelnut, pistachio, chocolate-dipped raspberry, and several other flavors at this bakery associated with the restaurant of the same name. The brownies, pastries, and other baked goods are equally alluring. ⊠ *6528 Washington St., at Yount St.* ☎ *707/944–2253* ⊕ *www.bouchonbakery.com.*

WORTH NOTING

Chimney Rock Winery. This winery is easily spotted from the road—unless the poplar trees surrounding it are in full leaf, hiding it from view. In the somewhat ornate Cape (as in Cape of Good Hope) Dutch style of the 17th century, it seems out of place amid the austere Stags Leap landscape. Most of the grapes grown at this winery owned by the Terlato family go into a Cabernet Sauvignon that's softer and more supple than most of its local counterparts. There are also a fine Sauvignon Gris wine (the grape is a clone of Sauvignon Blanc) and a dry Rosé of Cabernet Franc. The comfortable tasting room's decor mirrors the exterior, with high, wood-beamed ceilings and a fireplace that warms things up in winter. Tours are by appointment, but walk-ins are welcome as space permits. ⊠ *5350 Silverado Trail, at Capps Dr., Napa* ☎ *707/257–2641* ⊕ *www.chimneyrock. com* ⊠ *Tastings $20–$30, tours $50–$90* ☉ *Daily 10–5; tour by appointment.*

Clos du Val. A Napa Valley mainstay since the early 1970s, this austere winery doesn't seduce you with dramatic architecture or lush grounds. It doesn't have to: the wines, crafted by winemaker John Clews, have a wide following, especially among those who are patient enough to cellar them for a few years. Clews and his team make great Pinot Noir and Chardonnay wines from grapes grown in the nearby Carneros region, but Clos du Val's real claim to fame is its intense reserve Cabernet Sauvignon, made with fruit from the Stags Leap District. The few picnic tables, in a peaceful olive grove, fill up early on summer weekends, and anyone is welcome to try a hand at the boccie-style French game of pétanque. ⊠ *5330 Silverado Trail, just south of Capps Dr., Napa* ☎ *707/261–5251, 800/993–9463* ⊕ *www. closduval.com* ⊠ *Tasting $15–$30, tour $30* ☉ *Daily 10–5; tour 10:30 and 2:30 by appointment.*

Napa Valley Museum. For a brief but informative respite from wine tasting, drop by this small museum next to Domaine Chandon. A permanent exhibit documents Native American life, the pioneer period, and the modern wine-making era, and temporary exhibits showcase the works of artists from the Napa Valley and beyond. ⊠ *55 Presidents Circle, at California Dr., off Hwy. 29* ☎ *707/944–0500* ⊕ *www. napavalleymuseum.org* ⊠ *$5* ☉ *Tues.–Sun. 10–4.*

WHERE TO EAT

★ Fodor'sChoice 🍴 **Ad Hoc.** *Modern American.* When superstar
$$$$ chef Thomas Keller first opened this relatively casual spot, he meant to run it for six months until he launched a burger joint in the same space, but locals were so charmed by the homey food that they clamored for the stopgap to stay. Now a single, seasonal, fixed-price menu ($52) is offered nightly, with a small menu of decadent brunch items served on Sunday. The selection might include a juicy pork loin and buttery polenta, served family style, or a delicate *panna cotta* with a citrus glaze. The dining room is warmly low-key, with zinc-top tables, wine served in tumblers, and rock and jazz on the stereo. If you can't wait to know what's going be served before you visit, call a day in advance for the menu. [$] *Average main: $52* ✉ *6476 Washington St., at Oak Circle* ☎ *707/944–2487* 🌐 *www.adhocrestaurant.com* 🕒 *No lunch Mon.–Sat. No dinner Tues. and Wed.*

$$$$ 🍴 **Bottega.** *Italian.* The food at this lively trattoria is simultaneously soulful and inventive, transforming local ingredients into regional Italian dishes with a twist. The antipasti shine: you can order olives grown on chef Michael Chiarello's own property in St. Helena, house-made charcuterie, or incredibly fresh fish. Potato gnocchi might be served with pumpkin *fonduta* (Italian-style fondue) and roasted root vegetables, and hearty main courses like twice-cooked pork chops with peck seasoning might be accompanied by cinnamon stewed plums and crispy black kale. The vibe is more festive than formal, with exposed-brick walls, an open kitchen, and paper-topped tables, but service is spot-on, and the reasonably priced wine list offers lots of interesting choices from both Italy and California. [$] *Average main: $35* ✉ *6525 Washington St., near Mulberry St.* ☎ *707/945–1050* 🌐 *www.botteganapavalley.com* 🕒 *No lunch Mon.*

$$$ 🍴 **Bouchon.** *French.* The team that brought French Laundry to its current pinnacle is also behind this place, where everything—the lively and crowded zinc-topped bar, the elbow-to-elbow seating, the traditional French onion soup—could have come straight from a Parisian bistro. Roast chicken with mustard greens and fingerling potatoes and steamed mussels served with crispy, addictive *frites* (french fries) are among the hearty dishes served in the high-ceilinged room. ■ TIP→ A limited menu is served until midnight—a rarity in the Wine Country, where it's often difficult to find a place that's open after 10. [$] *Average main: $27* ✉ *6534 Washington St., near Humboldt St.* ☎ *707/944–8037* 🌐 *www.bouchonbistro.com.*

Ad Hoc, Thomas Keller's casual restaurant in Yountville

★ $$$$ Fodor's Choice 🍴 **Étoile.** *American.* Domaine Chandon's quietly elegant restaurant seems built for romance, with delicate orchids on each table and views of the wooded grounds from the large windows. Chef Perry Hoffman has racked up numerous awards for his sophisticated California cuisine. Such starters as terrine of duck and artichokes or oxtail aspic and sweet white corn play with a variety of textures, and succulent black mission figs might accompany main courses like Liberty Farms duck with Padrón peppers. Four- and six-course tasting menus can be ordered with or without wine pairings. The wine list features Domaine Chandon sparklers, but it's strong in wines from throughout California as well. $ *Average main: $34* ✉ *1 California Dr., at Solano Ave., west of Hwy. 29* ☎ *888/242–6366* 🌐 *www.chandon.com/etoile-restaurant* ⏲ *Closed Tues. and Wed.*

★ $$$$ Fodor's Choice 🍴 **French Laundry.** *American.* An old stone building laced with ivy houses the most acclaimed restaurant in Napa Valley—and, indeed, one of the most highly regarded in the country. The restaurant's two nine-course prix-fixe menus (both $270), one of which highlights vegetables, vary, but "oysters and pearls," a silky dish of pearl tapioca with oysters and white sturgeon caviar, is a signature starter. Some courses rely on luxe ingredients like *calotte* (cap of the rib eye), while others take humble foods like fava beans and elevate them to art. Many courses also offer the option of "supplements," such as sea urchin or black truffles. Reservations at French Laundry are hard-

DID YOU KNOW?

These tomatoes are headed for the kitchen of the French Laundry, one of the Napa Valley's most famous restaurants, where dinner will set you back $270 if you can get a reservation.

won, and not accepted more than two months in advance.
■ TIP➜ Call two months ahead to the day at 10 am, on the dot. Didn't
get a reservation? Call on the day you'd like to dine here to be considered if there's a cancellation. [S]*Average main: $270* ✉ *6640
Washington St., at Creek St.* ☎ *707/944–2380* ⊕ *www.
frenchlaundry.com* ⚑ *Reservations essential. Jacket required*
☉ *No lunch Mon.–Thurs.*

$$$ ✕ **Mustards Grill.** *American.* There's not an ounce of preten-
sion at Cindy Pawlcyn's longtime Napa favorite, despite the
fact that it's filled nearly every day and night with fans of
her hearty cuisine. The menu mixes updated renditions of
traditional American dishes (what the restaurant likes to call
"deluxe truck stop classics"), such as barbecued baby back
pork ribs and a lemon-lime tart piled high with browned
meringue, with a handful of more innovative choices such
as sweet corn tamales with tomatillo-avocado salsa and wild
mushrooms. A black-and-white marble tile floor and upbeat
artwork set a scene that one Fodors.com reader describes
as "pure fun, if not fancy." [S]*Average main: $27* ✉ *7399
St. Helena Hwy./Hwy. 29, 1 mile north of Yountville, Napa*
☎ *707/944–2424* ⊕ *www.mustardsgrill.com.*

★ **Fodor's**Choice ✕ **Redd.** *Modern American.* The minimalist
$$$ dining room seems a fitting setting for chef Richard Red-
dington's up-to-date menu. The culinary influences include
California, Mexico, Europe, and Asia, but the food always
feels modern and never fussy. The glazed pork belly with
apple purée, set amid a pool of soy caramel, is a prime
example of the East-meets-West style. The seafood preparations—among them petrale sole, mussels, and chorizo
poached in a saffron-curry broth—are deft variations on the
original dishes. Desserts like the butterscotch "sundae"—a
scoop of vanilla-rum ice cream served with an airy butterscotch cream and salted butter shortbread—put a novel
twist on the classics. For the full experience, consider the
five-course tasting menu ($80 per person, $125 with wine
pairing). ■ TIP➜ For a quick bite, order small plates and a cocktail
and sit at the bar. [S]*Average main: $29* ✉ *6480 Washington
St., at Oak Circle* ☎ *707/944–2222* ⊕ *www.reddnapavalley.
com* ⚑ *Reservations essential.*

$$ ✕ **Redd Wood.** *Italian.* Not to be confused with his ultrachic
Redd, chef Richard Reddington's more casual restaurant
specializes in thin-crust wood-fired pizzas and contemporary
variations on rustic Italian classics. The cool nonchalance
of the industrial decor mirrors the service (which at its best
provides an antidote to the fussiness found elsewhere) and
the cuisine itself. The glazed beef short ribs, for instance,

seem like yet another fancy take on a down-home favorite until you realize how cleverly the sweetness of the glaze plays off the creamy polenta and the piquant splash of salsa verde. Redd Wood does for Italian comfort food what nearby Mustards Grill does for the American version: it spruces it up but retains its innate pleasures. [$] *Average main: $22* ✉ *North Block Hotel, 6755 Washington St., at Madison St., Yountville* ☎ *707/299–5030* 🌐 *www.redd-wood.com.*

WHERE TO STAY

★ Fodor's Choice 🏨 **Bardessono.** *Resort.* Although Bardessono
$$$$ bills itself as the "greenest luxury hotel in America," there's nothing spartan about its accommodations. **Pros:** large rooftop lap pool; exciting restaurant; polished service. **Cons:** expensive; the view from many rooms is uninspiring. [$] *Rooms from: $500* ✉ *6526 Yount St.* ☎ *707/204–6000* 🌐 *www.bardessono.com* 🛏 *50 rooms, 12 suites* 🍴 *No meals.*

$ 🏨 **Maison Fleurie.** *B&B/Inn.* If you'd like to be within easy walking distance of Yountville's fine restaurants, and possibly score a great bargain, look into this casual, comfortable inn. **Pros:** smallest rooms are some of the most affordable in town; free bike rental; refrigerator stocked with free bottled water and soda. **Cons:** breakfast room can be crowded at peak times; bedding could be nicer. [$] *Rooms from: $175* ✉ *6529 Yount St.* ☎ *707/944–2056, 800/788–0369* 🌐 *www.maisonfleurienapa.com* 🛏 *13 rooms* 🍴 *Breakfast.*

$ 🏨 **Napa Valley Railway Inn.** *Hotel.* Budget-minded travelers and those with kids appreciate these very basic accommodations—inside actual railcars—just steps away from most of Yountville's best restaurants. **Pros:** central location; access to nearby gym. **Cons:** minimal service, since the office is often unstaffed; rooms on the parking-lot side get some noise. [$] *Rooms from: $125* ✉ *6523 Washington St.* ☎ *707/944–2000* 🌐 *www.napavalleyrailwayinn.com* 🛏 *9 rooms* 🍴 *No meals.*

$$$$ 🏨 **North Block Hotel.** *Hotel.* With a rustic-chic Tuscan style, this 20-room hotel has dark-wood furniture and soothing decor in brown and sage. **Pros:** extremely comfortable beds; attentive service; breakfast, included in rates, can be delivered to your room. **Cons:** outdoor areas get some traffic noise. [$] *Rooms from: $425* ✉ *6757 Washington St.* ☎ *707/944–8080* 🌐 *northblockhotel.com* 🛏 *20 rooms* 🍴 *Breakfast.*

★ Fodor's Choice 🏨 **Villagio Inn & Spa.** *Resort.* Quiet, refined luxury
$$$ is the hallmark of this relaxing haven built to resemble a Tuscan village. **Pros:** amazing buffet breakfast; no extra charge

for the spa facilities; steps away from many dining options. **Cons:** can be bustling with large groups; you can hear highway noise from many balconies or patios. [$] *Rooms from: $375* ✉ *6481 Washington St.* ☎ *707/944–8877, 800/351–1133* 🌐 *www.villagio.com* 🛏 *86 rooms, 26 suites* 🍴 *Breakfast.*

$$$ 🏨 **Vintage Inn.** *Resort.* Rooms in this elegant country-style inn are housed in two-story villas scattered around a lush, landscaped 3½-acre property. **Pros:** spacious bathrooms with spa tubs; lavish breakfast buffet; luscious bedding. **Cons:** highway noise is audible in some exterior rooms. [$] *Rooms from: $350* ✉ *6541 Washington St.* ☎ *707/944–1112* 🌐 *www.vintageinn.com* 🛏 *68 rooms, 12 suites* 🍴 *Breakfast.*

SPAS

Spa Villagio. With a Mediterranean style, this 13,000-square-foot spa has all the latest gadgets, including men's and women's outdoor hot tubs and showers with an extravagant number of showerheads. Huge spa suites—complete with flat-panel TV screens and wet bars—are perfect for couples and groups. The pièce de résistance, perhaps for the entire Napa Valley, is the Suite Sensations experience ($575), which combines treatments drawn from Asian, Mediterranean, and Middle-Eastern traditions and includes wine-and-food pairings matched to these cultural influences. The spa also provides the full array of services, including massages, body peels, facials, and manicures. ✉ *6481 Washington St., at Oak Circle* ☎ *707/948–5050, 800/351–1133* 🌐 *www.villagio.com/spavillagio* 🎫 *Treatments $75–$575.*

SPORTS AND THE OUTDOORS

BALLOONING

Napa Valley Aloft. The friendly Kimball family, longtime operators in the Napa Valley, take between 8 and 12 passengers for rides in balloons that launch from downtown Yountville's V Marketplace. Preflight refreshments and a huge breakfast are included in the rates. ✉ *V Marketplace, 6525 Washington St., near Mulberry St.* ☎ *707/944–4400, 855/944–4408* 🌐 *www.nvaloft.com* 🎫 *$195–$220.*

Napa Valley Balloons. Departing from Domaine Chandon, the valley's oldest balloon company offers trips that are elegant from start to finish. Satisfied customers include Chelsea Clinton and *Today* show host Matt Lauer. ✉ *Domaine Chandon, 6525 1 California Dr., at Solano Ave., west of Hwy. 29* ☎ *707/944–0228, 800/253–2224* 🌐 *www.napavalleyballoons.com* 🎫 *$215 per person.*

CLOSE UP

The Wine Country by Bicycle

Thanks to the scenic country roads winding through the region, bicycling is a nearly perfect way to get around the Wine Country (the lack of designated bike lanes notwithstanding). Whether you're interested in an easy spin to a few wineries or a strenuous haul up a mountainside, there's a way to make it happen.

Cycle shops in most towns will rent you a bike and helmet for the day. In addition to providing maps and advice on the least-trafficked roads, staffers can typically recommend a route based on your interests and fitness level.

If you're concerned about the logistics of your trip, consider joining a one-day or multiday bike tour, which includes lunch, a guide, and a "sag wagon" in case you tire before you reach your destination.

BICYCLING

★ **Fodor'sChoice Napa Valley Bike Tours.** Napa Valley Bike Tours will deliver bikes, which rent for $39 to $78 a day, to many hotels in the Napa Valley if you're renting at least two bikes for a full day. In addition to hourly rentals, guided and self-guided winery and other tours are available. ✉ *6795 Washington St., at Madison St., Yountville* ☎ *707/944–2953* ⊕ *www.napavalleybiketours.com.*

OAKVILLE

2 miles northwest of Yountville.

Barely a blip on the landscape as you drive north on Highway 29, Oakville is marked only by its grocery store. Oakville's small size belies the big mark it makes in the wine-making world. Slightly warmer than Yountville and Carneros to the south, but a few degrees cooler than Rutherford and St. Helena to the north, the Oakville area benefits from gravelly, well-drained soil. This allows roots to go deep—sometimes more than 100 feet deep—so that the vines produce intensely flavored grapes.

The winemakers who have staked their claim here are an intriguing blend of the old and the new. Big-name wineries such as Far Niente, Robert Mondavi, and Opus One have been producing well-regarded wines—mostly notably Cabernet Sauvignon—for decades. But upstarts such as PlumpJack are getting just as much press these days.

GETTING HERE AND AROUND

If you're driving along Highway 29, you'll know you've reached Oakville when you see the Oakville Grocery on the east side of the road. Here the Oakville Cross Road provides access to the Silverado Trail. Oakville wineries are scattered along Highway 29, Oakville Cross Road, and the Silverado Trail in roughly equal measure.

You can reach Oakville from the town of Glen Ellen in Sonoma County by heading east on Trinity Road from Highway 12. The twisting route, along the mountain range that divides Napa and Sonoma counties, eventually becomes the Oakville Grade. The views of both valleys on this drive are breathtaking, though the continual curves make it unsuitable for those who suffer from motion sickness.

EXPLORING

TOP ATTRACTIONS

★ **Fodor's Choice Far Niente.** Though the fee for the combined tour and tasting is at the high end, Far Niente is especially worth visiting if you're tired of elbowing your way through crowded tasting rooms and are looking for a more personal experience. Here you're welcomed by name and treated to a glimpse of one of the most beautiful Napa properties. Small groups are shepherded through the historic 1885 stone winery, including some of the 40,000 square feet of caves, for a lesson on the labor-intensive method for making Far Niente's two wines, a Cabernet blend and a Chardonnay. (The latter is made without undergoing malolactic fermentation, so it doesn't have that buttery taste that's characteristic of many California Chardonnays.) The next stop is the Carriage House, which holds a gleaming collection of classic cars. The tour concludes with a seated tasting of wines and cheeses. ✉ *1350 Acacia Dr., off Oakville Grade Rd.* ☎ *707/944–2861* ⊕ *www. farniente.com* ✆ *Tasting and tour $50* ⊙ *By appointment.*

Opus One. The combined venture of the late California winemaker Robert Mondavi and the late French Baron Philippe de Rothschild, Opus One produces only one wine: a big, inky Bordeaux blend that was the first of Napa's ultra-premium wines, fetching unheard-of prices before it was overtaken by cult wines like Screaming Eagle. The winery's futuristic limestone-clad structure, built into the hillside, seems to be pushing itself out of the earth. Although the tours, which focus on why it costs so much to produce this exceptional wine, can come off as "stuffy" (in the words of one Fodors.com reader), the facilities are undoubtedly impressive, with gilded mirrors, exotic orchids, and a large semicircular cellar modeled on the Château Mouton Rothschild winery in France. You can also taste the current vintage without the tour ($40), as long as you've called ahead for a reservation. ■TIP➜ Take your glass up to the rooftop terrace if you want to appreciate the views out over the vineyards. ✉ 7900 St. Helena Hwy./Hwy. 29 ☎ 707/944–9442, 800/292–6787 ⊕ www.opusonewinery.com ☜ Tasting $40, tours $60–$85 ☉ Daily 10–4; tasting and tour by appointment.

PlumpJack. If Opus One is the Rolls-Royce of the Oakville District—expensive, refined, and a little snooty—then PlumpJack is the Mini Cooper: fun, casual, and sporty. With its metal chandelier and wall hangings, the tasting room looks like it could be the stage set for a modern Shakespeare production. (The name "PlumpJack" is a nod to Shakespeare's Falstaff.) The reserve Chardonnay has a good balance of baked fruit and fresh citrus flavors, and a Merlot is blended with Cabernet Franc, Petit Verdot, and Cabernet Sauvignon, giving the wine sufficient tannins to ensure it can age another five years or more. ■TIP➜ If the tasting room is crowded, take a breather under the shady arbor on the back patio. ✉ 620 Oakville Cross Rd., off Hwy. 29 ☎ 707/945–1220 ⊕ www.plumpjack.com ☜ Tasting $15 ☉ Daily 10–4.

WORTH NOTING

QUICK BITES. **Oakville Grocery.** Built in 1881 as a general store, this popular spot carries unusual and high-end groceries and prepared foods. The place shines after a 2012 renovation, and the notoriously narrow aisles are now wider—helpful on busy summer weekends, when the grocery is often packed with customers stocking up on picnic provisions (meats, cheeses, breads, and hearty sandwiches). This is a fine place to sit on a bench and sip an espresso between winery visits. ✉ 7856 St. Helena Hwy./Hwy. 29, at Oakville Rd. ☎ 707/944–8802 ⊕ www.oakvillegrocery.com.

Far Niente ages its Cabernets and Chardonnays in 40,000 square feet of caves.

Robert Mondavi. The arch at the center of the sprawling Mission-style building perfectly frames the lawn and the vineyard behind, inviting a stroll under the lovely arcades. You can head straight for one of the two tasting rooms, but if you've never taken a winery tour before, the comprehensive Signature Tour and Tasting ($25), which concludes with a seated tasting, is a good way to learn about enology, as well as the late Robert Mondavi's role in California wine making. Those new to tasting and mystified by all that swirling and sniffing should consider the 45-minute Wine Tasting Basics experience ($20). Serious wine lovers should opt for the one-hour $55 Exclusive Cellar tasting, where a well-informed server pours and explains limited-production, reserve, and older-vintage wines. Concerts, mostly jazz and R&B, take place in summer on the lawn; call ahead for tickets. ⊠ *7801 St. Helena Hwy./Hwy. 29* ☎ *888/766–6328* ⊕ *www.robertmondaviwinery.com* ⊠ *Tastings and tours $15–$55* ⊙ *Daily 10–5; tour times vary.*

RUTHERFORD

2 miles northwest of Oakville.

You could drive through the tiny community of Rutherford, at the intersection of Highway 29 and Rutherford Road, in the blink of an eye, but this may well be one of the most important wine-related intersections in the United States.

Opus One produced the first of the Napa Valley's ultrapremium wines.

With its singular microclimate and soil, Rutherford is an important viticultural center, with more big-name wineries than you can shake a corkscrew at, including Beaulieu, Inglenook, Mumm Napa, and St. Supéry.

Cabernet Sauvignon is king here. The soil is ideal for those vines, and since this part of the valley gets plenty of sun, the grapes develop exceptionally intense flavors. Legendary winemaker André Tchelistcheff's famous claim that "it takes Rutherford dust to grow great Cabernet" is quoted by just about every winery in the area that produces the stuff. That "Rutherford dust" varies from one part of the region to another, but the soils here are primarily gravel, sand, and loam, a well-drained home for Cabernet Sauvignon grapes that don't like to get their feet wet.

GETTING HERE AND AROUND
Wineries around Rutherford are dotted along Highway 29 and the parallel Silverado Trail just north and south of Rutherford Road/Conn Creek Road, which connect these two major thoroughfares.

EXPLORING

TOP ATTRACTIONS

Beaulieu Vineyard. The Cabernet Sauvignon produced at the ivy-covered Beaulieu Vineyard is a benchmark of the Napa Valley. André Tchelistcheff, who helped define the California style of wine making, worked his magic here from 1938 until his death in 1973. This helps explain why Beaulieu's flagship, the Georges de Latour Private Reserve Cabernet Sauvignon, still garners high marks from major wine publications. The wines being poured in the main tasting room, which might include anything from a spry Pinot Gris to a lush Syrah, are always competent and sometimes surprise. Still, it's worth the $35 to $50 fee to taste that special Cabernet in the less-crowded reserve tasting room. The tour, an excellent overview of the wine-making process, includes a barrel tasting. ⊠ *1960 St. Helena Hwy./Hwy. 29* ☎ *707/967–5200, 800/373–5896* ⊕ *www.bvwines.com* 🍷 *Tasting $15–$50, tours $20* ⊙ *Daily 10–5.*

★ **Fodor'sChoice Frog's Leap.** John Williams, owner of Frog's
FAMILY Leap, maintains a goofy sense of humor about wine that translates into an entertaining yet informative experience— if you're a novice, this is the perfect place to begin your education. You'll also taste some fine Zinfandel, Cabernet Sauvignon, Merlot, Chardonnay, Sauvignon Blanc, Rosé, and Frögenbeerenauslese, a variation on the German dessert wine Trockenbeerenauslese. The winery includes a red barn built in 1884, 5 acres of organic gardens, an eco-friendly visitor center, and, naturally, a frog pond topped with lily pads. The fun tour ($20; call ahead) is highly recommended, but you can also just sample wines while seated on a porch overlooking the garden. ⊠ *8815 Conn Creek Rd.* ☎ *707/963–4704, 800/959–4704* ⊕ *www.frogsleap.com* 🍷 *Tasting $20, tour $20* ⊙ *Tasting daily 10–4 by appointment only; tours weekdays at 10:30 and 2:30.*

FAMILY **Honig Vineyard & Winery.** Sustainable farming is the big story at this family-run winery in the heart of Rutherford. Michael Honig, the grandson of founder Louis Honig, helped write the code of Sustainable Practices for the California Wine Institute and was a key player in developing the first certification programs for state wineries. Some of the modern applications of this mind-set: solar panels that generate a majority of the winery's power and an on-site bee colony that helps with pollination. Michael and his wife, Stephanie, produce nothing but Cabernet Sauvignon and

Sauvignon Blanc, and the awards they consistently win recognize the family's commitment to excellence. Because the Honigs have three young children, the winery is incredibly family friendly, with a special play area for toddlers. ✉ *850 Rutherford Rd.* ☎ *800/929–2217* ⊕ *www.honigwine.com* ✇ *Tasting $10* ⊙ *Daily 10–4:30; tastings by appointment.*

Inglenook. It's the house *The Godfather* built. Literally. Filmmaker Francis Ford Coppola began his wine-making career in 1975, when he bought part of the historic Inglenook estate. He eventually reunited the original Inglenook land and purchased the ivy-covered 19th-century château to boot. In 2006 he renamed the property Rubicon Estate, intending to focus on his premium wines, including the namesake Cabernet Sauvignon–based blend. Then, in 2011, he renamed the place Inglenook. Various tours cover the estate's history, the local climate and geology, and the sensory evaluation of wine. Two distinctly different tastings are held in an opulent, high-ceilinged tasting room. The Bistro, an on-site eatery, has seating in a picturesque courtyard. ✉ *1991 St. Helena Hwy./Hwy. 29* ☎ *707/968–1100, 800/782–4266* ⊕ *www.inglenook.com* ✇ *Tastings $25–$50, tours $45–$95* ⊙ *Daily 10–5; call for tour times.*

Mumm Napa. Although this is one of California's best-known sparkling-wine producers, enjoying the bubbly from the light-filled tasting room—available in either single flutes or by the flight—isn't the only reason to visit Mumm. An excellent gallery displays 30 Ansel Adams prints and presents temporary exhibits by local photographers. You can even take that glass of crisp Brut Rosé with you as you wander. For a leisurely tasting of library wines while seated on the Oak Terrace ($40), reserve in advance. ■TIP→ A two-for-one tasting coupon for the Salon or Patio is available on the winery's website. ✉ *8445 Silverado Trail* ☎ *707/967–7700, 800/686–6272* ⊕ *www.mummnapa.com* ✇ *Tastings $8–$40, tours free–$25* ⊙ *Daily 10–4:45; tours daily at 10, 11, 1, and 3.*

★ Fodor'sChoice **Round Pond Estate.** Sophisticated wines come from Round Pond, but the estate also produces premium olive oils, most from olives grown and crushed on the property. Informative olive-related seminars begin with a look at some trees and a tour of the high-tech mill, followed by tastings of the aromatic oils, both alone and with housemade red-wine vinegars. You'll also sip wines, but for a full tasting, head across the street to the winery. The basic tasting includes a suave Sauvignon Blanc and Round Pond's supple, well-rounded reds. The flagship Estate Cabernet Sauvignon has the structure and heft of the classic 1970s Rutherford Cabs, but gracefully acknowledges 21st-century palates with smoother, if still sturdy, tannins. The Estate Tasting ($45) pairs small morsels with the wines. ⊠ *875 Rutherford Rd., off Conn Creek Rd.* ☎ *707/302–2575, 888/302–2575* ⊕ *www.roundpond.com* ☞ *Wine tasting $20, tour and tasting $55; olive mill tour and tasting $35* ☉ *All tastings and tours by appointment 24–48 hrs in advance.*

Rutherford Hill Winery. This place is a Merlot lover's paradise in a Cabernet Sauvignon world. When the winery's founders were deciding what grapes to plant, they discovered that the climate and soil conditions resembled those of Pomerol, a region of Bordeaux where Merlot is king. Now owned by the Terlato family, the winery has some of the most extensive wine caves in California—nearly a mile of tunnels and passageways. You can get a glimpse of the tunnels and the 8,000 barrels inside on the tours, then cap your visit with a picnic amid oak or olive groves. ■ TIP→ With views over the valley from a perch high on a hill, the picnic grounds are more charming than many others in Napa. ⊠ *200 Rutherford Hill Rd., east of Silverado Trail* ☎ *707/963–1871* ⊕ *www. rutherfordhill.com* ☞ *Tastings $15–$30; call for tour prices* ☉ *Daily 10–5; tours daily at 11:30, 1:30, and 3:30.*

WORTH NOTING

Cakebread Cellars. Jack and Dolores Cakebread snapped up the property at Cakebread Cellars in 1973, after Jack fell in love with the area while visiting on a photography assignment. Since then, they've been making luscious Chardonnays, as well as Merlot, a great Sauvignon Blanc, and a beautifully complex Cabernet Sauvignon. You must make an appointment for a tasting, for which there are several different options. The most basic usually involves a stroll through the winery's barrel room and crush pad and past Dolores's kitchen garden before ending in a taste of six current releases. Other options focus on red wines, reserve wines, or the pairing of wine and food, and might take place in the winery's modern wing, where an elevator is crafted out of a stainless-steel fermentation tank and the ceiling is lined with thousands of corks. ⊠ *8300 St. Helena Hwy./Hwy. 29* ☎ *707/963–5222, 800/588–0298* ⊕ *www. cakebread.com* ☞ *Tastings $15–$45, tour $25* ☉ *Daily 10–4; tasting and tour by appointment.*

Caymus Vineyards. Winemaker Chuck Wagner, who started making wine on the property in 1972, runs this well-regarded winery. His family, however, had been farming in the valley since 1906. Though Caymus makes a fine Zinfandel and (occasionally) a Sauvignon Blanc, Cabernet Sauvignon is the winery's claim to fame, a ripe, powerful wine that's known for its consistently high quality. ■ TIP→ There's no tour, and you have to reserve to taste, but it's a great opportunity to learn about the valley's Cabernet artistry. ✉ *8700 Conn Creek Rd.* ☎ *707/967–3010* 🌐 *www.caymus.com* 🎟 *Tasting $30* ⏲ *Daily 10–4; tasting by appointment.*

St. Supéry Estate Vineyards & Winery. Major renovations in 2012 transformed the tasting experience at this Rutherford hot spot from exclusive to ultra-exclusive. The winery now offers several tastings and interactive wine classes showcasing estate-grown wines. The pours might include Sauvignon Blanc, Chardonnay, Cabernet Sauvignon, Merlot, and even winery-exclusive vintages such as Cabernet Franc or Petit Verdot. The tour provides a behind-the-scenes perspective of the entire wine-making process, from the vineyard to the glass. Outside, a small demonstration vineyard allows you to try your hand at the science of ampelography—identifying grapevines by observing the shape and color of their leaves. ✉ *8440 St. Helena Hwy./Hwy. 29* ☎ *707/963–4533, 800/942–0809* 🌐 *www.stsupery.com* 🎟 *Tastings $15–$50, tour $25* ⏲ *Daily 10–5; tours Mon., Thurs., Fri., and Sun. 10:30 and 1.*

WHERE TO EAT

★ Fodor's Choice ✕ **Restaurant at Auberge du Soleil.** *Modern American.* Possibly the most romantic roost for a dinner in all the Wine Country is a terrace seat at the Auberge du Soleil's illustrious restaurant, and the Mediterranean-inflected cuisine of chef Robert Curry more than matches the dramatic views over the vineyards. The menu, which relies largely on local produce, changes with the seasons but might include veal sweetbreads with chanterelles, apples, horseradish, and watercress, or northern halibut served with string and shell beans, bacon, and a basil broth. Service is as polished as you would expect for a restaurant of this stature, and the wine list is one of the most extensive around. ■ TIP→ The more casual Auberge Bistro & Bar serves lighter, less expensive fare nightly until 11. [$] *Average main: $98* ✉ *Auberge du Soleil, 180 Rutherford Hill Rd., off Silverado Trail* ☎ *707/963–1211, 800/348–5406* 🌐 *www.aubergedusoleil.com* ✍ *Reservations essential.*

$$$$

Round Pond Estate makes sophisticated wines and extra virgin olive oils.

WHERE TO STAY

★ Fodor'sChoice 🏨 **Auberge du Soleil.** *Resort.* Taking a cue from the olive-tree-studded landscape, this hotel with a renowned restaurant and spa cultivates a luxurious Mediterranean look—earth-tone tile floors, heavy wood furniture, and terra-cotta colors—and backs it up with such lavish amenities as flat-screen TVs (in both the rooms and bathrooms), private terraces, jetted soaking tubs, and extra-large showers. **Pros:** stunning views over the valley; spectacular pool and spa areas; the most expensive suites are fit for a superstar. **Cons:** stratospheric prices; least expensive rooms get some noise from the bar and restaurant. [$] *Rooms from: $650* ✉ *180 Rutherford Hill Rd., off Silverado Trail north of Hwy. 128* ☎ *707/963–1211, 800/348–5406* 🌐 *www.aubergedusoleil.com* 🛏 *31 rooms, 21 suites* 🍴 *Breakfast.*

$$$$

ST. HELENA

4 miles northwest of Oakville.

★ Fodor'sChoice Downtown St. Helena is a symbol of how well life can be lived in the Wine Country. Sycamore trees arch over Main Street (Highway 29), where chic-looking visitors flit between boutiques, cafés, and storefront tasting rooms housed in sun-faded redbrick buildings. Genteel St. Helena pulls in rafts of Wine Country tourists during the day, though like most Wine Country towns it more or less rolls up the sidewalks after dark.

Many visitors never get away from the Main Street magnets—dozens of great restaurants and boutiques selling women's clothing, food and wine, and upscale housewares—but you should explore a bit farther and stroll through the quiet residential neighborhoods. A few blocks west of Main Street you'll be surrounded by vineyards, merging into the ragged wilderness edge of the Mayacamas Mountains. Several blocks east of Main Street, off Pope Street, is the Napa River, which separates St. Helena from the Silverado Trail and Howell Mountain.

Around St. Helena the valley floor narrows between the Mayacamas and Vaca mountains. These slopes reflect heat onto the 9,000 or so acres below, and since there's less fog and wind, things get pretty toasty. In fact, this is one of the hottest AVAs in Napa Valley, with midsummer temperatures often reaching the mid-90s. Bordeaux varietals are the most popular grapes grown here—especially Cabernet Sauvignon but also Merlot. You'll also find Chardonnay, Petite Sirah, and Pinot Noir in the vineyards.

GETTING HERE AND AROUND

The stretch of Highway 29 that passes through St. Helena is called Main Street, and many of the town's shops and restaurants are clustered on two pedestrian-friendly blocks between Pope and Adams streets. Wineries are found both north and south of downtown along Highway 29 and the Silverado Trail, but some of the less touristy and more scenic spots are southwest of town on the slopes of Spring Mountain (to access Spring Mountain Road from Main Street, take Madrona Avenue or Elmhurst Avenue southwest a few blocks and turn right) and far east of downtown past Lake Hennessey off Highway 128.

EXPLORING

TOP ATTRACTIONS

Beringer Vineyards. Arguably the Napa Valley's most beautiful winery, the 1876 Beringer Vineyards is also the oldest continuously operating property. In 1884 Frederick and Jacob Beringer built the Rhine House Mansion to serve as Frederick's family home. Today it serves as the reserve tasting room, where you can sample wines surrounded by Belgian art nouveau hand-carved oak and walnut furni-

ST. HELENA HISTORY

Unlike many other parts of the Napa Valley, where milling grain was the primary industry until the late 1800s, St. Helena took to vines almost instantly. The town got its start in 1854, when Henry Still built a store. Still wanted company, and donated land lots on his town site to anyone who wanted to erect a business. Soon he was joined by a wagon shop, a shoe shop, hotels, and churches. Dr. George Crane planted a vineyard in 1858, and was the first to produce wine in commercially viable quantities. A German winemaker named Charles Krug followed suit a couple of years later, and other wineries soon followed.

In the late 1800s, phylloxera had begun to destroy France's vineyards, and Napa Valley wines caught the world's attention. The increased demand for Napa wines spawned a building frenzy in St. Helena. Many of the mansions still gracing the town's residential neighborhoods were built around this time. During the same period, some entrepreneurs attempted to turn St. Helena into an industrial center to supply specialized machinery to local viticulturists. Several stone warehouses were built near the railroad tracks downtown. Other weathered stone buildings on Main Street, mostly between Adams and Spring streets and along Railroad Avenue, date from the same era. Modern facades sometimes camouflage these old-timers, but you can study the old structures by strolling the back alleys.

ture and stained-glass windows. The assortment includes a limited-release Chardonnay, a few big Cabernets, and a luscious white dessert wine named Nightingale. A less expensive tasting takes place in the original stone winery. ■TIP➔ First-time visitors to the valley will learn a lot about the region's wine-making history on the introductory tour. Longer tours, which might pass through a demonstration vineyard or end with a seated tasting in the Rhine House, are also offered. ⊠ 2000 Main St./Hwy. 29, near Pratt Ave. ☎707/967–4412, 866/708–9463 ⊕ www.beringer.com ⊠ Tastings $20–$40, tours $25–$40 ⊙ June–Oct., daily 10–6; Nov.–May, daily 10–5; many tours daily, call for times.

★ **Fodor's Choice Culinary Institute of America.** The West Coast headquarters of the Culinary Institute of America, the country's leading school for chefs, are in the **Greystone Winery,** an imposing building that was the largest stone winery in the world when it was built in 1889. On the ground floor you can check out the quirky Corkscrew Museum and shop at a well-stocked store that tempts aspiring chefs with gleaming gadgets and an impressive selection of cookbooks. The adjacent Flavor Bar lets you sample certain types of ingredients (for example, chocolate or olive oil). Upstairs, if no special events are taking place, you can browse the Vintners Hall of Fame, where plaques fastened to 2,200-gallon redwood wine barrels commemorate winemakers past and present. Beguiling one-hour cooking demonstrations (reservations required) take place on weekends. ⊠ *2555 Main St./Hwy. 29* ☎ *707/967–1100* ⊕ *www.ciachef.edu* ⏎ *Museum and store free, cooking demonstrations $20, tastings $10–$15, tour $10* ⊙ *Museum and store daily 10:30–6; tour 11:45, 2:45, 5; restaurant Sun.–Thurs. 11:30–9, Fri. and Sat. 11:30–10.*

Duckhorn Vineyards. Merlot's moment in the spotlight may have passed, but you wouldn't know it at this winery, whose patrons gladly pay from $50 to nearly $100 a bottle for some of the world's finest wines produced from this varietal. In fact, Duckhorn fans can be so dedicated to their Merlots that they sometimes forget that some fine Sauvignon Blanc and Cabernet Sauvignon wines are made here as well. The winery's airy, high-ceilinged tasting room looks like a sleek restaurant; you'll be seated at a table and served by staffers who make the rounds to pour. In fair weather, you may do your sipping on a fetching wraparound porch overlooking a vineyard. ■TIP→ Reservations are recommended for the tasting of current releases ($30) and are required for the more elaborate tasting and tour experience ($50). ⊠ *1000 Lodi La., at Silverado Trail N* ☎ *707/963–7108* ⊕ *www.duckhorn.com* ⏎ *Tasting $30; tasting and tour $50* ⊙ *Daily 10–4; call for tour hrs.*

Hall. The award-winning Cabs, Merlots, and an impeccable Syrah produced here are works of art—and of up-to-the-minute organic-farming science and high technology. When a glass-wall tasting center opens here in late 2013, you'll see in action some of the technology winemaker Steve Leveque employs to craft wines that also include a Cabernet Franc and late-harvest Sauvignon Blanc dessert wines. The Production Tour and Barrel Tasting provides an even more in-depth look. ■TIP→ For an understatedly elegant experience, book an Artisan Tasting at Hall's Rutherford winery, where the hilltop vistas enthrall and even the stainless-steel aging tanks are dazzling. Tastings take place deep inside a dramatic brick-lined cave. ⊠ *401 St. Helena Hwy./Hwy. 29, near White*

The Culinary Institute's well-stocked Spice Islands store tempts aspiring chefs.

La., St. Helena ☎ 707/967–2626, 800/688–4255 ⊕ www. hallwines.com ☐ Tastings $25–$50; tours with tastings start at $40 ⊙ St. Helena daily 10–5:30; Rutherford by appointment only.

★ Fodor's Choice **Joseph Phelps Vineyards.** Although an appointment is required for tastings at the winery started by the legendary Joseph Phelps—his son Bill now runs the operation—it's well worth the effort. In fair weather, the casual, self-paced wine tastings are held on the terrace of a modern barnlike building with stunning views down the slopes over oak trees and orderly vines. Phelps makes fine whites, but the blockbuster wines are reds, particularly the Cabernet Sauvignon and the flagship Bordeaux-style blend called Insignia. The luscious-yet-subtle Insignia sells for more than $200 a bottle. Luckily, all tastings include the current vintage. The 90-minute seminars include one on wine-and-cheese pairing and another focusing on blending (both $75). In the latter you mix the various varietals that go into the Insignia blend. ✉ 200 Taplin Rd., off Silverado Trail ☎ 707/963–2745, 800/707–5789 ⊕ www.josephphelps.com ☐ Tastings $35–$75, seminars $75–$150 ⊙ Weekdays 9–5, weekends 10–4; tastings by appointment.

QUICK BITES. **Napa Valley Olive Oil Manufacturing Company.** "There's a crazy little shack beyond the tracks," the song goes, but in this case the barnlike building just east of the railroad

Joseph Phelps tasting seminars include a sip of the much-lauded Insignia blend.

tracks sells tickle-your-taste-buds olive oils and vinegars, along with cheeses, meats, breads, and other delectables you can take with you on the road or enjoy at picnic tables right outside. This is old Napa—no frills, cash only—with a shout-out to old Italy. It's a fun stop even if you're not buying, though something will likely tempt you. ✉ *835 Charter Oak Ave., off Main St.* ☎ *707/963–4173* ⊕ *oliveoilsainthelena.com.*

Spring Mountain Vineyard. Hidden off a winding road behind a security gate, the family-owned Spring Mountain Vineyard has the feeling of a private country estate, even though it's only a few miles from downtown St. Helena. Sauvignon Blanc, Pinot Noir, and Syrah wines are produced in limited quantities, but the calling card here is Cabernet Sauvignon—big and chewy, reflecting its mountain origin. A tasting of current releases ($25) gives you a good sense of these wines' charms, but consider opting for the estate tasting ($50), which includes a meander through the elegant property, from the 19th-century caves to the beautifully preserved 1885 mansion. Other tastings explore library vintages of Cabernet Sauvignon ($75) and a vertical selection of the signature Bordeaux blend, Elivette ($100). ✉ *2805 Spring Mountain Rd., off Madrona Ave.* ☎ *707/967–4188, 877/769–4637* ⊕ *www.springmountain-vineyard.com* 🍷 *Tastings $25–$100* ☉ *Daily 10–4; tastings by appointment only.*

St. Clement Vineyards. A boutique winery steeped in history, St. Clement Vineyards is blessed with such splendid views that you might drift into reverie even before tasting the signature Bordeaux-style blend, Oroppas. (That's Sapporo spelled backward, because the famous Japanese brewery owned this place for a time.) The restored Rosenbaum House, built by a wealthy merchant in 1878, has an intimate tasting room. You can also sip wine at café tables on the front porch while taking in views of nearby vineyards and the more distant Howell Mountain. Tours of the property reveal details about its colorful past, as well as the workings of the winery. Only a portion of the fruit for the wines is grown on the estate; instead, the winemakers purchase grapes from various vineyards to produce their Sauvignon Blanc, Chardonnay, Merlot, and Cabernet Sauvignon wines. ⊠ *2867 St. Helena Hwy. N/Hwy. 29* ☎ *707/963–7221, 866/877–5939* ⊕ *www.stclement.com* 🍷 *Tastings $20–$30, tour $20* ☉ *Wed.–Mon. 11–5; tour daily at 10:30 and 2:30 by appointment.*

WORTH NOTING

Bale Grist Mill State Historic Park. For a break from the winery whirlwind, slip north of St. Helena to this park whose water-powered mill was built in 1846 and partially restored in 1925. A short trail from the parking lot leads through the woods to the mill and granary, where exhibits open just on weekends explain the milling process and docents sometimes offer fascinating milling demonstrations. A trail leads from the park to Bothe–Napa Valley State Park, where you can pick up a number of hiking trails or linger for a picnic. ⊠ *3369 St. Helena Hwy./Hwy. 29, 3 miles north of St. Helena* ☎ *707/942–4575* ⊕ *www.napavalleystateparks. org* 🍷 *Free, mill buildings $5* ☉ *Weekends 10–5.*

Charles Krug Winery. The first winery founded in the Napa Valley opened in 1861 when Count Agoston Haraszthy lent Charles Krug a small cider press; today the family of Peter Mondavi (Robert's brother) runs the operation. The winery is best known for its lush red Bordeaux blends, but its Zinfandel is also good. Restoration of the valley's oldest winery building (1872) is scheduled for completion by late 2013. Several tasting lounges will be unveiled, along with a place to buy food and beverages to enjoy in the nearby picnic area, which has views of Mt. St. Helena. ⊠ *2800 Main St./Hwy. 29, across from Culinary Institute of America* ☎ *707/967–2200* ⊕ *www.charleskrug.com* 🍷 *Tastings $15–$25* ☉ *Daily 10:30–5.*

Domaine Charbay Winery and Distillery. Most people who have heard of Domaine Charbay know about its flavored vodkas, infused with such ingredients as blood oranges, Meyer lemons, and green tea, but there's much more going on at this rustic property uphill from St. Helena. On the casual, one-hour tour, you're likely to meet one or more members of the Karakasevic family, who have been in the distilling business for 13 generations. Their passions beyond vodka include crafting small batches of rum, whiskey, tequila, and pastis. Though most of the distilling is actually done in Mendocino County, on the tour here you'll learn the basics of distillation. Domaine Charbray makes some wines and ports, as well as excellent, not-too-sweet aperitifs, and its brandy has also been highly rated. By law, tastings of distilled spirits are not permitted, but the presentation concludes with a wine tasting. ✉ *4001 Spring Mountain Rd., 4.5 miles northwest of downtown (from Main St., take Madrona Ave. west 3 blocks to Spring Mountain Rd.)* ☎ *707/963–9327* ⊕ *www.charbay.com* ✑ *Tasting and tour $20* ⊙ *Daily 10–4, by appointment.*

WORD OF MOUTH. "The scenery in the Napa Valley is beautiful. You can spend loads of time taking pictures—or just drive around the valley. We like to go up the main road, wine taste, stop at St. Helena, walk around, and then cut over to the Silverado Trail." —Ronda

Franciscan Estate. Cabernet Sauvignon and Merlot predominate at this big winery, whose tasting-room staffers aim to educate you—if you're willing—about the wines. The best of winemaker Janet Myers's reds are bold yet smooth, with just enough tannins to build character but not overwhelm. These wines include the reserve Cabernet Sauvignon and her versions of Franciscan's Magnficat blend, among the first of the Napa Valley's now-familiar Meritage wines. You can learn about the blending process at one of two seminars ($50 each); a third explores how the sense of smell controls taste. In good weather, the education moves outdoors for vineyard tours ($25). Franciscan also pours the dense, complex wines—including the truly lofty Cabernet Sauvignon Elevation 1550—Myers produces for Mount Veeder Winery. ✉ *1178 Galleron Rd., at Hwy. 29* ☎ *707/967–3830* ⊕ *www.franciscan.com* ✑ *Tastings $15–$25, tour $25.*

Merryvale Vineyards. Chardonnay and Cabernet Sauvignon are this ivy-covered winery's claims to fame, though you'll

Franciscan Estate's Magnificat blend was among Napa's first Meritage wines.

also find Pinot Noir and Merlot. For the full Merryvale experience, reserve a spot in the weekend Wine Component Tasting seminar ($50). A walk through the winery concludes in the enchanting Cask Room, where guides focus on wine's essential components—sugar, alcohol, acid, and tannins—and discuss how the vintner achieves the perfect balance. The Historic Tour & Barrel Tasting ($35) provides insights into Napa Valley wine making following the repeal of Prohibition. ■TIP→ The red Meritage blend called Profile is the top-of-the-line wine, and it's worth asking if there is an open bottle around so you can taste it. ✉ *1000 Main St., at Charter Oak Ave.* ☎ *707/963–2225* ⊕ *www.merryvale.com* ☞ *Tastings $15–$75* ☉ *Daily 10–6:30; call for seminar hrs.*

Nichelini Family Winery. A scenic drive east of the Silverado Trail winds past Lake Hennessey to Nichelini, the oldest family-owned and operated winery in the Napa Valley. Erected in the late 1800s by Swiss-Italian immigrant Anton Nichelini, the old winery buildings, still in use, cling to a steep embankment where the road skirts a cliff. The wines to taste—they're made by Anton's great-great-granddaughter Aimée Sunseri—are the Zinfandel, its Italian cousin the Primitivo, and the extra-crisp old-vine Muscadelle. The last grape often finds its way into blends, but here it makes a delightful single-varietal white wine redolent of tropical fruit. ■TIP→ The winery is open for drop-in tastings on weekends, but if you call a few hours ahead, you can easily arrange a weekday

Tastings in Raymond's atmospheric Barrel Cellar include wines that are still aging.

appointment. ✉ *2950 Sage Canyon Rd./Hwy. 128, 8 miles east of Silverado Trail* ☎ *707/963–0717* ⊕ *www.nicheliniwinery.com* 🍷 *Tasting $10* ⊙ *Weekdays by appointment, weekends 11–5.*

Raymond Vineyards. All the world's a stage to Jean-Charles Boisset, Raymond's charismatic owner—even his vineyards, where his five-act Theater of Nature includes a well-executed series of gardens and displays that explain biodynamic agriculture. The theatrics continue indoors in the disco-dazzling Crystal Cellar tasting room (chandelier and other accoutrements by Baccarat), along with several other spaces, some sedate and others equally expressive. Despite goosing up the glamour—gal pals out for a fun afternoon love this place—Boisset and winemaker Stephanie Putnam, formerly of Hess and Far Niente, have continued the winery's tradition of producing reasonably priced premium wines. The Cabernet Sauvignons and Merlots often surprise. ■TIP→ Concerned about dogs being left in hot cars during tasting, Boisset established the on-site Frenchie Winery, where canines lounge in comfort while their guardians sip wine. ✉ *849 Zinfandel La., off Hwy. 29* ☎ *707/963–3141* ⊕ *www.raymondvineyards.com* 🍷 *Tastings $20–$40; tour and tasting $45* ⊙ *Daily 10–4.*

Robert Louis Stevenson Museum. If you have a soft spot for author Robert Louis Stevenson (*Treasure Island, Kidnapped*), drop by this small museum housing an impressive collection of memorabilia—rare manuscripts, first editions, photographs, childhood toys, and other artifacts—documenting Stevenson's life and literary career. One exhibit examines the months that Stevenson, at the time impoverished, spent in an abandoned mining town on the slopes of nearby Mt. St. Helena. The interlude later became the inspiration for the book *The Silverado Squatters.* ✉ *1490 Library La., at Adams St.* ☎ *707/963–3757* 🌐 *www.silveradomuseum.org* 🎟 *Free* 🕒 *Tues.–Sat. noon–4.*

RustRidge Winery. Secluded RustRidge is only a 20-minute drive from Napa, but it seems more like Colorado or Montana than the California Wine Country. Signs on Lower Chiles Valley Road point you toward the property, where you'll wind your way past barns and horse paddocks before reaching the tasting room. The property, in the Chiles Valley AVA, is a working thoroughbred-horse ranch, and owners Susan Meyer and husband Jim Fresquez also run a bed-and-breakfast. As for the winery, in their respective roles as winemaker and vineyard manager the couple collaborates on Sauvignon Blanc, Chardonnay, Cabernet Sauvignon, and Zinfandel, along with a Cab-Zin blend called RaceHorse Red (natch). All are poured at tastings, often by Susan or Jim. ✉ *2910 Lower Chiles Valley Rd., east of Silverado Trail* ☎ *707/965–9353* 🌐 *www.rustridge.com* 🎟 *Tastings $20–$50* 🕒 *Daily 10–4; tastings at 11, 1, and 3.*

3

WHERE TO EAT

★ Fodor's Choice ✕ **Cindy's Backstreet Kitchen.** *Modern American.*
$$ At her upscale-casual St. Helena outpost, Cindy Pawlcyn serves variations on the comfort food her iconic Mustards Grill made popular, but spices things up with dishes influenced by Mexican, Central American, and occasionally Asian cuisines. Along with mainstays like herb-marinated hanger steak, meat loaf with garlic mashed potatoes, and beef and duck burgers served with flawless fries, the menu might include a rabbit tostada or duck legs and thighs cooked in a wood oven to succulent perfection. Two dessert favorites are the high-style yet homey warm pineapple upside-down cake and the nearly ethereal parfait. ■ TIP→ If you can't snag a table, try Pawlcyn's Wood Grill and Wine Bar; ½ mile away, it also serves comfort food and many wines by the glass. [$] *Average main: $21* ✉ *1327 Railroad Ave., at Hunt St., 1 block east of Main St.* ☎ *707/963–1200* 🌐 *www.cindysbackstreetkitchen.com.*

$$$$ 🍴 **Farmstead at Long Meadow Ranch.** *Modern American.* Housed in a former barn, Farmstead revolves around an open kitchen where chef Stephen Barber cooks with as many local and organic ingredients as possible. Many of them—including grass-fed beef, fruits and vegetables, eggs, extra-virgin olive oil, wine, and honey—come from the property of parent company Long Meadow Ranch. Others are sourced from within a 30-mile radius. On Tuesday, three-course meals ($35) include such comfort food as chicken-fried grass-fed steak, slow-cooked ribs, or fried chicken and dessert. In warm weather, you can dine on an open-air patio among apple trees. Instead of charging a corkage fee, Farmstead collects $2 per bottle to donate to a local non-profit organization. [$] *Average main: $35* ✉ *738 Main St., at Charter Oak Ave.* ☎ *707/963–4555, 877/627–2645* 🌐 *www.longmeadowranch.com/Farmstead-Restaurant.*

★ $$$ Fodor's Choice 🍴 **Goose & Gander.** *Modern American.* At the clubby Goose & Gander, the pairing of food and drink is as likely to involve cocktails as it is wine. Main courses like Scottish salmon with wild-dandelion spaetzle work well with such starters as an heirloom chicory salad and a rich yet rustic cream of mushroom soup made from both wild and cultivated varieties. You might enjoy your meal with a top-notch Chardonnay or Pinot Noir—or a Manhattan made with three kinds of bitters and poured over a hand-carved block of ice. On cold days a fireplace warms the main dining room, and in good weather the outdoor patio is a splendid spot for dining alfresco. ■ TIP→ Year-round the basement bar is a great place for a drink, whether you're dining here or not. [$] *Average main: $24* ✉ *1245 Spring St., at Oak St.* ☎ *707/967–8779* 🌐 *www.goosegander.com.*

$ 🍴 **Gott's Roadside.** *American.* A slick 1950s-style outdoor hamburger stand goes upscale at this hugely popular spot whose customers brave long lines to order breakfast sandwiches, juicy burgers, root-beer floats, and garlic fries. You'll also find plenty of choices not available a half century ago, such as the ahi tuna burger and the chili spice–marinated chicken breast served with Mexican slaw. Try to arrive early or late for lunch, or all the shaded picnic tables on the lawn might be filled. [$] *Average main: $12* ✉ *933 Main St./Hwy. 29* ☎ *707/963–3486* 🌐 *www.gotts.com.*

$$ 🍴 **Market.** *American.* Comfort reigns at this understated-yet-modern eatery. Executive chef and owner Eduardo Martinez spruces up American classics such as crab Louis, made with local Dungeness crab, and fried chicken served with jalapeño corn bread. Sunday brunch is popular, with

locals frequently lining up outside the door. For the most relaxed experience, stroll in at lunchtime midweek and linger over local wine from the extensive list. [$] *Average main: $18* ✉ *1347 Main St., near Hunt Ave.* ☎ *707/963–3799* 🌐 *marketsthelena.com.*

★ $ **Fodor's Choice** ✕ **Model Bakery.** *Bakery.* Thanks to a Food Network plug by chef Michael Chiarello of Bottega, the English muffins here are so popular that takeout customers are sometimes limited to purchases of six—but the scones, croissants, breads, and other baked goods also dazzle. The menu expands for lunch to include soups, salads, pizzas, and sandwiches and paninis with such fillings as turkey and Brie with sautéed apples. After ordering at the counter you often have to wait for a table (inside or out), but you'll likely find the results worth the effort. [$] *Average main: $10* ✉ *1357 Main St., near Adams Ave.* ☎ *707/963–8192* 🌐 *www.themodelbakery.com* ⏲ *No dinner.*

$ ✕ **Pizzeria Tra Vigne.** *Pizza.* Early in the evening, families with kids flock to the outdoor tables at this casual pizzeria. Later on, young couples gather around the pool table or watch the game on the TV. At any time of day you'll find crisp, thin-crust pizzas, such as the unusual Positano, with sautéed shrimp, crescenza cheese, and fried lemons. Salads and pasta round out the menu. Service is friendly, if not particularly speedy, and the lack of a corkage fee makes it a good place to try out that bottle of Sangiovese you picked up at one of the wineries. [$] *Average main: $13* ✉ *1016 Main St., at Charter Oak Ave.* ☎ *707/967–9999* 🌐 *www.travignerestaurant.com* ✍ *Reservations not accepted.*

★ $$$$ **Fodor's Choice** ✕ **Press.** *Modern American.* Few taste sensations surpass the combination of a sizzling steak and a Napa Valley red, a union that the chef and sommeliers here celebrate with a reverence bordering on obsession. Beef from carefully selected local and international purveyors is the star—especially the rib eye for two—but chef Stephen Rogers also prepares pork chops and free-range chicken and veal on his cherry-and-almond-wood-fired grill and rotisserie. The cellar holds thousands of wines; if you recall having a great steak with a 1985 Mayacamas Mt. Veeder Cab, you'll be able to re-create, and perhaps exceed, the original event. The kitchen's attention to detail is matched by the efforts at the bar, whose tenders know their way around both rad and trad cocktails. [$] *Average main: $36* ✉ *587 St. Helena Hwy./Hwy. 29, at White La.* ☎ *707/967–0550* 🌐 *www.pressst helena.com* ✍ *Reservations essential* ⏲ *Closed Tues. No lunch.*

★ Fodor's Choice 🍴 **The Restaurant at Meadowood.** *Modern American.* Chef Christopher Kostow has garnered rave reviews for creating a unique dining experience that starts when you make your reservation. You and your guests will be interviewed about food likes and dislikes, allergies and aversions, and desired level of culinary adventure. Based on notes from these conversations, Kostow crafts a specific menu for your table, transforming seasonal local ingredients, some grown on or near the property, into elaborate, elegant Modern American fare. There are two options, a Chef's Tasting Menu ($225, $450 with wine pairings), composed of eight or nine courses, and a Chef's Counter Menu ($500, $850 with wine pairings). For the latter, you and up to three guests sit inside the kitchen and watch Kostow's team prepare your meal. The warm lighting and beautiful finishes in the dining room, renovated in 2012, make this a top choice for a romantic tête-à-tête. [$] *Average main: $225* ✉ *900 Meadowood La., off Silverado Trail N* ☎ *707/967–1205, 800/458–8080* 🌐 *www.meadowood.com* ⏲ *Closed Sun. No lunch.*

$$$$

★ Fodor's Choice 🍴 **Terra.** *Mediterranean.* For old-school romance and service, many diners return year after year to this quiet favorite in an 1884 fieldstone building. Since 1988, chef Hiro Sone has been giving an unexpected twist to Italian and southern French cuisine in such dishes as mussel soup with caramelized onions and garlic croutons, heavily perfumed with saffron. A few standouts, like the signature sake-marinated black cod in a *shiso* broth, draw on Sone's Japanese background. Homey yet elegant desserts, courtesy of Sone's wife, Lissa Doumani, might include a chocolate caramel tart topped with *fleur de sel* (a kind of sea salt). Next door, the livelier Bar Terra serves inventive cocktails, local wines, and a menu of smaller, lighter dishes, among them succulent fried rock shrimp with a chive-and-mustard sauce. [$] *Average main: $36* ✉ *1345 Railroad Ave., off Hunt Ave.* ☎ *707/963–8931* 🌐 *www.terrarestaurant.com* ⏲ *Closed Tues. No lunch.*

$$$$

$$$ 🍴 **Tra Vigne Restaurant.** *Italian.* It's hard to say whether this restaurant is most appealing spring, when the wildflowers in the small vineyard out front are in full bloom, or on a rainy winter day, when the bright decor, hearty food, and friendly staff warm the chill in your bones. The menu by chef Nash Cognetti changes frequently, but butternut squash ravioli, smoked and braised beef short ribs, and clay-pot roasted flounder have been among recent offerings. The desserts include well-executed traditional favorites like cannoli

The Restaurant at Meadowood's Christopher Kostow creates a specific meal for each party.

and the signature tiramisu. Sunday brunch is a colossal event throughout the year because of the dizzying array of options, from doughnuts to eggs Benedict to kale-and-farro salad. [$] *Average main: $25* ⊠ *1050 Charter Oak Ave., at Main St.* ☎ *707/963–4444* ⊕ *www.travignerestaurant.com.*

$$$ ✕ **Wine Spectator Greystone Restaurant.** *Mediterranean.* The Culinary Institute of America runs this place in the Greystone Winery, which once served as the Christian Brothers Winery. Century-old stone walls encase a spacious restaurant that bustles at both lunch and dinner, with several cooking stations in full view. On busy nights you may find the hard-at-work chefs more entertaining than your dining companions. The tables on the terrace, shaded by red umbrellas, are away from the action, but on fair days they're even more appealing, providing a panoramic view down the hillside. The menu has a Mediterranean spirit and emphasizes locally grown produce. Typical main courses include seared breast of Sonoma duck with a celery-root purée and house-made pasta with trumpet mushrooms and a sherry cream sauce. [$] *Average main: $26* ⊠ *2555 Main St./Hwy. 29* ☎ *707/967–1010* ⊕ *www.ciachef.edu.*

WHERE TO STAY

$$ 🏨 **Ambrose Bierce House.** *B&B/Inn.* Writer and professional curmudgeon Ambrose Bierce lived here until 1910, when he became bored with the peaceful wine valley and vanished into Pancho Villa's Mexico, never to be seen or heard from again. **Pros:** up-to-date amenities; free port and chocolates in each room; within walking distance of downtown and its many restaurants. **Cons:** breakfast served only at 9 am may be inconvenient for some guests; fire-station siren across the street occasionally goes off. [$] *Rooms from: $239* ✉ *1515 Main St.* ☎ *707/963–3003* 🌐 *www.ambrosebiercehouse.com* 🛏 *3 rooms, 1 suite* 🍴 *Breakfast.*

$$$$ 🏨 **Black Rock Inn.** *B&B/Inn.* Owner Jeff Orlik provides his guests such a gracious, thoughtful experience that they tend to gush poetic about his suites, his gourmet breakfasts, but most of all his passion for ensuring a memorable time for everyone. **Pros:** winning host; gorgeous retreat; a gourmet breakfast to remember. **Cons:** rooms fill up quickly in season; somewhat pricey. [$] *Rooms from: $450* ✉ *3100 N. Silverado Trail* ☎ *707/968–7893* 🌐 *www.blackrockinn.net* 🛏 *4 suites, 1 guest house* 🍴 *Breakfast.*

$ 🏨 **El Bonita Motel.** *Hotel.* Only in St.Helena would basic accommodations in a roadside motel cost around $150 a night in high season, but for budget-minded travelers the tidy rooms here are pleasant enough, and the landscaped grounds and picnic tables elevate this property over similar places. **Pros:** cheerful rooms; hot tub; microwaves and mini-refrigerators. **Cons:** road noise is a problem in some rooms. [$] *Rooms from: $149* ✉ *195 Main St./Hwy. 29* ☎ *707/963–3216, 800/541–3284* 🌐 *www.elbonita.com* 🛏 *38 rooms, 4 suites* 🍴 *Breakfast.*

$$$ 🏨 **Harvest Inn.** *Hotel.* Although this inn sits just off Highway 29, its patrons remain mostly above the fray, strolling 8 acres of landscaped gardens with views of adjoining vineyards, partaking in spa services, and drifting off to sleep in beds adorned with fancy linens and down pillows. **Pros:** garden setting; very spacious rooms; professional staff; plush furnishings. **Cons:** some lower-priced rooms lack elegance; high weekend rates; complimentary breakfast is serviceable, not memorable. [$] *Rooms from: $319* ✉ *1 Main St.* ☎ *707/963–9463, 800/950–8466* 🌐 *www.harvestinn.com* 🛏 *54 rooms, 20 suites* 🍴 *Breakfast.*

★ Fodor's Choice 🏨 **Meadowood Napa Valley.** *Resort.* A rambling
$$$$ lodge and several gray clapboard bungalows are scattered across this sprawling property, giving it an exclusive New

CLOSE UP

A Great Northern Napa Drive

Decadent **Dean & DeLuca** in St. Helena opens early, making it a fine starting point for a day of exploring the northern Napa Valley. Purchase your food and drink to fortify yourself, then drive north on Highway 29, turning east on Lincoln Avenue and driving through Calistoga to Tubbs Lane.

Turning left at Tubbs Lane, on your right you'll soon see the entrance to **Chateau Montelena** (which opens at 9:30). Enjoy the Beyond Paris & Hollywood wine tasting, then return to Highway 29 and turn left. The route winds steeply up the slopes of Mt. St. Helena until you reach the crest, where parking lots on either side of the road invite you to hike a bit in **Robert Louis Stevenson State Park,** named for the author who squatted here during a period of impoverishment.

Return to **Calistoga** on Highway 29 and enjoy lunch at **All Seasons Bistro** or **Bosko's Trattoria.** If you've made a reservation for one of the excellent tours at **Schramsberg** (the last one's at 2:30), head south on Highway 29 to Peterson Road, where you'll turn right and then quickly right again onto narrow Schramsberg Road. If sparkling wines aren't your thing or if you've a hankering for a medieval romp, opt for **Castello di Amorosa,** off Highway 29 a half-mile before Schramsberg. Either experience should leave you in a bubbly mood.

Return to Highway 29 and turn right to reach **St. Helena.** You'll have an hour or two to browse the shops along Main Street before they close for the evening. Numerous dining options await in St. Helena, but wherever you're going, stop beforehand at the handsome basement bar at **Goose & Gander** for a well-crafted cocktail.

3

England feel. **Pros:** site of one of Napa's best restaurants; lovely hiking trails on the property; the most gracious service in Napa. **Cons:** very expensive; far from downtown St. Helena. [$] *Rooms from: $525* ✉ *900 Meadowood La.* ☎ *707/963–3646, 800/458–8080* 🌐 *www.meadowood.com* 🛏 *85 rooms, suites, and cottages.*

$$ 🏨 **Wine Country Inn.** *B&B/Inn.* A pastoral landscape of vine-covered hills surrounds this retreat, which was styled after the traditional New England inns its owners visited in the 1970s. **Pros:** free shuttle to some restaurants (reserve early); rates include hearty buffet breakfast and afternoon wine and appetizers; lovely grounds; swimming pool is heated year-round. **Cons:** some rooms let in noise from

neighbors; some areas could use updating. [$] *Rooms from: $250* ✉ *1152 Lodi La., east of Hwy. 29* ☎ *707/963–7077, 888/465–4608* 🌐 *www.winecountryinn.com* 🛏 *24 rooms, 5 cottages* 🍴 *Breakfast.*

NIGHTLIFE AND THE ARTS

Cameo Cinema. The art nouveau Cameo Cinema, built in 1913 and now beautifully restored, screens first-run and art-house movies and occasionally hosts live performances. ✉ *1340 Main St., near Hunt Ave.* ☎ *707/963–9779* 🌐 *www.cameocinema.com.*

Cindy Pawlcyn's Wood Grill and Wine Bar. St. Helena rolls up the sidewalks early, but if you slip into this restaurant's bar before closing, around 9:30 on weekdays and 10 or so on weekends, you can enjoy a cocktail or some wine (huge by-the-glass list here), along with congenial chatter from the patrons and bartenders. ✉ *641 Main St., at Mills La.* ☎ *707/963–0700* 🌐 *cindypawlcynsgrill.com.*

SPAS

Health Spa Napa Valley. The focus at this local favorite is on health, wellness, and fitness, so there are personal trainers offering advice and an outdoor pool where you can swim laps in addition to the extensive regimen of massages and body treatments. The grape-seed mud wrap, during which you're slathered with mud mixed with crushed grape seeds, is a more indulgent, slightly less messy alternative to a traditional mud bath. Afterward you can take advantage of the sauna, hot tub, and eucalyptus steam rooms. The vibe here is upscale if mildly sterile, but everything runs like clockwork. **TIP→** Longtime patrons book treatments before noon to take advantage of the all-day access. ✉ *1030 Main St., at Pope St.* ☎ *707/967–8800* 🌐 *www.napavalleyspa.com* 🎫 *Treatments $15–$235* ⏰ *Weekdays 5:30 am–8 pm, weekends 6:45 am–7 pm; open daily until 8:30 pm June–Sept.*

SPORTS AND THE OUTDOORS

BICYCLING

St. Helena Cyclery. Rent bikes by the hour, as well as by the day (hybrids $37, road bikes $67) at this shop whose website links to a useful map of area bike routes. ✉ *1156 Main St., at Spring St.* ☎ *707/963–7736* 🌐 *www.sthelenacyclery.com.*

SHOPPING

St. Helena's coolest stores are clustered along bucolic Main Street, where 19th-century redbrick buildings recall the town's past and make it a particularly pleasant place to while away an afternoon window-shopping.

Dean & Deluca. The upscale chain's Napa Valley branch sells a variety of kitchenware and has a large wine selection, but most visitors come for the terrific produce and decadent deli items, all of which help you to picnic in style. ✉ 607 *St. Helena Hwy./Hwy. 29, at White La.* ☎ 707/967–9980 ⊕ *www.deandeluca.com.*

Footcandy. Precariously steep stilettos and high-heeled boots are raised to an art form here. You'll also find ultracool handbags and other accessories. ✉ *1239 Main St., at Hunt Ave.* ☎ *707/963–2040* ⊕ *www.footcandyshoes.com.*

I. Wolk Gallery. This airy gallery exhibits abstract and contemporary realist paintings, works on paper, and sculpture. ✉ *1354 Main St., near Adams St.* ☎ *707/963–8800* ⊕ *www. iwolkgallery.com.*

Jan de Luz. Fine French table linens and high-quality items for home and garden fill this shop. ✉ *1219 Main St., at Spring St.* ☎ *707/963–1550* ⊕ *www.jandeluz.com.*

Spice Islands Marketplace. This fun store sells cookbooks, kitchenware, and everything else related to cooking. ✉ *Culinary Institute of America, 2555 Main St./Hwy. 29* ☎ *888/424–2433, 707/967–2309* ⊕ *www.ciachef.edu.*

St. Helena Olive Oil Company. Famous Napa chefs have been known to drop in at this chic-looking store for its high-quality extra-virgin olive oil and vinegars. You'll also find artisanal honey, jams, herbs, mustards, and sauces, along with bath products made from all-natural ingredients. ✉ *1351 Main St., near Adams Ave.* ☎ *707/968–9260* ⊕ *www. sholiveoil.com.*

Woodhouse Chocolate. Elaborate confections made on the premises are displayed like miniature works of art at this lovely shop resembling an 18th-century Parisian salon. ✉ *1367 Main St., at Adams St.* ☎ *707/963–8413, 800/966–3468* ⊕ *www.woodhousechocolate.com.*

CALISTOGA

3 miles northwest of St. Helena.

False-fronted shops, 19th-century hotels, and unpretentious cafés lining the main drag of Lincoln Avenue give Calistoga a slightly rough-and-tumble feel that's unique in the Napa Valley. With Mt. St. Helena rising to the north and visible from downtown, it looks a bit like a cattle town tucked into a remote mountain valley. It's easier to find a bargain here than farther down the valley, making Calistoga's quiet, tree-shaded streets and mellow bed-and-breakfasts a relatively affordable base for exploring the surrounding vineyards and back roads.

Ironically, Calistoga was developed as a ritzy vacation getaway. In 1859 Sam Brannan—Mormon missionary, entrepreneur, and vineyard developer—learned about a place in the upper Napa Valley, called Agua Caliente by the settlers, that was peppered with hot springs and even had its own "old faithful" geyser. He snapped up 2,000 acres of prime property and laid out a resort. Planning a place that would rival New York's famous Saratoga Hot Springs, he built an elegant hotel, bathhouses, cottages, stables, observatory, and distillery (the last a questionable choice for a Mormon missionary). Brannan's gamble didn't pay off as he'd hoped, but Californians kept coming to "take the waters," supporting a sprinkling of small hotels and bathhouses built wherever a hot spring bubbled to the surface. Many of them are still going, and you can come for an old-school experience of a mud bath or a dip in a warm spring-fed pool.

GETTING HERE AND AROUND

To get here from St. Helena or anywhere else farther south, take Highway 29 north and then turn right on Lincoln Avenue. Alternately, you can head north on Silverado Trail and turn left on Lincoln.

EXPLORING

TOP ATTRACTIONS

Castello di Amorosa. Possibly the most astounding sight in Napa Valley is the Castello di Amorosa, built to resemble a medieval castle, complete with drawbridge and moat, chapel, stables, and secret passageways. Some of the 107 rooms contain replicas of 13th-century frescoes (cheekily signed [the-artist's-name].com), and the dungeon has an actual iron

The astounding Castello di Amorosa

maiden from Nuremberg, Germany. You must pay for the tour ($33 or $49, depending on the wine you taste) to see the most of Dario Sattui's extensive eight-level property, though basic tastings ($18 or $28) include access to a small portion of the complex. All include a sample of several Italian-style wines, including a "super Tuscan," a blend of Sangiovese and Merlot with Cabernet Sauvignon that has more heft than your average Italian red. ⌂ *4045 N. St. Helena Hwy./Hwy. 29* ☎ *707/967–6272* ⊕ *www.castellodiamorosa.com* 🍷 *Tastings $18–$28, tours $33–$49* ☉ *Mar.–Oct., daily 9:30–6; Nov.–Feb., daily 9:30–5; tour by appointment.*

Chateau Montelena. Set amid a bucolic northern Calistoga landscape, this winery helped establish the Napa Valley's reputation for high-quality wine making. At the legendary Paris tasting of 1976, the Chateau Montelena Chardonnay took first place, beating out four white Burgundies from France and five other California Chards. The 2008 movie *Bottle Shock* immortalized the event, and the winery honors its four decades of classic wine making with a special Beyond Paris & Hollywood tasting of the winery's Chardonnays ($40). You can also opt for a standard tasting ($20) of current releases and a library tasting ($40) that includes some stellar Cabernet Sauvignons and a limited-release Riesling. ⌂ *1429 Tubbs La., off Hwy. 29* ☎ *707/942–5105* ⊕ *www.montelena.com* 🍷 *Tastings $20–$40, tours $30–$50* ☉ *Daily 9:30–4; tours vary.*

An underground aging room at Schramsberg Vineyards

★ Fodor'sChoice **Schramsberg.** Founded in 1865, the venerable Schramsberg produces bubblies made using the traditional *méthode champenoise* (which means, among other things, that the wine undergoes a second fermentation in the bottle before being "riddled," or turned every few days, to nudge the sediment into the neck of the bottle). To taste, you first must tour, but what a tour: in addition to glimpsing the winery's historic architecture, you see the underground cellars dug in the late 19th century by Chinese laborers. A mind-boggling 2.7 million bottles are stacked in gravity-defying configurations. The tour ($45) includes generous pours of several very different sparkling wines, as well as tiny snacks to enhance the experience. To learn more about sparkling wines, consider the three-day **Camp Schramsberg.** In the fall sessions, you harvest grapes and explore riddling, food-and-wine pairing, and other topics. Spring camps focus on blending sparkling wines. ⊠ *1400 Schramsberg Rd., off Hwy. 29* ☎ *707/942–4558, 800/877–3623* ⊕ *www. schramsberg.com* 🖾 *Tasting and tour $45* ⊗ *Tours at 10, 11:30, 12:30, 1:30, and 2:30 by appointment.*

FAMILY **Sterling Vineyards.** The approach to Sterling Vineyards, perched on a hilltop about a mile south of Calistoga, is the most spectacular in the valley. Instead of driving to the tasting room, you board an aerial tram to reach pristine white buildings that recall those in the Greek islands. (The founder once lived on Mykonos.) The views from the winery are superb, although the quality of the wines doesn't necessarily match the vista. If you visit, pony up the extra $10 to $15 for VIP tastings that include reserve, single-vineyard, and limited-release wines. The short tram ride is one of the area's few kid-friendly attractions; it's $10 for those under 21. ✉ *1111 Dunaweal La., off Hwy. 29* ☎ *707/942–3300, 800/726–6136* ⊕ *www.sterlingvineyards.com* ⌐ *Tastings $25–$40* ⊙ *Weekdays 10:30–4:30, weekends 10–5.*

Storybook Mountain Vineyards. Tucked into a rock face in the Mayacamas range, Storybook occupies a picture-perfect site with rows of vines rising steeply in dramatic tiers. Zinfandel is king here, and there's even a Zin Gris, an unusual dry Rosé of Zinfandel grapes. (In Burgundy, Vin Gris—a pale Rosé—is made from Pinot Noir grapes.) Tastings are preceded by a low-key tour that includes a short walk up the hillside and a visit to the atmospheric tunnels, parts of which have the same rough-hewn look as they did when Chinese laborers painstakingly dug them around 1888. ✉ *3835 Hwy. 128, 4 miles northwest of town* ☎ *707/942–5310* ⊕ *www.storybookwines.com* ⌐ *Tasting and tour $25* ⊙ *Mon.–Sat. by appointment.*

WORTH NOTING

Clos Pegase. Designed by postmodern architect Michael Graves, the Clos Pegase winery is a one-of-a-kind "temple to wine and art" packed with unusual works from the art collection of owner and publishing entrepreneur Jan Shrem. After tasting the bright Sauvignon Blanc, fruity Chardonnays, and mellow Pinot Noirs, Merlots, and Cabernets—they're made in a soft, approachable style and meant to be drunk somewhat young—be sure to check out the surrealist paintings near the main tasting room, which include one by Jean Dubuffet that you may have seen on a Clos Pegase label. Better yet, bring a picnic and have lunch in the courtyard, where a curvaceous Henry Moore sculpture depicting Gaia (or Mother Earth) is one of about two dozen works of art. ✉ *1060 Dunaweal La., off Hwy. 29* ☎ *707/942–4981* ⊕ *www.clospegase.com* ⌐ *Tastings $20–$35, tour $20* ⊙ *Daily 10:30–5; tour daily at 11:30 and 2.*

Dutch Henry Winery. The tasting room at this winery is barely more than a nook in the barrel room between towering American and French oak barrels full of excellent Cabernet Sauvignon, Merlot, Pinot Noir, and Zinfandel wines.

The Sauvignon Blanc and charming Rosé also have their adherents. Most of Dutch Henry's output is sold on-site or through its wine club, which explains the simple facilities, but the wines are truly top-notch. Tasting-room staffers can occasionally be crotchety, but the lack of crowds and casual style at the pet-friendly winery make it a welcome change of pace from some of its overly serious neighbors. If you're lucky, you'll get a tour of the wine caves, which are less than a decade old but don't seem so. ✉ *4310 Silverado Trail, near Dutch Henry Canyon Rd.* ☎ *707/942–5771, 888/224–5879* ⊕ *www.dutchhenry.com* 🍷 *Tasting $20* ⊙ *Daily 10–5.*

Robert Louis Stevenson State Park. Encompassing the summit of Mt. St. Helena, this mostly undeveloped park is where Stevenson and his bride, Fanny Osbourne, spent their honeymoon in an abandoned bunkhouse of the Silverado Mine. This stay in 1880 inspired the writer's travel memoir *The Silverado Squatters,* and Spyglass Hill in *Treasure Island* is thought to be a portrait of Mt. St. Helena. A marble memorial marks the site of the bunkhouse. The 10-mile trail is steep and lacks shade in spots, but the summit is often cool and breezy. ■TIP➜ Bring plenty of water, and dress in layers. ✉ *Hwy. 29, 7 miles north of Calistoga* ☎ *707/942–4575* ⊕ *www.parks.ca.gov/?page_id=472* 🍷 *Free* ⊙ *Daily sunrise–sunset.*

Sharpsteen Museum of Calistoga History. Walt Disney animator Ben Sharpsteen, who retired to Calistoga, founded this museum whose centerpiece is an intricate diorama depicting the Calistoga Hot Springs Resort during its 19th-century heyday. One exhibit examines the indigenous Wappo people who once lived here, and another focuses on Sharpsteen's career as an animator. The adjacent Sam Brannan Cottage, built by the town's founder in 1862 and later moved to this site, has been furnished in lavish period detail. ✉ *1311 Washington St., at 1st St.* ☎ *707/942–5911* ⊕ *www.sharpsteen-museum.org* 🍷 *$3* ⊙ *Daily 11–4.*

WHERE TO EAT

$$ ✕ **All Seasons Bistro.** *American.* At this cheerful, sun-filled space, tables topped with flowers stand on an old-fashioned black-and-white checkerboard floor. The California-style bistro's seasonal menu might include risotto with seared scallops and shiitake mushrooms, fettuccine puttanesca, or flavorful lasagna. Among the homey desserts are a perfectly

executed vanilla-bean crème brûlée and a warm dark-chocolate torte. You can order reasonably priced wines from the extensive list, or buy a bottle at the attached shop and have it poured at your table. Attentive service contributes to the welcoming atmosphere. [$] *Average main: $20* ✉ *1400 Lincoln Ave., at Washington St.* ☎ *707/942–9111* 🌐 *www.allseasonsnapavalley.net* ⏲ *Closed Mon.*

$$ 🍴 **Barolo.** *Italian.* With red-leather seats, artsy lighting fixtures, and a marble bar indoors and café seating outside, this Italian-inflected wine bar is a stylish, modern spot for a glass of wine, including many from small producers you probably haven't heard of. Small plates that could have come straight from Tuscany—*polpettine* (braised pork-and-beef meatballs), risotto croquettes, a selection of *salumi* (dry-cured and other meats)—are great for sharing. Pastas, pizzas, and large plates such as chicken piccata and braised short ribs round out the menu. [$] *Average main: $19* ✉ *Mount View Hotel, 1457 Lincoln Ave., near Fair Way* ☎ *707/942–9900* 🌐 *www.barolocalistoga.com.*

$$ 🍴 **Bosko's Trattoria.** *Italian.* In a town where the cost of a meal has risen steeply in recent years—and where low-end dining can be a listless affair—Bosko's provides tasty Italian cuisine at a fair price. The specialties here are house-made pastas and thin-crust pizzas cooked in a wood-fired oven. Two of the hefty sandwiches worth trying are the free-range chicken breast sandwich on mildly garlicky focaccia and the Italian sausage on a sourdough roll. Both come with a salad or a bowl of minestrone or other soup. Nothing super-fancy here, just good value. [$] *Average main: $17* ✉ *1364 Lincoln Ave., at Washington St.* ☎ *707/942–9088* 🌐 *www.boskos.com* ✍ *Reservations not accepted.*

$$$$ 🍴 **JoLē.** *American.* Local produce plays a starring role here—not surprising, as chef Matt Spector is one of the area's biggest proponents of farm-to-table dining. Depending on when you visit, you might enjoy Mendocino-caught squid with crab stuffing; Forni, Brown & Welsh mixed greens with Asian pears; and chicken-fried quail with fig jam. The tasting-style menu is available à la carte, and there are four-, five-, and six-course prix-fixe options. No visit is complete without a slice of coconut cream pie, and pastry chef Sonjia Spector also makes scrumptious cupcakes you can take home. [$] *Average main: $50* ✉ *Mount View Hotel, 1457 Lincoln Ave., at Fair Way* ☎ *707/942–5938* 🌐 *www.jolerestaurant.com* ⏲ *No lunch.*

★ Fodor's Choice 🍴 **Solbar.** *Modern American.* Chef Brandon
$$$ Sharp is known around the region for his subtle and sophisticated take on Wine Country cooking. As befits a restaurant at a spa resort, the menu here is divided into "healthy, lighter" dishes and "hearty" fare. On the lighter side, grilled yellowfin tuna comes with baby artichokes and a prosciutto-mustard vinaigrette, with toasted farro replacing rice or potatoes as the starch. On the heartier side you might find confit of Niman Ranch pork shoulder served with bacon-roasted brussels sprouts, or the popular flatiron steak with Yukon-gold potato gnocchi and king trumpet mushrooms. The service at Solbar is uniformly excellent, and in summer the patio is a festive spot for breakfast, lunch, or dinner. The Sunday brunch is lighter than most in the valley. [$] *Average main: $29* ✉ *Solage Calistoga, 755 Silverado Trail, at Rosedale Rd.* ☎ *707/226–0850* 🌐 *www.solagecalistoga.com/solbar.*

WHERE TO STAY

★ Fodor's Choice 🏨 **Best Western Plus Stevenson Manor.** *Hotel.* Bud-
$ get travelers get what they pay for—and a little bit more—at this clean, well-run motel a few blocks from Calistoga's downtown. **Pros:** great price for region; friendly staff; nice pool area; complimentary full breakfast. **Cons:** decidedly lacking in glamour. [$] *Rooms from: $159* ✉ *1830 Lincoln Ave.* ☎ *707/942–1112, 800/780–7234* 🌐 *www.bestwestern.com* 🛏 *34 rooms* 🍽 *Breakfast.*

$$ 🏨 **Brannan Cottage Inn.** *B&B/Inn.* Inside the only one of Sam Brannan's 1860 resort cottages still standing on its original site, this inn, a pristine Victorian house with lacy white fretwork, large windows, and a shady porch, is on the National Register of Historic Places. **Pros:** innkeepers go the extra mile; most rooms have fireplaces; a five-minute walk from most of Calistoga's restaurants. **Cons:** beds may be too firm for some. [$] *Rooms from: $230* ✉ *109 Wapoo Ave., at Lincoln Ave.* ☎ *707/942–4200* 🌐 *www.brannancottageinn.com* 🛏 *6 rooms* 🍽 *Breakfast.*

★ Fodor's Choice 🏨 **Calistoga Ranch.** *Resort.* Spacious cedar-shin-
$$$$ gle lodges throughout this posh, wooded property have outdoor living areas, and even the restaurant, spa, and reception space have outdoor seating and fireplaces. **Pros:** almost half the lodges have private hot tubs on the deck; lovely hiking trails on the property; guests have reciprocal privileges at Auberge du Soleil and Solage Calistoga. **Cons:** innovative indoor-outdoor organization works better in fair

Almost half the lodgings at the posh Calistoga Ranch have private hot tubs.

weather than in rain or cold. [$] *Rooms from: $750* ✉ *580 Lommel Rd.* ☎ *707/254–2800, 800/942–4220* 🌐 *www.calistogaranch.com* 🛏 *48 rooms* 🍴 *No meals.*

$$ 🏨 **Cottage Grove Inn.** *B&B/Inn.* A long driveway lined with freestanding cottages, each shaded by elm trees and with rocking chairs on the porch, looks a bit like Main Street, USA, but inside the skylighted buildings are all the perks necessary for a romantic weekend getaway. **Pros:** loaner bicycles available; plenty of privacy; huge bathtubs. **Cons:** no pool; decor may seem too old-school for some. [$] *Rooms from: $300* ✉ *1711 Lincoln Ave.* ☎ *707/942–8400, 800/799–2284* 🌐 *www.cottagegrove.com* 🛏 *16 cottages* 🍴 *Breakfast.*

$$ 🏨 **Indian Springs Resort and Spa.** *Resort.* Stylish Indian Springs—operating as a spa since 1862—ably splits the difference between laid-back style and ultrachic touches. **Pros:** lovely grounds with outdoor seating areas; stylish for the price; enormous mineral pool; free touring bikes. **Cons:** lodge rooms are small; service could be more polished. [$] *Rooms from: $262* ✉ *1712 Lincoln Ave.* ☎ *707/942–4913* 🌐 *www.indianspringscalistoga.com* 🛏 *24 rooms, 17 suites* 🍴 *No meals.*

★ Fodor's Choice 🏨 **Meadowlark Country House.** *B&B/Inn.* Two
$$ charming European gents run this laid-back but sophisticated inn on 20 wooded acres just north of downtown. **Pros:** charming innkeepers; tasty sit-down breakfasts; welcoming vibe that attracts diverse guests. **Cons:** clothing-

optional pool policy isn't for everyone. [$] *Rooms from: $210* ✉ *601 Petrified Forest Rd.* ☎ *707/942–5651, 800/942–5651* 🌐 *www.meadowlarkinn.com* 🛏 *5 rooms, 3 suites, 1 cottage, 1 guesthouse* 🍴 *Breakfast.*

$$ 🏨 **Mount View Hotel & Spa.** *B&B/Inn.* Although it's in a 1912 building that's been designated a National Historic Landmark, the Mount View feels completely modern, with freshly painted rooms (some are a dramatic red and black), feather duvets, and high-tech touches like iPod docking stations. **Pros:** convenient location; excellent spa treatments; eco-friendly. **Cons:** ground-floor rooms are dark; mediocre continental breakfast; some bathrooms could use updating. [$] *Rooms from: $250* ✉ *1457 Lincoln Ave.* ☎ *707/942–6877, 800/816–6877* 🌐 *www.mountviewhotel.com* 🛏 *18 rooms, 13 suites and cottages* 🍴 *Breakfast.*

$$$$ 🏨 **Solage Calistoga.** *Resort.* The aesthetic at this 22-acre property is Napa Valley barn meets San Francisco loft, so the rooms have high ceilings, polished concrete floors, recycled walnut furniture, and all-natural fabrics in soothingly muted colors. **Pros:** great service; complimentary bikes; separate pools for kids and adults. **Cons:** the vibe may not suit everyone. [$] *Rooms from: $425* ✉ *755 Silverado Trail* ☎ *866/942–7442, 707/226–0800* 🌐 *www.solagecalistoga.com* 🛏 *83 rooms, 6 suites* 🍴 *No meals.*

NIGHTLIFE AND THE ARTS

Brannan's Grill. The talented mixologists behind the mahogany bar make Brannan's a good stop for after-dinner cocktails (it's also a fairly decent place to have your meal). While you sip, take a look at the vaulted ceiling, redwood beams, and hand-forged iron trestles; the building was constructed in 1903 as a garage. On Friday and Saturday night there's superb jazz. ✉ *1374 Lincoln Ave., at Washington St.* ☎ *707/942–2233* 🌐 *www.brannanscalistoga.com.*

SPAS

Dr. Wilkinson's Hot Springs Resort. Newer, fancier establishments may have eclipsed Calistoga's oldest spa, but loyal fans appreciate its reasonable prices and unpretentious vibe. The mud baths here are a mix of volcanic ash and Canadian peat, warmed by the spa's own hot springs. Fun fact: back in 1952, "The Works"—a mud bath, steam room, blanket wrap, and a massage—cost $3.50. The charge now is $139. You can also get a facial here. ✉ *1507 Lincoln Ave., at Fair*

Way ☎ *707/942–4102* ⊕ *www.drwilkinson.com* ☜ *Treat-ments $69–$179* ⊙ *Daily 8:30–5:30.*

Indian Springs Resort and Spa. Even before Sam Brannan constructed a spa on this site in the 1860s, the Wappo Indians were building sweat lodges over its thermal geysers. You can enjoy the volcanic-ash mud baths and other treatments, then relax in the small Zen-inspired garden. Clients have access to the Olympic-size mineral-water pool, kept at 92°F in summer and a toasty 102°F in winter. ✉ *1712 Lincoln Ave., at Wappo Ave.* ☎ *707/942–4913* ⊕ *www.indianspring-scalistoga.com* ☜ *Treatments $70–$380* ⊙ *Daily 9–8.*

★ Fodor'sChoice **Spa Solage.** This eco-conscious spa has rein-
$$ vented the traditional Calistoga mud and mineral water therapies. Case in point: the hour-long "Mudslide," a three-part treatment that includes a mud body mask (in a heated lounge), a soak in a thermal bath, and a power nap in a comfy sound/vibration chair. The mud here is a mix of clay, volcanic ash, and essential oils. Traditional spa services—combination Shiatsu-Swedish and other massages, full-body exfoliations, facials, and waxes—are available, as are fitness and yoga classes. ✉ *755 Silverado Trail, at Rosedale Rd.* ☎ *866/942–7442, 707/226–0825* ⊕ *www.solagecalistoga. com/spa* ☜ *Treatments $25–$335* ⊙ *Daily 8–8.*

SPORTS AND THE OUTDOORS

BICYCLING

Calistoga Bikeshop. You can rent regular and fancy bikes here, or you can opt for the self-guided Calistoga Cool Wine Tour ($80), which includes tastings at small wineries. If you've bought more wine than will fit into your bike's handy bottle carrier, the shop will pick it up for you. ✉ *1318 Lincoln Ave., near Washington St.* ☎ *707/942–9687* ⊕ *www. calistogabikeshop.net.*

SHOPPING

Shops and restaurants along Lincoln Avenue in downtown Calistoga tend to cater to locals rather than visitors; you'll find few of the high-priced boutiques that line the main street of St. Helena.

Calistoga Depot. An old train depot and its six restored railway cars house gift shops, a café where you can pick up picnic items, and a wineshop and tasting room. ✉ *1458 Lincoln Ave.*

DID YOU KNOW?

Silverado Trail runs parallel to Highway 29 from the town of Napa to Calistoga and is popular with bicyclists because it has a bit less traffic than the more heavily traveled highway.

Calistoga Pottery. You may recognize the dinnerware and other pottery sold by owners Jeff and Sally Manfredi— their biggest customers are the area's inns, restaurants, and wineries. Works by a few other potters are also sold here. ✉ *1001 Foothill Blvd., at Pine St.* ☎ *707/942–0216* ⊕ *www.calistogapottery.com.*

Enoteca Wine Shop. The extensive tasting notes posted alongside nearly all of the wines sold here—among them some hard-to-find bottles from Napa, Sonoma, and around the world—help you make a wise choice. ✉ *1348-B Lincoln Ave.* ☎ *707/942–1117* ⊕ *www.enotecawineshop.com.*

CARNEROS DISTRICT

THE PROXIMITY OF THE COMPACT LOS CARNEROS AVA
to San Francisco—it's less than an hour's drive away—
makes it a favorite of in-the-know day-trippers and lovers
of Pinot Noir and Chardonnay. This viticultural region,
also known as the Carneros District or just the Carneros,
stretches across the cool lower reaches of Sonoma and Napa
counties. *Carneros* means "ram" in Spanish, and the slopes
now covered with vines were once thought to be suitable
only as sheep-grazing pasture.

To understand how different Los Carneros is from the other
California wine-producing regions, notice how close it is
to the northern reaches of San Francisco Bay, at this point
called San Pablo Bay. On a gray day, the flat marshes and
low hills near the water look moody, more like a Scottish
moor than a typical California shore. During summer and
autumn, strong west winds blow in from the ocean every
afternoon, tempering the hot days.

The soil here is shallow and not particularly fertile, which
means that the vines struggle to produce fruit. Though
this would seem to be a drawback, it's in fact a plus. Vines
that grow slowly and yield less fruit tend to produce concentrated, high-acid grapes that are ideal for wine making. Growers in the mid-19th century recognized this and
planted vast tracts. Because of the low yields, some of
the land was returned to sheep pasture after phylloxera
destroyed the vines in the 1890s. But the reputation of the
grapes survived, and shortly after the repeal of Prohibition,
vines once again spread across the hills.

Pinot Noir and Chardonnay thrive on these exposed, windy
slopes, but these days, winemakers are also trying out
Merlot and Syrah, which are also well suited to the thin
soil, moderate temperatures, and low rainfall. (Carneros
generally gets less precipitation than elsewhere in Napa
and Sonoma.) Even such warm-climate grapes as Cabernet
Sauvignon can ripen well in favored Carneros locations.

GETTING AROUND CARNEROS

The Carneros District is closer to San Francisco than any
other part of the Wine Country. From San Francisco, travel
north on U.S. 101 to the city of Novato. Take the Highway
37 turnoff (Exit 460A) to the east, continuing for about 7
miles to Highway 121, the main route through the Carneros. Public transportation is either nonexistent or inconvenient for getting to the wineries in this area.

CLOSE UP

Best Bets for
Carneros District Wineries

WINE TASTING

Anaba Wines, Sonoma: This boutique winery's stalwarts are the Burgundian varietals (Chardonnay and Pinot Noir) that made the Carneros famous, but Anaba also makes single-vineyard Rhône wines.

Saintsbury, Napa. The straightforward tasting sessions at this Pinot Noir pioneer focus on the Carneros region's *terroir* and climate and how they combine to produce grapes that yield well-balanced wines.

Truchard Vineyards, Napa. Top-drawer Napa Valley wineries purchase grapes from family-owned Truchard, which produces worthy Chardonnays and Pinot Noirs of its own, along with Zinfandels, Syrahs, and several other varietals.

WINERY TOURING

Bouchaine Vineyards, Napa. On this winery's self-guided walking tour you're apt to see squirrels and other wildlife scurrying through the vineyards and hawks and other birds soaring high above.

Gloria Ferrer Caves and Vineyards, Sonoma. The sparkling-wine maker's tour takes in the aging caves and covers the winery's history and its contributions to wine science.

SETTING

Artesa Vineyards & Winery, Napa. The winery's high-style tasting room blends so discreetly into the surrounding landscape that visitors often gasp upon encountering the fountains, sculptures, and other contemporary artworks that flank the entrance.

Ram's Gate Winery, Sonoma. Wherever you perch yourself at ultracool Ram's Gate—at the tasting bar, several lounging spaces, or strategically positioned outdoor areas—you'll take in sweeping (and often windswept) vistas.

FOOD-WINE PAIRING

Domaine Carneros, Napa: The winery's sparklers are made in the classic style, and the tasting menu strikes a classic note: cheese and charcuterie plates, caviar, smoked salmon, and European-style pastries.

Etude Wines, Napa: At one of the region's most enlightening food-pairing seminars, you'll learn how sweetness, acidity, and other elements of food alter the tastes of the wines they accompany.

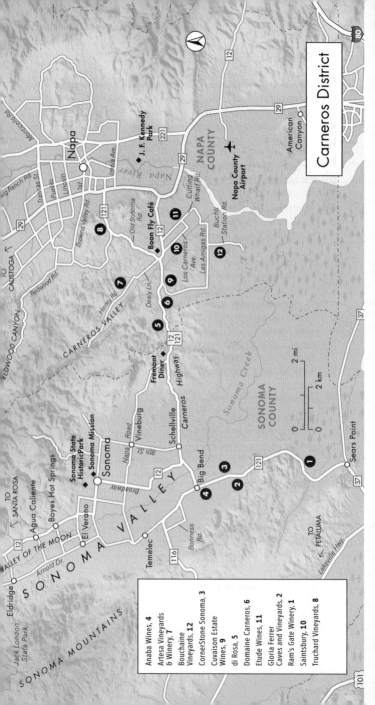

Carneros District

Anaba Wines, **4**
Artesa Vineyards & Winery, **7**
Bouchaine Vineyards, **12**
CornerStone Sonoma, **3**
Cuvaison Estate Wines, **9**
di Rosa, **5**
Domaine Carneros, **6**
Etude Wines, **11**
Gloria Ferrer Caves and Vineyards, **2**
Ram's Gate Winery, **1**
Saintsbury, **10**
Truchard Vineyards, **8**

WESTERN CARNEROS

37 miles from San Francisco.

A few gems hide in plain sight in the windswept western Carneros, among them the dramatic Ram's Gate Winery—a must for lovers of architecture, design, and well-balanced Pinot Noirs—and the enigmatic CornerStone Sonoma complex of shops and gardens. From either venue you'll see rows and rows of vines, nearly all of them Pinot Noir and Chardonnay grapes. Most become still wines, but about 20 percent are transformed into lively sparkling wines, like the crisp and citrusy ones you'll find at Gloria Ferrer Caves and Vineyards.

4

The western reaches of Los Carneros AVA, from the foot of the Sonoma Mountains to the breezy banks of San Pablo Bay, lie within Sonoma County and for the most part within the larger Sonoma Valley AVA. Just to complicate matters, a portion of the Sonoma Coast AVA overlaps the western Carneros, so don't be surprised if you're tasting a wine labeled Sonoma Coast and your pourer tells you that it was made from grapes from the vineyard just outside.

GETTING HERE AND AROUND

Most of the western Carneros wineries covered in this chapter are on or near Highway 121, often signed as the Carneros Highway, the Sonoma Highway, or Arnold Drive. The multiple names can lead to confusion. The Gloria Ferrer winery gives its address as 23555 Carneros Highway, for instance; the listed address of CornerStone, across the road, is 23570 Arnold Drive.

EXPLORING

TOP ATTRACTIONS

★ FodorsChoice **CornerStone Sonoma.** A huge blue Adirondack chair on the east side of the road marks the way to this willful jumble of galleries, tasting rooms, and design and gift shops set amid 9 acres of landscape installations and outdoor sculptures. The sight of brides and bridesmaids scurrying along dirt-and-gravel paths to the weddings and receptions often held here adds to the visual mix. Sometimes closed a bit early on weekends when there are special events, the gardens are worth a 20-minute stroll. Of the tasting rooms, Meadowcroft is the best (ask to sample the Mt. Veeder Cabernet). The Park 121 Café is a fine stop for coffee or for lunch. ■TIP→ The Sonoma Valley Visitors Bureau office, near Meadowcroft, has coupons for free or discounted tastings in the western Carneros. ⊠ *23570 Arnold Dr./Hwy. 121, across from Gloria Ferrer winery, Sonoma* ☎ *707/933–3010* ⊕ *www.cornerstonesonoma.com* ☜ *Free* ⊙ *Daily 10–5, gardens daily 10–4, sometimes later in summer.*

★ Fodor'sChoice **Ram's Gate Winery.** Stunning views, ultrachic architecture, and wines made from grapes grown by acclaimed producers make a visit to Ram's Gate an event. The welcoming interior spaces—think Restoration Hardware with an extra dash of high-style whimsy—give you a sense of the entire western Carneros, and on many days you'll experience (in comfort) the cooling breezes that sweep through the area. The attention to detail at this newcomer extends to the wines, mostly Pinot Noirs and Chardonnays, but also Sauvignon Blanc, Cabernet Sauvignon, Syrah, late-harvest Zinfandel, and even a sparkler. With grapes from the high-profile Sangiacomo and Lee Hudson vineyards and other noteworthy growing spots, the focus of winemaker Jeff Gaffner is on creating balanced vintages that express what occurred in nature that year. Jesse Fox, the affable assistant winemaker, conducts one-on-one tours on Thursday morning. ⊠ *28700 Arnold Dr./Hwy. 121, Sonoma* ☎ *707/721–8700* ⊕ *www. ramsgatewinery.com* ☜ *Tasting $15–$125; winemaker tour $85* ⊙ *Thurs.–Mon. 10–6; tour Thurs. at 10 by appointment.*

WORTH NOTING

Anaba Wines. With the greatest hits of Burgundy (Chardonnay, Pinot Noir) and the Rhône (Grenache, Mourvèdre, Syrah, Viognier), along with several blends, this relative newcomer tries to be all things to most wine drinkers—and generally succeeds. The Sonoma Coast and Gap's Crown Vineyard Pinot Noirs are the standouts, as is the Sun Chase Vineyard Chardonnay, but all the wines—Anaba also makes a white and a red Port and a late-harvest Viognier—are thoughtfully crafted. The bungalowlike tasting room sits at the intersection of highways 121 and 116 (turn west at the blinking red light). A side patio faces the vineyards; if you don't mind a little highway noise, on a sunny day it's not a bad spot for a picnic put together at the deli across the street. ⊠ *Bonneau Rd., off Hwy. 116/121, Sonoma* ☎ *707/996–4188, 877/990–4188* ⊕ *www.anabawines.com* ☜ *Tasting $10* ⊙ *Daily 10:30–5:30.*

DID YOU KNOW?

Howard Backen, one of
the Wine Country's most
acclaimed architects,
designed Ram's Gate Winery.

Tours at di Rosa include walks to view outdoor sculptures and installations.

QUICK BITES. Angelo's Wine Country Deli. Many Bay Area locals stop here during Wine Country treks to get their jerky fix (generous free samples) or to pick up cheese, charcuterie, and sandwiches (huge and reasonably priced). "Cavemen made jerky from buffalo, antelope, deer, elk, rabbit, or whatever else they could bring down," the company points out on its website, and though the sources today—cows and turkeys—are less exotic, the 10 types sold here are no less satisfying. ⊠ 23400 Arnold Dr./Hwy. 121, near Wagner Rd., Sonoma ☎ 707/938-3688 ⊕ angelossmoke-house.com/deli.htm ⊙ Daily 9–5.

Gloria Ferrer Caves and Vineyards. A tasting at Gloria Ferrer is an exercise in elegance: at tables inside the Spanish hacienda–style winery or outside on the terrace (no standing at the bar at Gloria Ferrer), you can take in vistas of gently rolling hills while sipping sparkling and still wines. The Chardonnay and Pinot Noir grapes from the surrounding vineyards are the product of old-world wine-making knowledge—the same family started the sparkling-wine maker Freixenet in 16th-century Spain—and contemporary soil management techniques and clonal research. The tour covers the winery's history and its staff's contributions to advancing wine science; you'll also visit the aging caves and see antique wine-making equipment. ⊠ 23555 Carneros Hwy./Hwy. 121, Sonoma ☎ 707/933-1917 ⊕ www.gloriaferrer.com ☎ Tastings $3–$25, tour $10 ⊙ Daily 10–5; tours at 11, 1, and 3.

WHERE TO EAT

★ Fodor'sChoice ✕ **Fremont Diner.** *Southern.* Locals mix with tour-
$$ ists at this retro-yet-au-courant diner, where the entire menu
consists of rock-around-the-clock Southern favorites. With
breakfasts like pancakes and bacon and fried oysters and
grits, no one leaves the Fremont hungry. Ditto for lunch,
at which oyster po'boys, the chicken-and-waffle combo,
and handmade hamburgers (no prefab patties here) fortify
patrons for the next round of wine tasting. Barbecue plat-
ters—chicken, beef spare ribs, and pork butt—come with
two large sides. There's no let-up at dinner, which you can
top off with butterscotch pudding, apple bourbon fried
pie, and other desserts of Dixie yore. ■TIP→ Service here can
be slow, so if you're pressed for time, pass this one by. $ *Average
main: $20* ✉ *2698 Fremont Dr., at Hwy. 121, Sonoma*
☎ *707/938–7370* ⊕ *www.thefremontdiner.com* ⚅ *Reserva-
tions not accepted* ☉ *No dinner Mon.–Wed.*

EASTERN CARNEROS

42 miles northeast of San Francisco.

Stretching from the Sonoma County line to the Napa River
in the town of Napa, the eastern half of the Carneros shares
the wine-growing climate and soils with the western half.
Though you'll find the same rustic, relatively undeveloped
atmosphere in eastern Carneros, wineries pop up more
frequently along this stretch of Highway 121.

To take a break from wine tasting, grab a picnic lunch and
take Cuttings Wharf Road south to the Napa River, stop
at the public boat ramp, and dangle your feet in the water.
Keep a lookout for white egrets, great blue herons, wood
ducks, and other waterfowl. But beware, as the waters
here are tricky and rise and fall with the tide. If the bleak
marshes to the south look familiar, this might be the rea-
son: Francis Ford Coppola used this landscape for some
of the Mekong Delta scenes for the film *Apocalypse Now.*

GETTING HERE AND AROUND

From the western Carneros, continue east on Highway 121
to reach the eastern Carneros wineries; some are on the
highway and most others are just off it. From San Francisco,
travel east over the San Francisco–Oakland Bay Bridge,
north on Interstate 80, west on Highway 37, and north on
Highway 29 to Highway 121, on which you continue west.

A Great Drive in Carneros

Starting in the western Carneros on Highway 37, head north along Highway 121, also known as the Carneros Highway. Stop at Ram's Gate Winery for an introduction to the Wine Country high life, 21st-century style, or continue on to Gloria Ferrer Caves and Vineyards for a more traditionally elegant experience. Across the highway from Gloria Ferrer is your next stop, the landscape gardens of CornerStone Sonoma, which also has a café and tasting rooms, shops, and galleries. From here, continue north and then east (at the Highway 116 junction) on Highway 121.

Wineries line the increasingly rolling hills on either side of the highway, and bits of shiny reflective tape, tied to the vines to keep the birds away,

flicker in the sunlight. When you see the grand French-style château on your right, turn onto Duhig Road into Domaine Carneros. On the terrace you can order caviar or a cheese plate accompanied by a glass of bubbly. Domaine Carneros also has still wines, as does Cuvaison Estate Wines just across the road; call to make a quick and easy appointment, or return to the Carneros Highway and continue east. At Old Sonoma Road, turn left. After about a third of a mile, turn left again onto Dealy Lane. It changes names to Henry Road before it takes you to Artesa Vineyards & Winery. After your visit, return to the Carneros Highway. For a meal or coffee, backtrack west to the Boon Fly Café or head east to Highway 29, the main thoroughfare through the Napa Valley.

EXPLORING

TOP ATTRACTIONS

★ Fodor'sChoice **Artesa Vineyards & Winery.** With its modern, minimalist architecture blending harmoniously into a Carneros hilltop, Artesa is a far cry from the region's many faux-French châteaus and Italian-style villas. It's surrounded by elegant outdoor sculptures and fountains. The winemaker, Mark Beringer—a great-great-grandson of the 19th-century Napa wine-making pioneer Jacob Beringer—focuses on Chardonnay and Pinot Noir, but also produces Cabernet Sauvignon and other limited-release wines such as Albariño and Tempranillo. Call ahead to reserve a spot on a wine-and-cheese pairing ($60), a wine-and-chocolate pairing ($45), and a tapas-and-wine tasting ($60). ⊠ *1345 Henry Rd., off Old Sonoma Rd. and Dealy La., Napa* ☎ *707/224–*

The main château at Domaine Carneros

1668 ⊕ www.artesawinery.com ✉ Tastings $10–$15, tour $20 ☉ Daily 10–5; tour daily at 11 and 2.

★ **Fodor's Choice di Rosa.** It's not unusual for Wine Country moguls to collect art and display it in their wineries, but the late Rene di Rosa took the practice one grand step further: in 1986 he sold his winery and used the proceeds to finance this 217-acre art preserve. Thousands of 20th-century artworks by Northern California artists crop up everywhere—in galleries, in the former di Rosa residence, on every lawn, in every courtyard, and even on the lake. Some of the works were commissioned especially for the preserve, such as Paul Kos's meditative *Chartres Bleu,* a video installation in a chapel-like setting that replicates a stained-glass window from the cathedral in Chartres, France. If you stop by without a reservation, you'll gain access only to the Gatehouse Gallery, where there's a small collection of riotously colorful figurative and abstract sculptures and paintings, as well as rotating modern-art exhibits. ∎TIP→ To see the rest of the property, sign up for one of the various tours of the grounds. ✉ *5200 Sonoma Hwy./Hwy. 121, Napa* ☎ *707/226–5991* ⊕ *www.dirosaart.org* ✉ *Gatehouse Gallery $5, tours $12–$15* ☉ *May–Oct., Wed.–Sat. 10–6; Nov.–Apr., Wed.–Sat. 10–4.*

★ **Fodor's Choice Domaine Carneros.** A visit to this majestic château is an opulent way to enjoy the Carneros District—especially in fine weather, when the vineyard views are spectacular.

The château was modeled after the Château de la Mar-
quetterie, an 18th-century mansion owned by the Taittinger family near Epernay, France. Carved into the hillside
beneath the winery, the cellars produce delicate sparkling
wines reminiscent of those made by Taittinger, using only
Los Carneros AVA grapes. The winery sells full glasses,
flights, and bottles of its wines, which also include such
still wines as Pinot Noir, Merlot, and Chardonnay. Enjoy
them all them with cheese and charcuterie plates, caviar,
or smoked salmon. Seating is in the Louis XV–inspired
salon or on the terrace overlooking the vines. The tour at
Domaine Carneros covers traditional methods of making
sparkling wines, from the vineyard to the bottle. ⊠ *1240
Duhig Rd., at Hwy. 121, Napa* ☎ *707/257–0101, 800/716-
2788* ⊕ *www.domainecarneros.com* 🍷 *Tastings $7.50–$85,
tour $30* ☉ *Daily 10–6; tour daily at 11, 1, and 3.*

Etude Wines. The well-conceived wine and food seminars
are a big draw, but perhaps the most seductive part of a
visit to Etude is tasting the suave Pinot Noirs. Though the
handsome, modern winery is in Napa County, its flagship
Carneros Estate Pinot Noir comes from grapes grown
in the Sonoma County portion of Los Carneros, as does
the rarer Heirloom Carneros Pinot Noir. Both are gentle,
sophisticated wines whose smooth tannins linger on the
palate. Pinot Noir accounts for much of Etude's production, but the winery also makes Pinot Gris, Chardonnay,
Cabernet Sauvignon, and a few other wines. Some of them
are paired with small bites of food at informative tasting
seminars ($35). ■TIP→ Don't leave without stopping to survey
the landscape. You're apt to see (or hear) geese, hawks, egrets, and
other wildlife. ⊠ *1250 Cuttings Wharf Rd., 1 mile south of
Hwy. 121, Napa* ☎ *877/586–9361* ⊕ *www.etudewines.com*
🍷 *Tastings $15–$35* ☉ *Daily 10–4:30.*

WORTH NOTING

Bouchaine Vineyards. Tranquil Bouchaine lies just north
of the tidal sloughs of San Pablo Bay—to appreciate the
setting, have your tasting on the back patio and scan the
skies for hawks and golden eagles soaring above the vineyards. Patio tastings ($35) include cheeses, almonds, and
olives. The alternately breezy and foggy weather in this part
of the Carneros works well for the Burgundian varietals
Pinot Noir and Chardonnay. These account for most of
Bouchaine's excellent wines, but also look for Pinot Gris,
Riesling, and Syrah. Tastings may end with the silky-sweet
late-harvest Chardonnay called Bouche d'Or. ■TIP→ Pick up

California poppies at Bouchaine Vineyards

a brochure if you're interested in taking a self-guided ¾-mile walking tour through the vineyards. ✉ *1075 Buchli Station Rd., off Duhig Rd., south of Hwy. 121, Napa* ☎ *707/252–9065* ⊕ *www.bouchaine.com* ✐ *Tastings $20–$35* ⊗ *Mid-Mar.–Oct., daily 10:30–5:30; Nov.–mid-Mar., daily 10:30–4:30.*

Cuvaison Estate Wines. The flagship Carneros Chardonnay—a crisp and classic rendition of the white wine this region does best—is the star at Cuvaison (pronounced coo-vay-ZON), which also makes Sauvignon Blanc, Pinot Noir, Syrah, Cabernet Sauvignon, and Zinfandel. Taste them all in the slick, modern tasting room constructed from inventively recycled materials. Some of the wine can be purchased only at the winery, or sometimes online; the fruit-forward yet smooth estate Pinot Noirs and excellent Zinfandels often sell out. All tastings are sit-down style, either indoors or, in good weather, on an outdoor patio whose lounge chairs and vineyard views encourage you to take the time to savor the wines. ■TIP→ You must make an appointment to visit, but even on the shortest of notice you can usually get in. ✉ *1221 Duhig Rd., at Hwy. 121, Napa* ☎ *707/942–2455* ⊕ *www.cuvaison.com* ✐ *Tasting $20, tour $30 (includes tasting)* ⊗ *Daily 10–5, by appointment; tour weekends at 9:30 by appointment.*

Saintsbury. This Carneros pioneer helped disprove the conventional wisdom that only the French could produce great Pinot Noir. Back in 1981, when Saintsbury released its first

DID YOU KNOW?

Boon Fly Café at the Carneros Inn may look casual, but it's one of the region's best restaurants, focusing on the local agricultural bounty. It has a great wine bar, too.

Pinot, the region had yet to earn its current reputation as a setting in which the often finicky varietal could prosper. If you still have doubts, try Saintsbury's earthy, intense Brown Ranch Pinot Noir. The other Pinot Noirs tend to be lighter in style and more fruit-forward. Named for the English author and critic George Saintsbury (he wrote *Notes on a Cellar-Book*), the winery also makes Chardonnays, Syrahs, and a delightful Vin Gris. ✉ *1500 Los Carneros Ave., south off Hwy. 121 and left on Withers Rd., Napa* ☎ *707/252–0592* ⊕ *www.saintsbury.com* 🍷 *Tasting $25* ☉ *Mon.–Sat. by appointment only.*

Truchard Vineyards. Diversity is the name of the game at this family-owned winery on prime acreage in the region's rolling hills. Although major Napa Valley vintners purchase most of the grapes grown on the property, some of the best are held back for estate-only wines—the Chardonnays and Pinot Noirs the region is known for, along with Roussannes, Zinfandels, Merlots, Syrahs, Cabernet Sauvignons, and a few others. You must call ahead to tour or taste, but if you do, you'll be rewarded with a casual but informative experience tailored to your interests. The tour takes in the vineyards and the wine cave. ■TIP→ Climb the small hill near the winery for a photo-op view of the pond and the pen of Angora goats over the ridge. ✉ *3234 Old Sonoma Rd., off Hwy. 121, Napa* ☎ *707/253–7153* ⊕ *www.truchardvineyards.com* 🍷 *Tasting $20* ☉ *Mon.–Sat., by appointment only.*

WORD OF MOUTH. "I would choose the Carneros Inn. The food is fabulous and they have a great spa. We visited three great wineries all very close by—we even rode bikes they loan from the hotel to one of the wineries."—Travelgirlsf

WHERE TO EAT

★ Fodor'sChoice ✕ **Boon Fly Café.** *Modern American.* Part of the
$$ Carneros Inn west of downtown Napa, this small spot melds rural charm with industrial chic. Outside, swings occupy the porch of a modern red barn; inside, things get sleek with high ceilings and galvanized-steel tabletops. The menu of three squares a day updates American classics, with such dishes as Dungeness crab cakes with a citrus salad, roasted pork chop with sweet potatoes, and chicken and waffles. The flatbread topped with bacon, Point Reyes blue cheese, and portobello mushrooms is a local favorite. If there's a wait for a table, never fear:

belly up to the bar, where you'll find a good selection of wines by the glass. Reservations are a good idea at dinner. ■ TIP→ One of the rare Wine Country restaurants open all day, Boon Fly makes a convenient morning or midday stop. [$] *Average main: $18* ✉ *4048 Sonoma Hwy., Napa* ☎ *707/299–4870* 🌐 *www.theboonflycafe.com.*

WHERE TO STAY

★ Fodor's Choice 🏨 **Carneros Inn.** *Resort.* Freestanding board-
$$$$ and-batten cottages with rocking chairs on each porch are simultaneously rustic and chic at this luxurious property. **Pros:** cottages have lots of privacy; beautiful views from the hilltop pool and hot tub; heaters on each private patio encourage lounging outside in the evening. **Cons:** a long drive from destinations up-valley; smallish rooms with limited seating options. [$] *Rooms from: $600* ✉ *4048 Sonoma Hwy./Hwy. 121, Napa* ☎ *707/299–4900, 888/400–9000* 🌐 *www.thecarnerosinn.com* ⇨ *76 cottages, 10 suites.*

SONOMA VALLEY

ALTHOUGH THE SONOMA VALLEY may not have quite the cachet of the neighboring Napa Valley, wineries here entice with their unpretentious attitude and, in some cases, smaller crowds. Sonoma's landscape seduces, too, its roads gently climbing and descending on their way to wineries hidden from the road by trees.

That's not to suggest that the Sonoma Valley, the birthplace (in the mid-1800s) of California wine making as we know it, is exactly undiscovered territory. On the contrary, along the main corridor through the Sonoma Valley, Highway 12 from the town of Sonoma to the city of Santa Rosa, you'll spot sophisticated inns and spas between the ubiquitous wineries. In high season the towns of Glen Ellen and Kenwood are filled with well-heeled wine buffs. Still, the pace of life is a bit slower here than in Napa—on some days you'll see as many bicyclists as limo drivers zipping from one winery to the next. And the historic Sonoma Valley towns offer glimpses of the past. The town of Sonoma, with its atmospheric central plaza, is rich with 19th-century buildings. Glen Ellen, meanwhile, has a special connection with the author Jack London.

Bounded by the Mayacamas Mountains on the east and Sonoma Mountain on the west, this scenic valley extends north from San Pablo Bay nearly 20 miles to the eastern outskirts of Santa Rosa. The varied terrain, soils, and climate—cooler in the south because of the bay influence and hotter toward the north—allow grape growers to raise cool-weather varietals such as Chardonnay and Pinot Noir as well as Zinfandel, Merlot, Cabernet Sauvignon, and other heat-seeking vines.

GETTING AROUND SONOMA VALLEY

Highway 12, also called the Sonoma Highway, is the main thoroughfare through the Sonoma Valley, running north–south through Sonoma, Glen Ellen, and Kenwood into Santa Rosa. Except for some summer weekends, traffic tends to move fairly smoothly along this route. To get to Highway 12 from the city of Napa, take Highway 29 south to Highway 121 west. From Oakville, head west over the Mayacamas range on the highly scenic—but slow and winding—Oakville Grade Road, which turns into Trinity Road before it reaches Highway 12. From Calistoga, travel north a few miles on Highway 29/128 and then west on Petrified Forest Road and later Calistoga Road to reach Highway 12 in Santa Rosa. From there, head south into the valley.

SONOMA VALLEY APPELLATIONS

Although Sonoma *County* is a large (as big as Rhode Island), diverse growing region encompassing several different appellations, the much smaller Sonoma *Valley*, at the southern end of Sonoma County, is comparatively compact and consists mostly of the **Sonoma Valley AVA**, which stretches from southeast of Santa Rosa toward San Pablo Bay. The weather and soils here are unusually diverse. Pinot Noir and Chardonnay vineyards are most likely to be found in the southernmost parts of the AVA—which overlaps with the Sonoma County portions of the Los Carneros AVA, the sections cooled by fog from San Pablo Bay. Zinfandel, Cabernet Sauvignon, and Sauvignon Blanc grapes are more plentiful farther north, near Glen Ellen and Kenwood, both of which tend to be a few degrees warmer.

The **Sonoma Mountain AVA** rises to the west of Glen Ellen on the western border of the Sonoma Valley AVA. Benefiting from a sunny mountain location and rocky soil, the vineyards here produce deep-rooted vines and intensely flavored grapes that are made into unique, complex red wines, especially hearty Cabernet Sauvignons.

The tiny **Bennett Valley AVA**, also part of the Sonoma Valley AVA, falls within the city of Santa Rosa *(⇨ Chapter 6)*.

SONOMA

14 miles west of Napa; 45 miles northeast of San Francisco.

★ **Fodor's Choice** One of the few towns in the valley with many attractions not related to food and wine, Sonoma has plenty to keep you busy for a couple of hours before you head out to tour the wineries. You needn't leave town to taste wine. There are more than a dozen and a half tasting rooms within steps of the plaza, some of which pour wines from more than one winery. The "Sonoma Plaza WineWalk" brochure, available at the visitor center on the plaza's eastern side, has a map pointing the way.

The valley's cultural center, Sonoma is the oldest town in the Wine Country. Founded in 1835, when California was still part of Mexico, it is built around a large, tree-filled plaza. If you arrive from the south, on wide Broadway (Highway 12), you'll be retracing the last stretch of what was once California's most important road—El Camino Real, or "royal road," the only overland route through

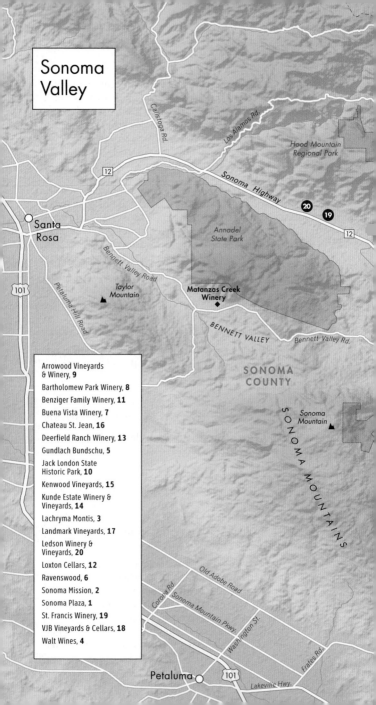

Sonoma Valley

Arrowood Vineyards
& Winery, **9**

Bartholomew Park Winery, **8**

Benziger Family Winery, **11**

Buena Vista Winery, **7**

Chateau St. Jean, **16**

Deerfield Ranch Winery, **13**

Gundlach Bundschu, **5**

Jack London State
Historic Park, **10**

Kenwood Vineyards, **15**

Kunde Estate Winery &
Vineyards, **14**

Lachryma Montis, **3**

Landmark Vineyards, **17**

Ledson Winery &
Vineyards, **20**

Loxton Cellars, **12**

Ravenswood, **6**

Sonoma Mission, **2**

Sonoma Plaza, **1**

St. Francis Winery, **19**

VJB Vineyards & Cellars, **18**

Walt Wines, **4**

The buildings and grounds please the eye at Bartholomew Park Winery.

the state. During California's Spanish and Mexican periods, it ran past all of the state's 21 missions: beginning at San Diego de Alcala (1769) and ending at Mission San Francisco Solano (1823). This last mission still sits in the center of Sonoma.

GETTING HERE AND AROUND
To get to the town of Sonoma from San Francisco, cross the Golden Gate Bridge, then head north on U.S. 101, east on Highway 37 toward Vallejo, and north on Highway 121, aka the Carneros Highway (Los Carneros AVA begins here). At Highway 12, head north; several blocks before the highway dead-ends at Sonoma Plaza, the street's name changes to Broadway. There are two-hour unmetered parking spaces until you get close to the plaza; if you're coming from this direction, parking south of Broadway or one block west on 1st Street West is sometimes easier than looking for metered parking space on the plaza. Once you've parked, a pleasant stroll takes you past many of the town's restaurants, shops, and tasting rooms. High-profile and boutique wineries can be found a mile or so east; arrow-shaped signs on East Spain Street and East Napa Street direct you.

CLOSE UP

Best Bets for Sonoma Valley Wineries

WINE TASTING

Deerfield Ranch Winery, Kenwood. You have to walk deep into the underground caves here to find the tasting room, where you'll sip "clean" red wines low in histamines and sulfites.

Loxton Cellars, Glen Ellen. Go retro at Loxton, where the personable owner-winemaker is often on the premises and the experience is down-home low-tech.

Walt Wines, Sonoma. At this tasting room just north of Sonoma Plaza, it's all Pinot Noir all the time, with grapes sourced from Oregon's Willamette Valley to California's Central Coast.

WINERY TOURING

Benziger Family Winery, Glen Ellen. On this winery's tram tour, you'll learn about its unique microclimates and deep commitment to biodynamic farming principles.

Buena Vista Winery, Sonoma. On some days, 19th-century wine pioneer Count Agoston Haraszthy (played by a local actor) leads tours.

Kunde Estate Winery & Vineyards, Kenwood. The Mountain Top Tastings passenger-van tour winds

1,400 feet above the valley floor. On a shaded deck you'll enjoy memorable vistas while sipping reserve wines.

SETTING

Bartholomew Park Winery, Sonoma. Come for the wines and stay for the grounds, which include a woodsy picnic spot and miles of hiking trails.

Chateau St. Jean, Kenwood. Something's always in bloom in this winery's formal gardens, inspired by their rustic counterparts in Italy and France.

Gundlach Bundschu, Sonoma. The hills of "GunBun" are alive with the sounds of happy picnickers all summer; year-round the vineyard views enchant, as do the sunsets.

FOOD-WINE PAIRING

Arrowood Vineyards & Winery, Glen Ellen. Distinguished Chardonnays, Syrahs, and age-worthy Cabs are paired with locally made artisanal cheeses at this laid-back winery's entertaining and educational tasting event.

St. Francis Winery, Kenwood. The executive chef's small-dish pairings are among the Sonoma Valley's better deals. Local cheeses and meats are served by the fireplace in winter and on a patio in summer.

5

EXPLORING

TOP ATTRACTIONS

★ Fodor'sChoice **Bartholomew Park Winery.** Although this certified organic winery was founded in 1994, grapes were grown in some of its vineyards as early as the 1830s. The emphasis here is on handcrafted, single-varietal wines—Cabernet, Merlot, Zinfandel, Syrah, Chardonnay, and Sauvignon Blanc. The wines alone make this a worthwhile stop, but another reason to visit is the small museum, with vivid exhibits about the history of the winery and the Sonoma region. Yet another plus is the beautiful, slightly off-the-beaten-path location in a 375-acre private park about 2 miles from downtown Sonoma (head east on East Napa Street and follow the signs). Pack a lunch to enjoy on the woodsy grounds, one of the prettier picnic spots in Sonoma, or hike 3 miles on the property's marked trails. ✉ *1000 Vineyard La., off Castle Rd.* ☎ *707/935–9511* ⊕ *www.bartpark.com* ▧ *Tasting $10, tour $20* ☉ *June–Oct., daily 11–5:30; Nov.–May, daily 11–4:30; tour Fri. and Sat. at 11:30 and 2, Sun. at 2, by reservation.*

Buena Vista Winery. The ebullient Jean-Charles Boisset, whose family owns wineries in France and elsewhere, purchased Buena Vista in 2011 and quickly set about transforming the site where modern California wine making got its start into an entertaining homage to the accomplishments of 19th-century wine pioneer Count Agoston Haraszthy. Tours, sometimes conducted by the count himself—as channeled by actor George Webber and others—pass through the original aging caves dug deep into the hillside by Chinese laborers. Tastings take place in the former press house (used for pressing grapes into wine), which was built in 1862 and stylishly renovated in 2012. The best wines here are the Chardonnays and Pinot Noirs from Los Carneros AVA. ■TIP→ On the mezzanine above the tasting room you can view reproductions of period photographs and prints of the winery. ✉ *18000 Old Winery Rd., off Napa Rd.* ☎ *800/926–1266* ⊕ *www.buenavistawinery.com* ▧ *Tasting $10; tours $10–$30* ☉ *Daily 10–5; tours by appointment 1–2 days in advance.*

QUICK BITES. **Crisp Bake Shop.** Only in the Wine Country would your local pastry chef, in this case Andrea Koweek, have honed her skills at the French Laundry. Much of what she bakes—croissants, cupcakes, mini-Bundt cakes, brioche sweet buns with ricotta

Wine-making Pioneer

Count Agoston Haraszthy arrived in Sonoma in 1857 and set out to make fine wine commercially. He planted European vinifera varietals rather than mission grapes (the varietals Spanish missionaries brought to the Americas) and founded Buena Vista Winery the year he arrived.

Haraszthy deserves credit for two breakthroughs. At Buena Vista, he grew grapes on dry hillsides, instead of in the wetter lowlands, as had been customary in the Mission and Rancho periods. His success demonstrated that Sonoma's climate was moist enough to sustain grapes without irrigation. The innovative count was also the first to try aging his wine in redwood barrels, which were much less expensive than oak barrels. More affordable barrels made it feasible to ratchet up wine production. For almost 100 years, redwood barrels would be the California wine industry's most popular storage method (even

though redwood can impart an odd flavor).

Despite producing inferior wines, the prolific mission grapes were preferred by California growers over better varieties of French, German, and Italian vinifera grapes through the 1860s and into the 1870s. But Haraszthy's success had begun to make an impression. A new red-wine grape, the Zinfandel, was becoming popular, both because it made excellent Claret (as good red wine was then called) and because it had adapted to the area's climate.

By this time, however, Haraszthy had disappeared, literally, from the scene. After a business setback during the 1860s, the count lost control of Buena Vista and ventured to Nicaragua to restore his fortune in the sugar and rum industries. While crossing a stream infested with alligators, the count lost his balance and plunged into water below. The body of modern California wine making's first promoter and pioneer was never recovered.

Buena Vista Winery and the nearby Bartholomew Park Winery now occupy Haraszthy's former land, and both have small museums with exhibits celebrating the count's legacy. At Buena Vista, an actor portraying the count gives tours of "his" winery and caves.

and blueberries, chocolate sea-salt cookies—is so cute, it's hard to take that first bite. Bacon, egg, cheese, and potato pies for breakfast and sandwiches for lunch are among the more savory fare, which is overseen by executive chef Moaya Scheiman (also Andrea's husband). Crisp is seven blocks west of Sonoma Plaza, but it's worth the walk or drive. ⊠ *720 W. Napa St./Hwy. 12, at 7th St. W* ☎ *707/933-9999* ⊕ *www.crispbakeshop.com* ☉ *Mon.-Sat. 7:30-4:30, Sun. 7:30-2.*

★ Fodor'sChoice **Gundlach Bundschu.** Wine Country visitors may mispronounce this winery's name (it's gund-lak bund-shoe), but still they flock here to sample ultrapremium wines served by some of the friendliest pourers in Sonoma County. Most of the winery's land has been in the Bundschu family since the 1850s. The Cabernet Sauvignon, Cabernet Franc, Merlot, Tempranillo, and Chardonnay wines are worth trying, and all are included in the standard $10 tasting. For a more comprehensive experience that also includes a tasting, consider the cave tour ($20) or the vineyard excursion ($40; available only between May and October). ■TIP➔ In summer you can taste outdoors at tables with splendid vineyard views. ⊠ *2000 Denmark St., at Bundschu Rd., off 8th St. E* ☎ *707/938-5277* ⊕ *www.gunbun.com* ☜ *Tastings $10–$15, tours $20–$40* ☉ *June–mid.-Oct., daily 11–5:30; mid.-Oct.–May, daily 11–4:30.*

WORD OF MOUTH. "We too love the town and square of Sonoma, and the area around it. It is not only cute/historic/Victorian themed but has some very good restaurants. One of our favorite wineries is Gundlach Bundschu, with a rich history (the oldest family winery in California)." —Tomsd

Sonoma Mission. The northernmost of the 21 missions established by Franciscan friars in California, Sonoma Mission was founded in 1823 as Mission San Francisco Solano. It serves as the centerpiece of **Sonoma State Historic Park,** which includes several other sites in Sonoma and nearby Petaluma. Some early structures were destroyed, but all or part of several remaining buildings date to the days of Mexican rule over California. These include the **Sonoma Barracks,** a block west of the mission at 20 East Spain Street, which housed troops under the command of General Mariano Guadalupe Vallejo, who controlled vast tracks of land in the region. The modest museum contains displays about the missions and information about the other historic sites. ⊠ *114 E. Spain St., at 1st*

Sonoma Mission was the last of California's 21 missions.

St. E ☎ *707/938–9560* ⊕ *www.parks.ca.gov/?page_id=479* ✉ *$3, includes same-day admission to other historic sites* ⊙ *Daily 10–5 (weekday hrs sometimes vary).*

Sonoma Plaza. Dating from the Mission era, central Sonoma Plaza is surrounded by 19th-century adobes, atmospheric hotels, and the swooping marquee of the Depression-era Sebastiani Theatre. A statue on the plaza's northeastern side marks the spot where California proclaimed its independence from Mexico on June 14, 1846. But despite its historical roots, the plaza is not a museum piece. On summer days it's a hive of activity, with children blowing off steam in the playground, couples enjoying picnics from gourmet shops, and groups listening to live music at the small amphitheater. The stone **City Hall** is also here. If you're wondering why the 1906 structure looks the same from all angles, here's why: its four sides were purposely made identical so that none of the plaza's merchants would feel that City Hall had turned its back to them. ■ TIP➔ Explore the courtyards on the streets bordering the plaza's eastern and southern sides, where cafés and boutiques line the passageways. ✉ *North end of Broadway/Hwy. 12, bordered by E. Napa St., 1st St. E, E. Spain St., and 1st St. W.*

★ **Fodor'sChoice Walt Wines.** You could spend a very full day sampling wines in the tasting rooms bordering Sonoma Plaza, but the one place not to miss is Walt Wines, which specializes in Pinot Noir. Fruit-forward yet subtle, these

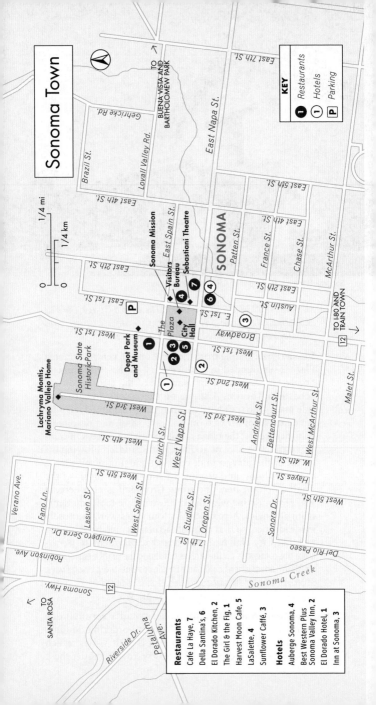

Sonoma Town

KEY
- **1** Restaurants
- **(1)** Hotels
- **P** Parking

Lachryma Montis,
Mariano Vallejo Home

Sonoma State
Historic Park

Depot Park
and Museum

The
Plaza

City
Hall

Sonoma Mission

Visitors
Bureau

Sebastiani Theatre

SONOMA

TO
BUENA VISTA AND
BARTHOLOMEW PARK

TO I80 AND
TRAIN TOWN

TO
SANTA ROSA

Sonoma Creek

Restaurants
Cafe La Haye, **7**
Della Santina's, **6**
El Dorado Kitchen, **2**
The Girl & the Fig, **1**
Harvest Moon Cafe, **5**
LaSalette, **4**
Sunflower Caffé, **3**

Hotels
Auberge Sonoma, **4**
Best Western Plus
Sonoma Valley Inn, **2**
El Dorado Hotel, **1**
Inn at Sonoma, **3**

wines win over even the purists who pine for the genre's days of lighter, more perfumey vintages. Walt is a good place to compare the Pinots one winemaker crafts from local grapes with others from grapes grown in Mendocino County (just north of Sonoma County), California's Central Coast, and even Oregon's Willamette Valley. Critics routinely bestow high ratings on all these wines. ⊠ *380 1st St. W, at W. Spain St.* ☎ *707/933–4440* ⊕ *www.waltwines. com* 🍷 *Tasting $10.*

WORTH NOTING

Lachryma Montis. General Mariano G. Vallejo commissioned this 1852 Victorian Gothic home that sits on several serene acres a few blocks west of Sonoma Plaza. It's a great place to picnic amid enormous cacti and learn about one of the region's early VIPs. The home blends Mexican and American styles and has opulent furnishings, including white-marble fireplaces and a French rosewood piano. Another building holds a small museum. Occasional weekend tours are conducted by docents. ⊠ *W. Spain St., at 3rd St. W* ☎ *707/938–9559* 🍷 *$3, including same-day admission to Sonoma Mission* ⊗ *Fri.–Wed. 10–5.*

Ravenswood. The punchy motto here is "no wimpy wines," and the winery generally succeeds, especially with its signature big, bold Zinfandels, which are sometimes blended with other varietals grown in the same field (this is called a "field blend"). Ravenswood also produces Bordeaux-style blends, early-harvest Gewürztraminer, and lightly sparkling Moscato. Tours focusing on viticultural practices, held daily at 10:30, include a barrel tasting of wines in the cellar. To learn even more about the wine-making process, make an appointment for one of the wine-blending sessions ($50), held on Friday and Saturday at 11. ⊠ *18701 Gehricke Rd., off E. Spain St.* ☎ *707/938–1960, 888/669–4679* ⊕ *www. ravenswoodwinery.com* 🍷 *Tasting $15, tour $15* ⊗ *Daily 10–4:30; tour daily at 10:30.*

WHERE TO EAT

★ Fodor's Choice ✕ **Cafe La Haye.** *American.* In a postage-stamp-
$$ size open kitchen, the skillful chef turns out main courses that star on a small but worthwhile seasonal menu emphasizing local ingredients. Chicken, beef, pasta, and fish get deluxe treatment without fuss or fanfare. The daily roasted chicken and the risotto specials are always good. Butterscotch pudding is a homey signature dessert. The

El Dorado Kitchen's chef Armando Navarro crafts flavorful dishes full of subtle surprises.

dining room is compact, but the friendly owner, always there to greet diners, maintains a particularly welcoming vibe. $ *Average main: $22* ✉ *140 E. Napa St., at 1st. St. E* ☎ *707/935–5994* ⊕ *www.cafelahaye.com* ⊗ *Closed Sun. and Mon. No lunch.*

$$ ╳ **Della Santina's.** *Italian.* Its owners hail from Lucca, Italy, which may be why this longtime favorite serves the most authentic Italian food in town. The heated patio out back adds to the setting's down-to-earth charms. Daily fish and veal specials join such classic northern Italian dishes as linguine with pesto and lasagna Bolognese. Of special note are the roasted meat dishes and, when available, petrale sole and sand dabs. Enoteca Della Santina, the casual wine bar and retail shop next door, also serves dinner nightly. $ *Average main: $19* ✉ *133 E. Napa St., near 1st St. E* ☎ *707/935–0576* ⊕ *www.dellasantinas.com.*

★ Fodors Choice ╳ **El Dorado Kitchen.** *Modern American.* The
$$$ visual delights at this winning restaurant include its clean lines and handsome decor, but the eye inevitably drifts westward to the open kitchen, where chef Armando Navarro and his diligent crew craft flavorful dishes full of subtle surprises. Pumpkin seeds and spiced marshmallows top the popular butternut squash soup, for instance, adding a crunchy-sweet piquancy that plays well off the dish's predominantly savory sentiments. Focusing on locally sourced ingredients, the menu might include Petaluma duck breast enlivened by the tangy flavors of parsnip puree, braised

endive, roasted turnips, persimmons, and huckleberries. Even a simple dish like truffle-oil fries, liberally sprinkled with Parmesan cheese, charms with its combination of tastes and textures. The noteworthy desserts include an apple tart tatin, banana crisp with lime curd, and molten chocolate cake. $ *Average main: $26* ✉ *El Dorado Hotel, 405 1st St. W, at W. Spain St.* ☎ *707/996–3030* 🌐 *www.eldoradosonoma.com/restaurant.*

$$$ 🍴 **The Girl & the Fig.** *French.* Chef Sondra Bernstein has transformed the historic bar room of the Sonoma Hotel into a hot spot for inventive French cooking. You can always find a dish with the signature figs on the menu, whether it's a fig-and-arugula salad or an aperitif blending sparkling wine with fig liqueur. Also look for duck confit with sweet potato Lyonnaise, a burger with matchstick fries, or wild flounder meunière. The wine list is notable for its emphasis on Rhône varietals, and a counter in the bar area sells artisanal cheese platters for eating here as well as cheese by the pound to go. The indulgent Sunday brunch includes rib-sticking chorizo and eggs, and potato pancakes with smoked salmon, dill crème fraiche, and caviar. On weekend nights the kitchen serves until 11. $ *Average main: $24* ✉ *Sonoma Hotel, 110 W. Spain St., at 1st St. W* ☎ *707/938–3634* 🌐 *www.thegirlandthefig.com.*

5

★ Fodor's Choice 🍴 **Harvest Moon Cafe.** *American.* It's easy to feel
$$ like one of the family at this little restaurant with an odd, zigzagging layout. Diners seated at one of the two tiny bars chat with the servers like old friends, but the husband-and-wife team in the kitchen is serious about the food, much of which relies on local produce. The ever-changing menu might include homey dishes like grilled pork loin with crispy polenta and artichokes, Niman Ranch rib-eye steak with a red-wine sauce, or shepherd's pie with rabbit ragout. Everything is so perfectly executed and the vibe is so genuinely warm that a visit here is deeply satisfying. A spacious back patio with tables arranged around a fountain more than doubles the seating; a heated tent keeps this area warm in winter. $ *Average main: $22* ✉ *487 1st St. W, at W. Napa St.* ☎ *707/933–8160* 🌐 *www.harvestmooncafesonoma.com* ⊗ *Closed Tues. No lunch Mon.–Sat.*

★ Fodor's Choice 🍴 **Hot Box Grill.** *Modern American.* Comfort
$$$ foods aren't often described as *nuanced*, but the term aptly describes the locally sourced preparations chef Norm Owens conjures up at his modest roadside restaurant. Take the fries (but not too many): long and not at all lean, they're cooked in duck fat and served with malt-vinegar

aioli, lending them a richness that lingers pleasingly in your memory. There's lots of frying going on here—of chicken, of course, but even the Cornish game hen gets the treatment. The corn-bread pudding on the side is creamy good. Up against these dishes, the daily-changing pasta offerings almost seem light, and the appetizers—think spicy ahi tuna with a ponzu sauce and persimmon "carpaccio"—downright dainty. [$] *Average main: $24* ✉ *18350 Sonoma Hwy./Hwy. 12* ☎ *707/939–8383* 🌐 *www.hotboxgrill.com* ⏲ *Closed Mon. and Tues. No lunch.*

$$$ ✕ **LaSalette.** *Portuguese.* Born in the Azores and raised in Sonoma, chef-owner Manuel Azevedo serves dishes inspired by his native Portugal in this warmly decorated spot. The best seats are on a patio along an alleyway off Sonoma Plaza. Such boldly flavored dishes as pork tenderloin *recheado,* stuffed with olives and almonds and topped with a port sauce, might be followed by a dish of rice pudding with Madeira-braised figs or a port from the varied list. The daily seafood specials are also well worth a try. [$] *Average main: $24* ✉ *452 E. 1st St., between E. Spain and E. Napa Sts.* ☎ *707/938–1927* 🌐 *www.lasalette-restaurant.com.*

★ Fodor'sChoice ✕ **Santé.** *American.* This elegant dining room has
$$$$ gained a reputation as a destination restaurant through its focus on seasonal and locally sourced ingredients. The room is understated, with drapes in rich earth tones and softly lighted chandeliers, but the food is anything but. Dishes such as truffled organic *poussin* (spring chicken)—poached breast, braised leg, stuffed thigh—served with brussels sprouts, butternut squash, and black-truffle bread, are complex without being fussy. Others, like the butter-poached Maine lobster pot-au-feu, served with Parisian gnocchi, black trumpet mushrooms, delicata squash, pickled pearl onions, and lobster bouillabaisse, are pure decadence. The restaurant offers a seasonal tasting menu ($125). [$] *Average main: $75* ✉ *Fairmont Sonoma Mission Inn & Spa, 100 Boyes Blvd./Hwy. 12, 2.5 miles north of Sonoma Plaza, Boyes Hot Springs* ☎ *707/938–9000* 🌐 *www.fairmont.com/sonoma* ⏲ *No lunch.*

$ ✕ **Sunflower Caffé.** *American.* This casual eatery's menu, composed mostly of salads and sandwiches, is simple but satisfying. Highlights include the smoked duck breast sandwich, served on a baguette and slathered with caramelized onions. A meal of soup and local cheeses is a good option if you just want to nibble. Both the pretty patio, which is in the back, and the sidewalk seating area facing Sonoma

Plaza are equipped with heating lamps and get plenty of shade, so they're comfortable in all but the most inclement weather. On dreary days, cheerful artworks brighten up the interior, where locals hunker over their computers and take advantage of the free Wi-Fi. Omelets and waffles are the stars at breakfast. [$] *Average main: $13* ✉ *421 1st St. W, at W. Spain St.* ☎ *707/996–6645* 🌐 *www.sonomasunflower.com* ⏲ *No dinner.*

$ 🍴 **Taqueria Los Primos.** *Mexican.* The ambience here is decidedly downscale, but the food is downright tasty—and there's plenty of it. Locals (including chefs from Sonoma's fancy restaurants) rave about the barbecue goat, the carnitas, and the chicken, beef, and pulled-pork tacos for lunch and dinner. The breakfast burritos, egg plates, and other morning fare will fortify you for a day of wine tasting. ■ TIP→ The easiest place to park is south of the restaurant on Hawthorne Avenue. [$] *Average main: $10* ✉ *18375 Hwy. 12, at Hawthorne Ave.* ☎ *707/935–3546.*

5

WHERE TO STAY

$$$ 🏨 **Auberge Sonoma.** *Rental.* If you are traveling in a group of three or four, or just prefer lodgings that feel more like home, consider the two-bedroom suites at this charmer just off Sonoma Plaza. **Pros:** good value for couples traveling together; beautifully appointed; close to Sonoma Plaza shops, restaurants, and tasting rooms. **Cons:** two-night minimum (three on summer weekends). [$] *Rooms from: $340* ✉ *151 E. Napa St.* ☎ *866/700–3648 voice mail* 🌐 *www.aubergesonoma.com* 🛏 *3 suites* 🍽 *Breakfast.*

$ 🏨 **Best Western Plus Sonoma Valley Inn.** *Hotel.* This motel just off Sonoma Plaza has enthusiastic staffers who provide fine service, and public areas, including the lobby and a pool and spa, that are inviting, if not elegant. **Pros:** good value; complimentary continental breakfast; coupons for complimentary tastings at local wineries; within walking distance of Sonoma Plaza shops and restaurants. **Cons:** small fitness center; public areas nicer than the rooms; convention facilities and rooms in front can be noisy. [$] *Rooms from: $179* ✉ *550 2nd St. W* ☎ *800/334–5784, 707/938–9200* 🌐 *www.sonomavalleyinn.com* 🛏 *73 rooms, 7 suites* 🍽 *Breakfast.*

$$ 🏨 **El Dorado Hotel.** *B&B/Inn.* Rooms in this remodeled 1843 building strike a spare, modern pose with their pristine white bedding, but the Mexican-tile floors hint at Sonoma's Mission-era past. **Pros:** stylish for the price; hip on-site restaurant; good café for breakfast; central location. **Cons:**

rooms are small; lighting could be better; noisy. $ *Rooms from: $200* ✉ *405 1st St. W* ☎ *707/996–3220* 🌐 *www.eldoradosonoma.com/hotel* 🛏 *27 rooms* 🍴 *No meals.*

$$$$ 🏨 **Fairmont Sonoma Mission Inn & Spa.** *Resort.* The real draw at this Mission-style resort is the extensive, swanky spa, easily the biggest in Sonoma, with a vast array of massages and treatments, some using locally sourced grape and lavender products. **Pros:** enormous spa; excellent restaurant; free shuttle to downtown. **Cons:** standard rooms on the smaller side; not as intimate as some similarly priced places. $ *Rooms from: $439* ✉ *100 Boyes Blvd./Hwy. 12, 2.5 miles north of Sonoma Plaza, Boyes Hot Springs* ☎ *707/938–9000* 🌐 *www.fairmont.com/sonoma* 🛏 *166 rooms, 60 suites* 🍴 *No meals.*

$$ 🏨 **Inn at Sonoma.** *B&B/Inn.* They don't skimp on the little luxuries here: wine and cheese is served every evening in the lobby, and the cheerfully painted rooms are warmed by gas fireplaces. **Pros:** last-minute specials are a great deal; free soda available in the lobby; free Wi-Fi. **Cons:** on a busy street rather than right on the plaza. $ *Rooms from: $220* ✉ *630 Broadway* ☎ *707/939–1340, 888/568–9818* 🌐 *www.innatsonoma.com* 🛏 *19 rooms* 🍴 *Breakfast.*

$ 🏨 **Sonoma Creek Inn.** *B&B/Inn.* The small but cheerful rooms
FAMILY at this roadside inn with a sunny yellow exterior are individually decorated with painted wooden armoires, cozy quilts, and brightly colored contemporary artwork, elevating this bargain option well above your average motel. **Pros:** clean, well-lighted bathrooms; a lot of charm for the low price. **Cons:** office not staffed 24 hours a day; a 10-minute drive from Sonoma Plaza. $ *Rooms from: $145* ✉ *239 Boyes Blvd., off Hwy. 12* ☎ *707/939–9463, 888/712–1289* 🌐 *www.sonomacreekinn.com* 🛏 *16 rooms.*

NIGHTLIFE AND THE ARTS

Aside from the hotel and restaurant bars, the nightlife scene in Sonoma is pretty subdued. The bar inside the El Dorado Kitchen is a good spot for a drink, as is the bar at the Ledson Hotel across Sonoma Plaza. The Epicurean Connection hosts live jazz from Thursday through Saturday (and sometimes on other nights) from about 7:30 to 10.

Sebastiani Theatre. This theater, built on Sonoma Plaza in 1934 by Italian immigrant and entrepreneur Samuele Sebastiani, schedules first-run films, as well as occasional musical and theatrical performances. ✉ *476 1st St. E, near W. Spain St.* ☎ *707/996–2020* 🌐 *www.sebastianitheatre.com.*

DID YOU KNOW?

The Fairmont Sonoma Mission Inn is best known for its spa, which has both indoor and outdoor thermal pools fed by the hot mineral springs that run under the property.

The tram tour is a highlight of a visit to Benziger Family Winery.

Swiss Hotel. Old-timers head to the hotel's old-timey bar for a blast of Glariffee, a cold and potent cousin to Irish coffee that loosens the tongue. ✉ *18 W. Spain St., at 1st St. W* ☎ *707/938–2884* ⊕ *www.swisshotelsonoma.com.*

SHOPPING

★ **Fodor's Choice Chateau Sonoma.** The fancy furniture, lighting fixtures, and objets d'art at this upscale shop make it a dangerous place to enter: after just a few minutes you may find yourself reconsidering your entire home's aesthetic. The owner's keen eye for style and sense of whimsy make a visit here a delight. ✉ *153 W. Napa St., near 2nd St. W* ☎ *707/935–8553* ⊕ *www.chateausonoma.com.*

The Epicurean Connection. Food-lover alert: In addition to selling Delice de La Vallee, her award-winning artisanal cheese made from triple-cream cow and goat milk, owner Sheana Davis offers jams, sauces, tapenades, and other toppings from local producers. You can also buy sandwiches and sweets, and in the evening from Thursday through Saturday (and sometimes other days) you can hear good live jazz. ✉ *122 W. Napa St., at 1st St.* ☎ *707/935–7960* ⊕ *www.theepicureanconnection.com.*

Sign of the Bear. This locally owned shop sells the latest and greatest in kitchenware and cookware, as well as a few Wine Country–theme items, such as lazy Susans made from wine barrels. ⊠ *435 1st St. W, near W. Spain St.* ☎ *707/996–3722.*

Sonoma Cheese Factory. The town's touristy cheese shop offers samples of many local types. The store has everything you need for a picnic, from sandwiches to wine to home-made fudge. ⊠ *2 E. Spain St., near 1st St. E* ☎ *800/535–2855* ⊕ *www.sonomacheesefactory.com.*

★ Fodors Choice **Sonoma Valley Certified Farmers Market.** To dis-cover just how bountiful the Sonoma landscape is—and how talented its farmers and food artisans are—head to Depot Park, just north of the Sonoma Plaza, on Friday morning. From April through October, the market gets extra play on Tuesday evening in Sonoma Plaza. ⊠ *Depot Park, 1st St. W, at Sonoma Bike Path* ☎ *707/538–7023* ⊕ *www.svcfm.org.*

Vella Cheese Company. A bit north and east of Sonoma Plaza, this old-world Italian cheese shop has been making superb cheeses, including raw-milk cheddars and several varieties of jack, since 1931. A bonus: plenty of free samples. ⊠ *315 2nd St. E, ½ block north of E. Spain St.* ☎ *707/938–3232, 800/848–0505* ⊕ *vellacheese.com.*

SPAS

Willow Stream Spa at Fairmont Sonoma Mission Inn & Spa. With 40,000 square feet and 30 treatment rooms—making it by far the largest spa in the Wine Country—Willow Stream offers every amenity you could possibly want, including several pools and hot tubs fed by local thermal springs. Although the spa bustles with patrons in summer and on some weekends, the vibe here is always soothing. The sig-nature bathing ritual includes an exfoliating shower, dips in two mineral-water soaking pools, an herbal steam, a dry sauna, and cool-down showers. Guests experience this ritual on their own or in conjunction with other treatments such as the warm ginger-oil float, which involves relaxation in a weightless environment, and the perennially popular caviar facial. The most requested room among couples is outfitted with a two-person copper bathtub. ⊠ *100 Boyes Blvd./Hwy. 12, 2.5 miles north of Sonoma Plaza, Boyes Hot Springs* ☎ *707/938–9000* ⊕ *www.fairmont.com/sonoma* ⊡ *Treatments $65–$485.*

5

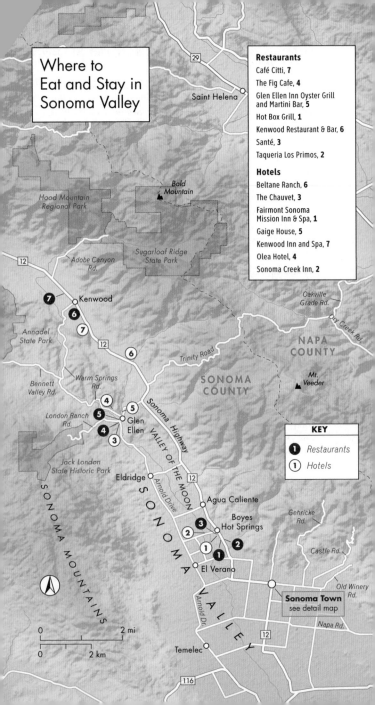

Where to Eat and Stay in Sonoma Valley

Restaurants

Café Citti, **7**

The Fig Cafe, **4**

Glen Ellen Inn Oyster Grill
and Martini Bar, **5**

Hot Box Grill, **1**

Kenwood Restaurant & Bar, **6**

Santé, **3**

Taqueria Los Primos, **2**

Hotels

Beltane Ranch, **6**

The Chauvet, **3**

Fairmont Sonoma
Mission Inn & Spa, **1**

Gaige House, **5**

Kenwood Inn and Spa, **7**

Olea Hotel, **4**

Sonoma Creek Inn, **2**

KEY

❶ *Restaurants*

① *Hotels*

GLEN ELLEN

7 miles north of Sonoma.

Craggy Glen Ellen epitomizes the difference between the Napa and Sonoma valleys. Whereas small Napa towns like St. Helena get their charm from upscale boutiques and restaurants lined up along well-groomed sidewalks, in Glen Ellen the crooked streets are shaded with stands of old oak trees and occasionally bisected by the Sonoma and Calabasas creeks. Tucked among the trees of a narrow canyon, where Sonoma Mountain and the Mayacamas pinch in the valley floor, Glen Ellen looks more like a town of the Sierra foothills gold country than a Wine Country village.

Wine has been part of Glen Ellen since the 1840s, when a French immigrant, Joshua Chauvet, planted grapes and built a winery and the valley's first distillery. The winery machinery was powered by steam, and the boilers were fueled with wood from local oaks. In 1881 Chauvet built a stone winery to house his operations. Other valley farmers followed Chauvet's example, and grape growing took off. Wine was even made during Prohibition, when the locals took a liberal view of the 200 gallons each family was allowed to produce for personal consumption. There are still dozens of wineries in the area that beg to be visited, but sometimes it's hard not to succumb to Glen Ellen's slow pace and simply lounge poolside at your lodging or linger over a leisurely picnic. The renowned cook and food writer M. F. K. Fisher, who lived and worked in Glen Ellen for 22 years until her death in 1992, would surely have approved.

Glen Ellen's most famous resident, however, was Jack London, who epitomized the town's rugged spirit.

GETTING HERE AND AROUND

To get to Glen Ellen from Sonoma, drive west on Spain Street. After about a mile, take Highway 12 for 7 miles to Arnold Drive, which deposits you in the middle of town. Many of Glen Ellen's restaurants and inns are along a half-mile stretch of Arnold Drive.

EXPLORING

TOP ATTRACTIONS

★ Fodor'sChoice **Benziger Family Winery.** One of the best-known Sonoma County wineries sits on a sprawling estate in a bowl with 360-degree sun exposure, the benefits of which are explored on popular tram tours that depart several times daily. Guides explain Benziger's biodynamic farming practices and give you a glimpse of the extensive cave system. The regular tram tour costs $20; another costing $40 concludes with a seated tasting. Benziger is noted for its Merlot, Pinot Noir, Cabernet Sauvignon, Chardonnay, and Sauvignon Blanc wines. Bring a picnic lunch, as the grounds are lovely. ■TIP→ Reserve a seat on the tram tour through the winery's website or arrive early in the day on busy summer weekends and during the harvest. ✉ *1883 London Ranch Rd., off Arnold Dr.* ☎ *707/935–3000, 888/490–2739* ⊕ *www. benziger.com* ✑ *Tastings $10–$20, tours $20–$40* ⊙ *Daily 10–5; tours daily at 11:15, 12:45, 2:15.*

★ Fodor'sChoice **Jack London State Historic Park.** The pleasures are both pastoral and intellectual at the beloved former ranch of the late author Jack London. You could easily spend the afternoon hiking along the edge of vineyards and through stands of oaks. Several manuscripts and a handful of personal effects are on view at the House of Happy Walls Museum, which provides a tantalizing overview of the author's life and literary passions. A short hike away lie the ruins of Wolf House, which mysteriously burned down just before the writer was to move in. Also open to the public are a few restored farm outbuildings and the Cottage, a wood-framed building where he penned many of his later works. London is buried on the property. ✉ *2400 London Ranch Rd., off Arnold Dr.* ☎ *707/938–5216* ⊕ *jacklondon-park.com* ✑ *Parking $10, includes admission to museum; cottage $4* ⊙ *Thurs.–Mon. park 9:30–5, museum 10–5, cottage noon–4.*

Loxton Cellars. Back in the day, when tasting rooms were low-tech and the winemaker often poured the wines, the winery experience unfolded pretty much the way it does at Loxton Cellars today. The personable owner, Chris Loxton, honed his skills at nearby Wellington, where he helped produce some of that winery's finest vintages. Full-bodied Zinfandels, Syrahs, and a Cabernet Sauvignon are the standouts at this operation, though some regulars swear by the more delicate Pinot Noir from Russian River Valley grapes and the seductively smooth Syrah Port. If you schedule the Walkabout with the Winemaker tour, you're sure to meet Loxton, but even if he's working elsewhere, one of his equally pleasant staffers will convey his passion for these wines. ✉ *11466 Dunbar Rd., at Hwy. 12, Glen Ellen* ☎ *707/935–7221* 🌐 *www.loxtonwines.com* 🎫 *Tasting free, tour $15* ⏲ *Daily 11–5; tours by appointment.*

WORTH NOTING

Arrowood Vineyards & Winery. Although it's neither as famous nor as old as some of its neighbors, Arrowood produces well-regarded wines, especially the Chardonnays, Syrahs, and age-worthy Cabernets. Except on summer weekends and at harvesttime, the pace here can be more relaxing, too. A wraparound porch with wicker chairs invites you to linger outside the tasting room, built to resemble a New England farmhouse. If you're more interested in lounging than a full-on tasting, you can buy a glass of wine to enjoy outside. Winery tours conclude with a seated tasting; there's also a tasting ($35) that pairs the signature wines with locally made gourmet cheeses. ✉ *14347 Sonoma Hwy./Hwy. 12* ☎ *707/935–2600, 800/938–5170* 🌐 *www.arrowoodwinery.com* 🎫 *Tastings $15–$35, tour $25* ⏲ *Daily 10–4:30; tours daily 10:30 and 2.*

5

WHERE TO EAT

★ Fodor's Choice 🍴 **The Fig Cafe.** *French.* Pale sage walls, a sloping
$$ ceiling, and casual but very warm service set a sunny mood in this little bistro run by the same team behind Sonoma's Girl & the Fig. The compact menu focuses on California and French comfort food—pot roast and duck confit, for instance, as well as thin-crust pizza. Steamed mussels are served with terrific crispy fries, which also accompany the sirloin burger. Weekend brunch brings out locals and tourists for French toast, pizza with applewood-smoked bacon and poached eggs, corned-beef hash, and other delights. ■ TIP→ The unusual no-corkage-fee policy makes this a great place to drink the wine you discovered down the road. [$] *Average main: $19* ✉ *13690 Arnold Dr., at O'Donnell La.* ☎ *707/938–2130* 🌐 *www.thefigcafe.com* ✍ *Reservations not accepted* ⏲ *No lunch weekdays.*

$$ 🍴 **Glen Ellen Inn Oyster Grill & Martini Bar.** *Eclectic.* Tucked inside a creekside 1940s cottage, this cozy restaurant exudes romance, especially if you sit in the shady garden or on the patio strung with tiny lights. After taking the edge off your hunger with some oysters on the half shell and an

A grilled sirloin burger at the Fig Café

ice-cold martini, order from a menu that plucks elements from California, French, and other cuisines. You might find ginger tempura calamari with grilled pineapple salsa, or dry-aged rib-eye steak with chimichurri sauce and a heaping side of country-style fries. Desserts tend toward the indulgent; witness the warm cinnamon-pecan bread pudding with a chocolate center that sits in a puddle of brandy sauce. $ *Average main: $20* ⊠ *13670 Arnold Dr., at O'Donnell La.* ☎ *707/996–6409* ⊕ *www.glenelleninn. com* ⊗ *No lunch Wed.*

WHERE TO STAY

★ **Fodor'sChoice** 🏨 **Beltane Ranch.** *B&B/Inn.* On a slope of the
$ Mayacamas range a few miles from Glen Ellen, this 1892 ranch house, shaded by magnificent oak trees, contains charmingly old-fashioned rooms, each individually decorated with antiques and original artwork by noted artists. **Pros:** casual, friendly atmosphere; reasonable prices; beautiful grounds with ancient oak trees. **Cons:** downstairs rooms get some noise from upstairs rooms; ceiling fans instead of air-conditioning. $ *Rooms from: $175* ⊠ *11775 Sonoma Hwy./Hwy. 12* ☎ *707/996–6501* ⊕ *www.beltaneranch.com* ⇆ *3 rooms, 2 suites, 1 cottage* ⊚ *Breakfast.*

$$$$ 🏨 **The Chauvet.** *Rental.* Opened as a hotel in 1906, this yellow-brick building in downtown Glen Ellen is listed on the National Register of Historic Places. **Pros:** spacious accom-

CLOSE UP

Jack London Country

The rugged, rakish author and adventurer Jack London is perhaps best known for his travels to Alaska and his exploits in the Pacific, which he immortalized in tales such as *Call of the Wild, White Fang,* and *South Sea Tales.* But he loved no place so well as the hills of eastern Sonoma County, where he spent most of his thirties and where he died in 1916 at the age of 40.

Between 1905 and 1916 London bought seven parcels of land totaling 1,400 acres, which he dubbed Beauty Ranch. When he wasn't off traveling, he dedicated most of his time to cultivating the land and raising livestock. He also maintained a few acres of wine grapes for his personal use.

DREAMS AND MYSTERIES

In 1913, London rhapsodized about his beloved ranch near Glen Ellen, writing, "The grapes on a score of rolling hills are red with autumn flame. Across Sonoma Mountain wisps of sea fog are stealing. The afternoon sun smolders in the drowsy sky. I have everything to make me glad I am alive. I am filled with dreams and mysteries."

Much of Beauty Ranch is now preserved as Jack London State Historic Park, worth visiting not only for its museum and other glimpses into London's life but also for the trails that skirt vineyards and meander through a forest of Douglas fir, coastal redwoods, oak, and madrones. London and his wife spent two years here constructing their dream house, Wolf House, before it burned down one hot August night in 1913, just days before they were scheduled to move in.

A look at the remaining stone walls and fireplaces gives you a sense of the building's grand scale. Within, a fireproof basement vault was to hold London's manuscripts. Elsewhere in the park stands the unusually posh pigsty that London's neighbors called the Pig Palace.

Outside the park, London-related attractions are relatively few. Downhill from the park entrance is the Jack London Saloon, which first opened in 1905 and has walls covered with photographs and other London memorabilia.

Parts of Beauty Ranch are still owned by London's descendants, who grow Cabernet Sauvignon, Zinfandel, and Merlot. For a taste of the wines made from these grapes, head a few miles north to Kenwood Vineyards, which uses them to produce Jack London Vineyard reserve wines.

5

The Olea Hotel is both sophisticated and down-home casual.

modations; local artwork adorns exposed-brick walls; short uphill walk to Jack London State Historic Park. **Cons:** no services. [$] *Rooms from: $600* ✉ *13756 Arnold Dr.* ☎ *415/823–4570, 855/242–8838* 🌐 *www.chauvetcondominium.com* 🛏 *6 condos* ☞ *2-night minimum stay.*

★ $$$ Fodor's Choice 🏨 **Gaige House.** *B&B/Inn.* Gorgeous Asian objets d'art and leather club chairs cozied up to the lobby fireplace are just a few of the graceful touches in this luxurious but understated bed-and-breakfast. **Pros:** beautiful lounge areas; lots of privacy; excellent service; full breakfasts, afternoon wine and appetizers. **Cons:** sound carries in the main house; the least expensive rooms are on the small side. [$] *Rooms from: $345* ✉ *13540 Arnold Dr.* ☎ *707/935–0237, 800/935–0237* 🌐 *www.gaige.com* 🛏 *10 rooms, 13 suites* 🍴 *Breakfast.*

★ $$ Fodor's Choice 🏨 **Olea Hotel.** *B&B/Inn.* The husband-and-wife team of Ashish and Sia Patel gave an extreme makeover to a run-down former B&B, and after a year's labor unveiled a boutique lodging that's at once sophisticated and down-home country casual. **Pros:** beautiful style; welcoming staff; chef-prepared breakfasts; handsome grounds. **Cons:** fills up quickly on weekends; away from downtown Glen Ellen; minor road noise in some rooms. [$] *Rooms from: B257* ✉ *5131 Warm Springs Rd., west off Arnold Dr., Glen Ellen* ☎ *707/996–5131* 🌐 *www.oleahotel.com* 🛏 *10 rooms, 2 cottages* 🍴 *Breakfast.*

KENWOOD

4 miles north of Glen Ellen.

Tiny Kenwood consists of little more than a few restaurants, shops, tasting rooms, and a historic train depot, now used for private events. But hidden in this pretty landscape of meadows and woods at the north end of Sonoma Valley are several good wineries, most just off the Sonoma Highway. Among the varietals grown here at the foot of the Sugarloaf Mountains are Sauvignon Blanc, Chardonnay, Zinfandel, and Cabernet Sauvignon.

GETTING HERE AND AROUND

To get to Kenwood from Glen Ellen, head northeast on Arnold Drive and north on Highway 12.

EXPLORING

TOP ATTRACTIONS

Chateau St. Jean. At the foot of the Mayacamas Mountains stretch the impeccably groomed grounds of Chateau St. Jean, an old-country estate. Pick up a map in the tasting room: it will identify many of the flowers, trees, and hedges lining the neat pathways in the formal gardens. After a spin around the grounds, whose style harmonizes with the sprawling Mediterranean-style villa, step inside for a tasting of fine whites like Chardonnay and Fumé Blanc and reds that include Pinot Noir, Cabernet Sauvignon, Merlot, and Syrah. The unusually large gift shop sells clothing and housewares, including a fully equipped picnic backpack. Daily tours (weather permitting) focus on the garden. ✉ *8555 Sonoma Hwy./Hwy. 12* ☎ *707/833–4134* ⊕ *www.chateaustjean.com* 🍷 *Tastings $15–$25, tour $20* ☉ *Daily 10–5; tours daily at 11 and 1.*

Deerfield Ranch Winery. The focus at Deerfield is on producing "clean wines"—ones low in histamines and sulfites—the better to eliminate the headaches and allergic reactions some red-wine drinkers experience. Winemaker Robert Rex accomplishes this goal with no loss of flavor or complexity. Deerfield wines are bold, fruit-forward wines with a long finish. The lush DRX and Meritage Bordeaux-style blends invite contemplation about the vineyards, weather, and wine-making skills involved in their creation, whereas the pleasures of the Red Rex blend revolve chiefly around its friskiness. To taste these and other vintages (Rex also makes white wines), you walk deep into a 23,000-square-

DID YOU KNOW?

Guests staying at Beltane Ranch can take advantage of the loop hiking trail that winds through the olive orchards and vineyards.

foot cave. Standard tastings ($15) include five wines; for an additional $5, you can sample more, including one from the reserve list. ✉ *10200 Sonoma Hwy./Hwy. 12* ☎ *707/833–5215* ⊕ *www.deerfieldranch.com* ✎ *Tastings $15–$20* ⊘ *Daily 10:30–4:30.*

Kunde Estate Winery & Vineyards. On your way into Kunde you pass a terrace flanked with fountains, virtually coaxing you to stay for a picnic with views over the vineyard. The winery is perhaps best known for its toasty Chardonnays, although tastings might also include Sauvignon Blanc, Cabernet Sauvignon, Merlot, and Zinfandel. For insight into the winery's approach to sustainable wine making, take a few minutes to wander around the demonstration vineyard outside the tasting room. The free basic tour of the grounds includes the extensive caves, some of which stretch 175 feet below a vineyard. ■TIP→ Reserve ahead for the Mountain Top Tasting, a tour that ends with a sampling of reserve wines ($40). ✉ *9825 Sonoma Hwy./Hwy. 12* ☎ *707/833–5501* ⊕ *www.kunde.com* ✎ *Tastings $10–$40, tours free–$50* ⊘ *Daily 10:30–5; tours daily at various times.*

WORD OF MOUTH. "In Kenwood, you must do the Mountain Top Tasting at Kunde—the view is spectacular."—juliecav

Landmark Vineyards. High-quality Chardonnays have always been Landmark's claim to fame, led by the flagship Overlook wine, with grapes from multiple vineyards going into each vintage. Winemaker Greg Stach has also earned high praise for his Sonoma Coast Grand Detour Pinot Noir, Steel Plow Grenache, and Kivelstadt Syrah. Stop here to sample the wines, relax in the picnic area, and play a game of boccie ball. Local cheeses, meats, and crackers are available for purchase in the gift shop. On Saturday, Landmark offers "Blending the Rules" seminars ($55, by appointment only) at which you can craft your own blends. ✉ *101 Adobe Canyon Rd., at Hwy. 12* ☎ *707/833–0218* ⊕ *www.landmarkwine.com* ✎ *Tasting $15, tour $25* ⊘ *Daily 10–4:30; tour by appointment.*

Ledson Winery & Vineyards. The outrageously ornate French Normandy–style castle visible from the highway might persuade you to visit Ledson Winery even before you know it produces lovely wines, all of which are available only at the estate and at the wine bar at the Ledson Hotel & Centre Du Vin in downtown Sonoma. Although the winery's total production is only about 30,000 cases a year, Ledson offers several dozen largely single-varietal wines—everything from

The food-and-wine pairings at St. Francis Winery are a delicious value.

California standbys such as Zinfandel to Rhône varietals such as Syrah and Mourvèdre. The castle, intended as the Ledson family's home when its construction began in 1989, is now a warren of tasting rooms, special-event spaces, and a small market selling a good selection of cheeses and other picnic supplies. ✉ *7335 Sonoma Hwy./Hwy. 12* ☎ *707/537–3810* ⊕ *www.ledson.com* 🍷 *Tastings $15–$25; $35 for private tasting* ☉ *Daily 10–5.*

St. Francis Winery. Nestled at the foot of Mt. Hood, this winery occupies one of the most scenic locations in Sonoma. With its red-tile roof and dramatic bell tower, the visitor center, a marvelous evocation of the California Mission style, completes the pastoral picture. The charm of the surroundings is matched by the wines, most of them red, including rich, earthy Zinfandels from both the Russian River and Sonoma valleys. Executive chef David Bush, formerly of the Girl and the Fig, creates five-to-seven-course food-and-wine pairings—cassoulet with Merlot, for example—that are an excellent value at $42. They're offered from Thursday through Monday (reservations recommended), but $25 cheese-and-charcuterie pairings are available daily. Tours costing $30 explore the winery and barrel room and end with reserve-wine tastings. ✉ *100 Pythian Rd., off Hwy. 12* ☎ *888/675–9463, 707/833–6146* ⊕ *www.stfranciswine.com* 🍷 *Tastings $10–$42, tour $30* ☉ *Daily 10–5; tour by appointment.*

WORTH NOTING

Kenwood Vineyards. The best of the Kenwood wines—Cabernet Sauvignons, Zinfandels, Syrahs, and Merlots—come from Jack London's old vineyard, in the Sonoma Mountain AVA. Many of these, along with some value-priced reds and whites, are poured in a tasting room housed in one of the property's original barns. The crisp Sauvignon Blanc, though, is what wins the winery its highest accolades. Fine on its own, especially on a hot summer day, it pairs well with oysters, chicken, light fish, and vegetarian dishes. ✉ *9592 Sonoma Hwy./Hwy. 12* ☎ *707/833–5891* 🌐 *www.kenwoodvineyards.com* 🎫 *Tasting $5* 🕒 *Daily 10–4:30.*

VJB Vineyards & Cellars. In 2012, the Belmonte family, VJB's Italian owners, opened a Tuscany-tinged courtyard marketplace with tasting spaces and food shops. Although it's unlikely that many patrons will feel transported to *Toscana* (the 21st-century sheen needs to age a bit first), this is a fine spot to sip value-priced wines, enjoy a pizza or a deli sandwich, or just relax. The wines, most from Italian varietals (some rare in these parts), are like the complex, which is to say less rustic than in the old country and clearly adapted for contemporary American tastes. This isn't always a bad thing, and the best vintages—the Barbera, the Sangiovese, and the Primitivo—are lively and clean on the palate. ■ TIP→ For gourmet dolci, check out Wine Truffle Boutique, which sells chocolates, Italian gelato, and wine-infused sorbets. ✉ *60 Shaw Ave., off Hwy. 12* ☎ *707/833–2300* 🌐 *www.vjbcellars.com* 🎫 *Tastings $10–$15* 🕒 *Daily 10–5.*

WHERE TO EAT AND STAY

$ 🍴 **Café Citti.** *Italian.* Classical music in the background and a friendly staff (as well as a roaring fire when the weather's cold) keep this no-frills roadside café from feeling too spartan. Order dishes such as roast chicken and slabs of tiramisu from the counter and they're delivered to your table, indoors or on an outdoor patio. The array of prepared salads and sandwiches means the café does a brisk business in takeout for picnic packers, but you can also choose pasta made to order. [$] *Average main: $13* ✉ *9049 Sonoma Hwy./Hwy. 12* ☎ *707/833–2690* 🌐 *www.cafecitti.com.*

$$$ 🍴 **Kenwood Restaurant and Bar.** *American.* This restaurant with a sloping wood-beamed ceiling is at its best on warm afternoons and evenings, when you can sit on the patio and bask in the views of the Kunde vineyards and the Sug-

CLOSE UP

A Great Drive in Sonoma Valley

It's easy to zip through the Sonoma Valley in a day—the drive from Sonoma at the south end to Kenwood to the north can be done in half an hour—but once you begin stopping at the historic sites and wineries, your visit could easily be spread over two days.

To hit the highlights, start in the town of Sonoma. Have breakfast at Sunflower Caffé or El Dorado Corner Cafe. After your coffee kicks in, take a quick spin around historic **Sonoma Plaza,** ending at either the Epicurean Connection or the Sonoma Cheese Factory, where you can pick up *picnic supplies.* Return to your car and drive east on East Napa Street. Turn south on East 8th Street and west onto Denmark Street to reach **Gundlach-Bundschu Winery.** After a tasting, hike up the GunBun hill for your alfresco lunch.

Back in the car, drive west on Spain Street until you run into Highway 12, where you'll head north for about 20 minutes. At the northern end of Kenwood, the grand French Normandy–style castle of **Ledson Winery** gleams in the sun. Stop here or the nearby **St. Francis Winery,** an equally photogenic spot and a must for red-wine fans. Heading back south on Highway 12, look for **Kunde Estate** a few minutes down the road. If you've managed to wrap up your wine tasting before 3 pm, continue south on Highway 12 and take Arnold Drive into the picturesque town of Glen Ellen. Turn right on London Ranch Road and wind your way uphill for a few minutes to reach **Jack London State Historic Park.** Take a short stroll through the grounds and a gander at some of the historic buildings near the parking area before the park closes at 4 pm (5 pm on weekends). Dine in Glen Ellen or return to Sonoma.

5

arloaf Mountains. The same scene also unfolds through the French doors of the airy dining room, where longtime patrons savor competently prepared French-inspired dishes such as cassoulet and beef bourguignon, along with pork tenderloin piccata, hearty hamburgers, and oysters on the half shell. The walnut tart and the flourless Swiss chocolate cake with raspberry coulis are popular for dessert. The wine list is very good, especially when it comes to local bottlings, and you can also order cocktails from the full bar. $ *Average main: $23* ⊠ *9900 Sonoma Hwy./Hwy. 12, at Kunde Winery Rd.* ☎ *707/833–6326* ⊕ *www.kenwoodrestaurant. com* ☉ *Closed Mon. and Tues.*

★ Fodor's Choice 🏨 **Kenwood Inn and Spa.** *B&B/Inn.* Buildings
$$$$ resembling graceful old haciendas and the mature fruit trees shading the courtyards make it seem like this inn has been here for more than a century (it was actually built in 1990). **Pros:** large rooms; lavish furnishings; extremely romantic. **Cons:** Wi-Fi can be spotty in some areas; expensive. [$] *Rooms from: $450* ✉ *10400 Sonoma Hwy./Hwy. 12* ☎ *707/833–1293, 800/353–6966* 🌐 *www.kenwoodinn.com* 🛏 *25 rooms, 4 suites* 🍴 *Breakfast.*

SHOPPING

Figone's Olive Oil Co. At this family-owned roadside shop you can sample extra-virgin olive oils (the porcini-mushroom blend is outstanding), zest-infused olive oils (blood-orange, Meyer lemon, Persian lime), and balsamic vinegars (pomegranate, fig, and several other winners). Figone's also carries cookbooks and tabletop accessories. From late spring to early fall, the outdoor Kenwood Farmers Market takes place here on Sunday morning. ✉ *9580 Sonoma Hwy./Hwy. 12, at Warm Springs Rd.* ☎ *707/282–9092* 🌐 *www.figoneoliveoil.com.*

SPAS

Spa at Kenwood Inn. A pretty setting, expert practitioners, and rejuvenating French therapies make a visit to the Spa at Kenwood Inn a marvelously ethereal experience. The wine-based Vinothérapie treatments and beauty products from the French line Caudalíe combine in the delicious-sounding Honey Wine Wrap, which involves a warming, full-body slathering of wine yeast and honey, the better to rehydrate your parched and neglected skin. The Crushed Cabernet Scrub, designed to stimulate and soften your skin, raises the sweetness ante by adding brown sugar to the honey, along with crushed grape seeds and grape-seed oil. The spa's other services include massages and facials using the products and treatments by iS Clinical and Intraceuticals. ✉ *10400 Sonoma Hwy./Hwy. 12* ☎ *707/833–1293, 800/353–6966* 🌐 *www.kenwoodinn.com* 💆 *Treatments $125–$390.*

NORTHERN SONOMA COUNTY

NORTHERN SONOMA COUNTY is a study in contrasts. In urban Santa Rosa, bypassed by most Wine Country visitors, bland office parks outnumber vineyards. Less than 20 miles to the north, the ritzy little town of Healdsburg buzzes with hip tasting rooms, luxe hotels, and some of the Wine Country's hottest restaurants. Rolling hills surround these towns, with only the occasional horse ranch, apple or peach orchard, or stand of oak trees interrupting the vineyards.

Healdsburg is the most convenient base for exploring the northern reaches of Sonoma County. Not only does it have an easily walkable town center, swanky hotels, and a remarkable restaurant scene, but it's at the confluence of the Russian River, Dry Creek, and Alexander valleys, three of Northern Sonoma's blockbuster appellations. The wineries here produce some of the country's best Pinot Noirs, Cabernet Sauvignons, Zinfandels, and Chardonnays. In Santa Rosa and the smaller towns of Sebastopol, Forestville, and Guerneville, high-style lodgings and fine dining are in shorter supply. All of them have a few charmers, however, along with wineries worth seeking out. The western reaches of Sonoma County, extending all the way to the Pacific Ocean, are more sparsely populated, although more and more vineyards are popping up where there used to be orchards or ranches.

Each of Northern Sonoma's regions claims its own microclimates, soil types, and most-favored varietals, but all have something in common: peace and quiet. Northern Sonoma is less crowded than the Napa Valley and southern Sonoma. Healdsburg, in particular, is hardly a stranger to overnight visitors, but you'll find less company in most of the region's tasting rooms.

GETTING AROUND NORTHERN SONOMA COUNTY

From San Francisco, the quickest route to Northern Sonoma is north on U.S. 101 to Santa Rosa and Healdsburg. Highway 116 (also called the Gravenstein Highway), heads west from U.S. 101, taking you through Sebastopol and the hamlets of Graton and Forestville before depositing you along the Russian River near Guerneville. Traffic can be slow on U.S. 101, especially around Petaluma and Santa Rosa around rush hour and on summer weekends.

NORTHERN SONOMA COUNTY APPELLATIONS

Covering about 329,000 acres, the sprawling **Northern Sonoma AVA** is divided into about a dozen smaller subappellations. Three of the most important subappellations meet at Healdsburg: **Russian River Valley AVA**, which runs southwest along the river; **Dry Creek Valley AVA**, which runs northwest of town; and **Alexander Valley AVA**, which extends to the east and north. The Knights Valley and Chalk Hill AVAs are also in this region, although many of the wineries here are not open for tasting.

The cool climate of the low-lying **Russian River Valley AVA** is perfect for fog-loving Pinot Noir grapes as well as Chardonnay. Although 20 years ago this was a little-known appellation, with as many farms, orchards, and redwood stands as vineyards, in recent years vines have sprouted up all over, and this is now one of Sonoma's most-recognized growing regions—with a significant subappellation of its own, the **Green Valley of the Russian River Valley AVA**, in the Forestville-Sebastopol area.

Although it's a small region—only about 16 miles long and 2 miles wide—**Dry Creek Valley AVA** is well known by Zin lovers. The coastal hills temper the cooling influence of the Pacific Ocean, making it ideal for such warm-climate grapes as Zinfandel. Even more acres are planted with Cabernet Sauvignon, and you'll find a smattering of Merlot, Chardonnay, Sauvignon Blanc, Syrah, and several other varietals growing in the diverse soils and climates (it's warmer in the north and cooler in the south).

The **Alexander Valley AVA** is an up-and-comer, still being planted with vines (you're apt to see orchards and pastures between vineyards). Winemakers continue to experiment to determine which varietals grow best in the relatively warm climate and diverse soils, but so far Chardonnay, Sauvignon Blanc, Zinfandel, and Cabernet Sauvignon seem to do well.

The classic combination of hot summer days and cooling evening fog and breezes (in some spots even cooler than the Russian River Valley) inspired major wine-making operations, including the Napa Valley's Joseph Phelps Vineyards, to invest in acreage in the **Sonoma Coast AVA**. The hunch paid off for Phelps and other area winemakers, whose Pinots and Chardonnays have been the darlings of national wine critics for nearly a decade. The attention is only likely to intensify now that the Phelps vineyards were rebranded as the Joseph Phelps Freestone Vineyards in late 2012.

6

Alexander Valley Vineyards, **15**

Armstrong Woods State Natural Reserve, **28**

The Barlow, **32**

Charles M. Schulz Museum, **37**

Copain Wines, **25**

David Coffaro Estate Vineyard, **3**

DeLoach Vineyards, **35**

Dry Creek Peach & Produce, **4**

Dry Creek Vineyard, **8**

Ferrari-Carano Winery, **1**

Foppiano Vineyards, **20**

Francis Ford Coppola Winery, **10**

Gary Farrell Winery, **26**

Hartford Family Winery, **29**

Healdsburg Museum & Historical Society, **19**

Iron Horse Vineyards, **30**

J Vineyards & Winery, **22**

Jimtown Store, **14**

Jordan Vineyard and Winery, **12**

Joseph Phelps Freestone Vineyards Guest Center, **31**

Korbel Champagne Cellars, **27**

La Crema, **17**

Locals Tasting Room, **5**

Luther Burbank Home and Gardens, **38**

Lynmar Estate, **34**

Martinelli Winery, **36**

Matanzas Creek Winery, **39**

Merry Edwards Winery, **33**

Papapietro Perry, **6**

Preston of Dry Creek, **2**

Quivira, **7**

Ridge Vineyards, **9**

Rochioli Vineyards and Winery, **24**

Rodney Strong Vineyards, **21**

Safari West, **23**

Seghesio Family Vineyards, **16**

Stryker Sonoma, **13**

Thumbprint Cellars Tasting Lounge, **18**

Trentadue Winery, **11**

Luther Burbank Home and Gardens

With only 650 acres planted with vines, the idyllic **Bennett Valley AVA**—technically part of Sonoma Valley AVA, but within the city of Santa Rosa—is one of California's smallest appellations. Surrounded by the mountains on three sides but cooled by coastal breezes that sneak through the wind gap at Crane Canyon, it's ideal for such cooler-weather grapes as Pinot Noir and Chardonnay, but also does well with Syrah, Cabernet Sauvignon, and Sauvignon Blanc.

SANTA ROSA

52 miles north of San Francisco; 8 miles northwest of Kenwood.

Urban Santa Rosa isn't as popular with tourists as many Wine Country destinations—not surprising, because there are more office parks than wineries within its limits. However, this hardworking town is home to a couple of interesting cultural offerings and a few noteworthy restaurants and vineyards. The city's chain motels and hotels can be handy if you're finding that everything else is booked up, especially since Santa Rosa is roughly equidistant from Sonoma, Healdsburg, and the western Russian River Valley, three of Sonoma County's most popular wine-tasting destinations.

Best Bets for Northern Sonoma County Wineries

WINE TASTING

Joseph Phelps Freestone Vineyards Guest Center, Freestone. A tasting here provides a splendid introduction to the cool Sonoma Coast and the austere Chardonnays and Pinot Noirs its rocky soils yield.

Locals Tasting Room, Geyserville. The flights are all of your own fancy at this room that pours the wines of small-lot producers. Sample Zins or Cabs, then decide which ones best suit your palate.

Merry Edwards Winery, Sebastopol. You can't amble up to the tasting bar—there isn't one—but you can drop by for informative sessions at which you'll sample fine Pinot Noirs.

WINERY TOURING

DeLoach Vineyards, Santa Rosa. The owner's commitment to sustainable, organic, and biodynamic farming practices is the focus of a tour that takes in the estate vineyards and includes a visit to the culinary garden.

Ferrari-Carano Winery, Healdsburg. Tours of the winery's over-the-top Italian villa take in the wine-making facilities, underground cellar, and meticulously manicured gardens.

Korbel Champagne Cellars, Guerneville. The pioneering efforts of the brothers Korbel and the making of sparkling wines using the French *méthode champenoise* are the topics of their winery's tour.

SETTING

Francis Ford Coppola Winery, Geyserville. A day at the film director's party palazzo unreels like a movie scene, and a glamorous one at that: lounge poolside in the summer, and sip rustic wines year-round.

Hartford Family Winery, Forestville. The opulent main winery and patio with views of vineyards and towering trees provide a gorgeous backdrop on a sunny summer day and even in the dead of winter.

Rochioli Vineyards and Winery, Healdsburg. Stop at Healdsburg's Oakville Grocery to pick up food for a picnic, then drive to Rochioli to enjoy the views and serenity.

FOOD-WINE PAIRING

J Vineyards and Winery, Healdsburg. At these food-wine pairing sessions, J's best sparkling and still wines are paired with marvelous morsels in the plush Bubble Room.

Lynmar Estate, Sebastopol. Artisanal cheeses are carefully chosen for the way they call attention to the subtleties of Lynmar's Chardonnays, Pinot Noirs, and single-vineyard Syrah.

6

GETTING HERE AND AROUND

To get to Santa Rosa from San Francisco, cross the Golden Gate Bridge and continue north on U.S. 101 to the downtown Santa Rosa exit. To get to Santa Rosa from Sonoma Valley, take Highway 12 north. Santa Rosa's hotels, restaurants, and wineries are spread over a wide area; factor in extra time when driving around the city, especially during morning and evening rush hour.

EXPLORING

TOP ATTRACTIONS

★ Fodor's Choice **Matanzas Creek Winery.** The visitor center at Matanzas Creek sets itself apart with an understated Japanese aesthetic, extending to a tranquil fountain and a koi pond. Best of all, huge windows overlook a vast field of lavender where you can wander on your own or on a tour of the grounds ($10). The winery specializes in Sauvignon Blanc, Chardonnay, and Merlot, although it also produces Syrah, a rich Bordeaux blend called Journey, and a late-harvest Sauvignon Blanc dessert wine. A second tour concludes with a taste of limited-production and library wines paired with artisanal cheeses. ■TIP→ The ideal time to visit is in May and June, when the lavender perfumes the air. ✉ 6097 Bennett Valley Rd., at Lafranconi Rd. ☎ 707/528–6464, 800/590–6464 ⊕ www.matanzascreek.com ✑ Tastings $10–$20, tours $10–$35 ⊙ Daily 10–4:30; estate tour daily at 10:30, others by appointment.

FAMILY **Safari West.** An unexpected bit of wilderness in the Wine Country, this African wildlife preserve covers 400 acres on the outskirts of Santa Rosa. A visit begins with a stroll around enclosures housing lemurs, cheetahs, giraffes, and many varieties of rare birds, like the brightly colored scarlet ibis. Next, climb onto open-air vehicles that spend about two hours combing the expansive property, where more than 80 species—including African Cape buffalo, gazelles, wildebeests, and zebras—make their homes on the hillsides. All the while you're accompanied by guides who inform you about the animals, their behavior, and the threats they face in the wild. If you'd like to extend your stay, lodging in well-equipped tent cabins is available. ✉ 3115 Porter Creek Rd., off Mark West Springs Rd. ☎ 707/579–2551, 800/616–2695 ⊕ www.safariwest.com ✑ $78–$80.

Matanzas Creek Winery is the star of the tiny Bennett Valley AVA.

WORTH NOTING

FAMILY **Charles M. Schulz Museum.** Fans of Snoopy and Charlie Brown will love the Charles M. Schulz Museum, dedicated to the cartoonist who lived in Santa Rosa for the last 30 years of his life, until his death in 2000. Permanent installations like a re-creation of the artist's studio share space with temporary exhibits that often focus on a particular theme in Schulz's work. Children and adults can take a stab at creating cartoons in the Education Room or wander through the labyrinth in the form of Snoopy's head. ⊠ *2301 Hardies La., at W. Steele La.* ☎ *707/579–4452* ⊕ *www.schulzmuseum.org* ⊑ *$10* ⊙ *Labor Day–Memorial Day, Wed.–Fri. and Mon. 11–5, weekends 10–5; Memorial Day–Labor Day, weekdays 11–5, weekends 10–5.*

DeLoach Vineyards. Slightly off the beaten track in western Santa Rosa, DeLoach is best known for its Russian River Valley Pinot Noirs, among them the much-lauded Pennacchio Vineyard edition and the Estate Collection Pinot Noir. The winery also produces old-vine Zinfandels, Chardonnays, and a handful of other varietals. Some of the reds are made using open-top wood fermentation vats that are uncommon in Sonoma but have been used in France for centuries to intensify a wine's flavor. The history-rich tour focuses on the estate vineyards outside the tasting-room door, where you can learn about the winery's labor-intensive biodynamic and organic farming methods. ⊠ *1791 Olivet*

A familiar-looking hat provides shade aplenty at the Charles M. Schulz Museum.

Rd., off Guerneville Rd. ☎ *707/526–9111* ⊕ *www.deloach-vineyards.com* 🖘 *Tastings $10–$50, tour and tasting $15* ⊙ *Daily 10–5; tour at 11.*

Luther Burbank Home & Gardens. Renowned horticulturist Luther Burbank lived and worked on these grounds and made great advances using the modern techniques of selection and hybridization. The 1.6-acre garden and greenhouse showcase the results of some of Burbank's experiments to develop spineless cactus and such flowers as the Shasta daisy. Instructions for the free self-guided garden tour, which uses your cell phone, are posted near the carriage house. In the music room of Burbank's home, a modified Greek Revival structure, a dictionary lies open to a page on which the verb *burbank* is defined as "to modify and improve plant life." Docent-led tours, required to see the house, take place from April through October. ✉ *204 Santa Rosa Ave., at Sonoma Ave.* ☎ *707/524–5445* ⊕ *www.lutherburbank.org* 🖘 *Gardens free, tour $7* ⊙ *Gardens daily 8–dusk; home and gift shop Apr.–Oct., Tues.–Sun. 10–4; docent tours every half hr.*

Martinelli Winery. In a century-old hop barn with the telltale triple towers, Martinelli has the feel of a traditional country store, but the sophisticated wines here are anything but old-fashioned. The winery's reputation rests on its big, complex Pinot Noirs, Syrahs, and Zinfandels, including the $120-a-bottle Jackass Hill Vineyard Zin. Most of these acclaimed wines are produced in such small lots that they're rarely poured in the tasting room (though you can always ask). A typical tasting begins with a Chardonnay, followed by a sampling of three reds—often among them the playful, luscious Lolita Ranch Pinot Noir—and finishing with a muscat that tastes like sweet honeysuckle. Winemaker Bryan Kvamme, whose mentors include the renowned Helen Turley, likes to bring the fruit forward, and most of his wines do the Russian River Valley AVA proud. ✉ *3360 River Rd., east of Olivet Rd., Windsor* ☎ *707/525–0570, 800/346–1627* 🌐 *www.martinelliwinery.com* 🎟 *Tasting $5* 🕒 *Daily 10–5.*

WHERE TO EAT

$$$$ 🍴 **Stark's Steak & Seafood.** *Steakhouse.* The low lighting, well-spaced tables, and gas fireplaces at this restaurant in Santa Rosa's Railroad Square area create a congenial setting for dining on generous slabs of steak, seafood from the raw bar, and sustainable fish. With entrées like the 20-ounce, dry-aged rib eye and the 32-ounce porterhouse for two, there's not a chance that meat eaters will depart unsated, and such nonsteak options as the tamarind barbecue prawns and the sea bass with charred baby leeks are a cut above those at your average temple to beef. The full menu is available in the adjoining lounge, which is renowned for its happy hour (3 to 6, except Sunday). [$] *Average main: $34* ✉ *521 Adams St., at 7th St.* ☎ *707/546–5100* 🌐 *starkssteakhouse.com* 🕒 *No lunch weekends.*

★ **$$$** Fodor's Choice 🍴 **Willi's Wine Bar.** *Eclectic.* Don't let the name fool you: instead of a sedate spot serving flights of bubbly with delicate nibbles, you'll find a cozy warren of rooms where boisterous crowds snap up small plates from the globe-trotting menu. Such dishes as the pork-belly pot stickers with shiitake mushrooms represent Asia, and Moroccan-style lamb chops and roasted flatbread with caramelized onions and feta are some of the Mediterranean-inspired foods. The delectable "fish-and-chips" plate of Monterey Bay sardines with garlic potato chips is among the many using California-sourced ingredients. Wines are available in 2-ounce pours, making it easier to pair each of your little plates with a different glass. ■ TIP→ The din inside can be deafening on busy nights, so consider a table on the covered patio. [$] *Average main: $28* ✉ *4404 Old Redwood Hwy., at Ursuline Rd.* ☎ *707/526–3096* 🌐 *williswinebar.net* 🕒 *No lunch Sun. and Mon.*

Martinelli Winery's reputation rests on big, complex reds.

WHERE TO STAY

$ 🏨 **Flamingo Conference Resort & Spa.** *Resort.* If Don Draper from the hit show *Mad Men* popped into Santa Rosa, he'd probably park himself in this 1950s-style resort just beyond downtown; the rooms have been updated since the property opened in 1957, but they've still got high ceilings and that old-school flair. **Pros:** cool pool; retro vibe; good value. **Cons:** noise travels through the walls; longish walk to downtown; dated, small bathrooms in some rooms. [$] *Rooms from: $119* ✉ *2777 4th St.* ☎ *707/545–8530, 800/848–8300* 🌐 *www.flamingoresort.com* 🛏 *170 rooms* 🍴 *No meals.*

$$ 🏨 **Vintners Inn.** *Hotel.* The owners of Ferrari-Carano Vineyards operate this oasis set amid 80 acres of vineyards that's known for its comfortable lodgings. **Pros:** spacious rooms with comfortable beds; jogging path through the vineyards; online deals pop up year-round. **Cons:** occasional noise from adjacent events center; some decor seems dated. [$] *Rooms from: $265* ✉ *4350 Barnes Rd., Santa Rosa* ☎ *707/575–7350, 800/421–2584* 🌐 *www.vintnersinn.com* 🛏 *38 rooms, 6 suites* 🍴 *No meals.*

NIGHTLIFE AND THE ARTS

Russian River Brewing Company. It's all about Belgian-style ales in this popular brewery's large pub. The legendary lineup includes Pliny the Elder (and Younger, but only in February), Blind Pig I.P.A., Mortification (nuances of clove, toffee, and roasted malts), and so many more. The prices are reasonable, too. ⊠ *725 4th St., near D St.* ☎ *707/545–2337* ⊕ *www.russianriverbrewing.com.*

SPORTS AND THE OUTDOORS

Up & Away Ballooning. Being so close to the coast means that if the balloon you're in gets high enough, you'll have ocean views on a sunny day. You'll also take in plenty of vineyard vistas. Journeys conclude with a sparkling-wine brunch at Kendall-Jackson Winery. ⊠ *Sonoma County Airport, 3200 Airport Blvd.* ☎ *707/836–0171, 800/711–2998* ⊕ *www. up-away.com* ✉ *$235 per person.*

HEALDSBURG

17 miles north of Santa Rosa.

★ **Fodor's Choice** Just when it seems that the buzz about Healdsburg couldn't get any bigger, there's another article published in a glossy food or wine magazine about properties such as the swingin' Spoonbar or the posh Hotel Les Mars. But you don't have to be a tycoon to enjoy Healdsburg. For every ritzy restaurant there's a great bakery serving reasonably priced sandwiches, and luxe lodgings are matched by modest bed-and-breakfasts.

Healdsburg is ideally located at the confluence of the Dry Creek Valley, Russian River Valley, and Alexander Valley AVAs, but you could easily spend a day or more exploring downtown. Around its old-fashioned plaza you'll find fashionable boutiques, art galleries, spas, hip tasting rooms, and some of the best restaurants in the Wine Country.

Walking downtown, you realize that locals haven't been pushed aside to make way for tourists. This isn't by accident. For example, free summer concerts used to be held in Healdsburg Plaza on Sunday, but when they became so popular that locals stopped coming, the city moved the performances to Tuesday. The concerts are quite fine, by the way—you might hear anything from bluegrass to military marches. Set amid the plaza's fragrant trees and flowers, the scene is as pretty as a Norman Rockwell painting.

The countryside around Healdsburg is the sort you dream about when you're planning a Wine Country vacation, with orderly rows of vines alternating with beautifully overgrown hills. Set alongside relatively untrafficked roads, country stores and roadside farm stands offer just-plucked fruits and vine-ripened tomatoes. The wineries here are barely visible, since they're tucked behind groves of eucalyptus or hidden high on fog-shrouded hills.

GETTING HERE AND AROUND

To get to Healdsburg from San Francisco, cross the Golden Gate Bridge and continue north on U.S. 101. About 65 miles from San Francisco, take the Central Healdsburg exit and follow Healdsburg Avenue a few blocks north to the town's central plaza. Many hotels and restaurants are on or around the scenic town square. From Santa Rosa, the drive along U.S. 101 takes about 15 minutes in light traffic. Wineries bearing Healdsburg addresses can be as far apart as 20 miles, so unless you plan to sample wines only at the many in-town tasting rooms, you'll need a car. Both Dry Creek Valley AVA and Russian River Valley AVA are west of U.S. 101; most of the Alexander Valley AVA is east of the freeway.

GETTING TO THE WINERIES

For wineries along Westside Road, head south on Center Street, then turn right at Mill Street. After Mill Street crosses under U.S. 101, the road's name changes to Westside Road. After about ½ mile, veer south to continue on Westside Road to reach the Russian River Valley wineries. Roughly following the curves of the Russian River, Westside Road passes vineyards, woods, and meadows along the way.

The route to wineries on Old Redwood Highway and Eastside Road is less scenic. Follow Healdsburg Avenue south to U.S. 101. Hop on the freeway, exiting after a mile at Old Redwood Highway. Veer right as you exit, and continue south. Just past the driveway that serves both Rodney Strong and J Vineyards, turn southwest to merge onto Eastside Road.

To reach the wineries along Dry Creek Road and West Dry Creek Road, head north on Healdsburg Avenue. After about a mile, turn west on Dry Creek Road. West Dry Creek Road, which runs roughly parallel to Dry Creek Road, is accessible by the cross streets Lambert Bridge Road and Yoakim Bridge Road.

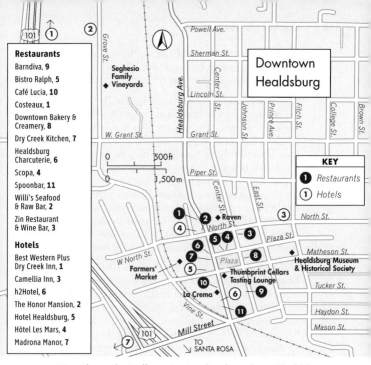

Restaurants

Barndiva, **9**
Bistro Ralph, **5**
Café Lucia, **10**
Costeaux, **1**
Downtown Bakery & Creamery, **8**
Dry Creek Kitchen, **7**
Healdsburg Charcuterie, **6**
Scopa, **4**
Spoonbar, **11**
Willi's Seafood & Raw Bar, **2**
Zin Restaurant & Wine Bar, **3**

Hotels

Best Western Plus Dry Creek Inn, **1**
Camellia Inn, **3**
h2Hotel, **6**
The Honor Mansion, **2**
Hotel Healdsburg, **5**
Hôtel Les Mars, **4**
Madrona Manor, **7**

Downtown Healdsburg

KEY

1 Restaurants
① Hotels

For Alexander Valley wineries, head north on Healdsburg Avenue. Reach Alexander Valley Vineyards by heading east on Alexander Valley Road. For Seghesio Family Vineyard, head west and then north onto Grove Street.

EXPLORING

TOP ATTRACTIONS

★ **Fodor'sChoice Copain Wines.** Wells Guthrie, Copain's wine-maker, is the kind of guy who spends his vacation working in a French vineyard, the better to understand how sun, soil, climate, and time-honored agricultural techniques combine to create great wines. This single-mindedness serves him well: his restrained yet accessible Chardon-nays, Pinot Noirs, and Syrahs are marvelous examples of intuitive craftsmanship supported by deep knowledge. The Copain wines are among the most "European" ones produced in Sonoma County. The grapes come from else-where, mostly Mendocino and Monterey counties, and the wines produced here have understated flavors that reflect the cool climate and rocky coastal terrain. ■TIP→ This win-ery occupies a hillside perch that begs you to sit, sip, and bask in the view. ⊠ *7800 Eastside Rd.* ☏ *707/836–8822* ⊕ *www. copainwines.com* ⌑ *Tasting $15* ⊘ *Thurs.–Sat. 10:30–4:30, Sun.–Wed. by appointment.*

Dry Creek Vineyard. Fumé Blanc is king at Dry Creek, where the refreshing white wine is made in the style of those in Sancerre, France. The winery also makes well-regarded Zinfandels, a zesty dry Chenin Blanc, a Pinot Noir, and a handful of Cabernet Sauvignon blends. Since many wines are priced below $30 a bottle (some less than $20), it's a popular stop for wine lovers looking to stock their cellars for a reasonable price. You can picnic on the lawn next to a flowering magnolia tree. Conveniently, a general store and deli is close by. ⊠ *3770 Lambert Bridge Rd., off Dry Creek Rd.* ☏ *707/433–1000, 800/864–9463* ⊕ *www.dry-creekvineyard.com* ⌑ *Tastings $5–$45, tour $15* ⊘ *Daily 10:30–4:30; tour 11 and 1 by appointment.*

Ferrari-Carano Winery. Known for its Disneyesque Italian villa, which has as many critics as it does aficionados for its general over-the-topness, this winery produces mostly Chardonnays, Fumé Blancs, Zinfandels, and Cabernet Sauvignons. Though whites have traditionally been the specialty here, the reds are now garnering more attention. Tours cover not only the wine-making facilities and underground cellar but also the truly splendid manicured gardens, where you can see a cork oak tree and learn about how cork is harvested. ∎TIP→ For a more relaxed experience, head downstairs to the reserve tasting room. ⊠ *8761 Dry Creek Rd., at Yoakim Bridge Rd.* ☏ *707/433–6700* ⊕ *www.ferrari-carano. com* ⌑ *Tastings $5–$35, tour free* ⊘ *Daily 10–5; reserve room daily 10–4:30, tour by appointment.*

QUICK BITES. **Flying Goat Coffee.** Healdsburg locals are as obsessive about coffee as they are about wine. The hot stop for a cup of joe these days is FGC, whose earthy and potent Espresso No. 9 blend, redolent of molasses and milk chocolate, makes for a exceptionally satisfying cappuccino or latte. The El Salvador Santa Sofia is another town favorite. ∎TIP→ A to-go-only satellite location is a block away at 419 Center Street. ⊠ *324 Center St., near Plaza St.* ☏ *707/433–3599* ⊕ *www.flyinggoatcoffee. com* ⊘ *Daily 7–7.*

J Vineyards and Winery. The dry sparkling wines made here, all from Pinot Noir and Chardonnay grapes planted in Russian River vineyards, have wonderfully complex fruit and floral aromas and good acidity. Best known for its sparklers, J also makes fine still wines, often from Pinot and Chardonnay grapes, as well as a brandy-fortified dessert wine and a pear eau-de-vie. You can sample just the wines at the tasting bar, enjoy a private reserve tasting in the Legacy Lounge, or indulge yourself in the Bubble Room (reservations required), where top-end still and sparkling wines are paired with food. Half-hour tours take place twice daily. ⊠ *11447 Old Redwood Hwy., at Eastside Rd.* ☎ *707/431–3646* ⊕ *www.jwine.com* ⊠ *Tastings $20–$75, tour free* ⊙ *Daily 11–5; tours 11:30 and 2:30.*

★ **Fodor'sChoice** **Preston of Dry Creek.** The long driveway at this winery, flanked by vineyards and punctuated by the occasional olive tree, winds down to some farmhouses encircling a shady yard with picnic tables. In summer a small selection of organic produce grown in the winery's gardens is sold at an impromptu stand on the front porch, and house-made bread and olive oil are available year-round. Owners Lou and Susan Preston are committed to organic growing techniques and use only estate-grown grapes in their wines, which include Sauvignon Blanc and such Rhône varietals as Syrah and Viognier. The family's down-home style is particularly in evidence on Sunday, the only day of the week that tasting-room staffers sell a 3-liter bottle of Guadagni Red, a primarily Zinfandel blend filled from the barrel right in front of you. ⊠ *9282 W. Dry Creek Rd., at Hartsock Rd. No. 1* ☎ *707/433–3372* ⊕ *www.prestonvineyards.com* ⊠ *Tasting $10* ⊙ *Daily 11–4:30.*

WORD OF MOUTH. "I thought of another recommendation, Merry Edwards, in Sebastopol. She is one of the originals in the valley, and her Pinots are very robust, spicy, and earthy. Oh, and Preston on Dry Creek Road is a charmer, great wines (especially their Pinot Gris), and they bake their own sourdough using decades-old starter, and bottle their own olive oil to go with it."—NewbE

Quivira Vineyards and Winery. An unassuming winery in a modern wooden barn topped by solar panels, Quivira produces some of the most interesting wines in Dry Creek Valley. It's known for its dangerously drinkable reds, including a knockout Syrah, and a few hearty Zinfandels. The excellent tour provides information about the winery's biodynamic and organic farming practices and offers a glimpse of the beautiful garden and the pigs, chickens, and beehives

DID YOU KNOW?

Preston of Dry Creek is a fully organic winery whose wines are all made from grapes grown on just 110 acres.

on the property. You can also take a free self-guided tour through the garden. ⊠ *4900 W. Dry Creek Rd., near Wine Creek Rd.* ☎ *707/431–8333, 800/292–8339* ⊕ *www.quivirawine.com* ⊠ *Tasting $10, tours $20–$30* ⊙ *Daily 11–5; tours by appointment.*

★ **Fodor's Choice** **Ridge Vineyards.** Ridge stands tall among California wineries, and not merely because one of its 1971 Cabernet Sauvignons placed first in a 2006 re-creation of the 1976 Judgment of Paris tasting. The winery built its reputation on Cabernet Sauvignons, Zinfandels, and Chardonnays of unusual depth and complexity, but you'll also find blends of Rhône varietals. Although Ridge makes wines using grapes from several California locales—including Dry Creek Valley, Sonoma Valley, Napa Valley, and Paso Robles—the focus is on single-vineyard estate wines such as the exquisitely textured Lytton Springs Zinfandel blend from grapes grown near the tasting room. The $20 tasting option includes a pour of the top-of-the-line Monte Bello Cabernet Sauvignon blend from grapes grown in the Santa Cruz Mountains. ■TIP→ Before or after you taste, pause at the picnic tables outside to appreciate the rolling vineyard hills. ⊠ *650 Lytton Springs Rd., off U.S. 101* ☎ *707/433–7721* ⊕ *www.ridgewine.com* ⊠ *Tastings $5–$20, tour $30* ⊙ *Daily 11–4.*

★ **Fodor's Choice** **Rochioli Vineyards and Winery.** Claiming one of the prettiest picnic sites in the area, with tables overlooking the vineyards, this winery also has an airy little tasting room hung with modern artwork. Production is small and fans on the winery's mailing list snap up most of the bottles, but the winery is still worth a stop. Because of the cool growing conditions in the Russian River Valley, the flavors of the Chardonnay and Sauvignon Blanc are intense and complex. It's the Pinot Noir, though, that is largely responsible for the winery's stellar reputation; it helped cement the Russian River's status as a Pinot powerhouse. ■TIP→ Rochioli is one of the few wineries of its stature that still doesn't charge for tastings. ⊠ *6192 Westside Rd.* ☎ *707/433–2305* ⊕ *www.rochioliwinery.com* ⊠ *Tasting free* ⊙ *Early Jan.–mid-Dec., Thurs.–Mon. 11–4, Tues. and Wed. by appointment.*

Ridge tastings include wines from its Sonoma and Santa Cruz Mountains wineries.

WORTH NOTING

Alexander Valley Vineyards. The 1841 homestead of Cyrus Alexander, for whom the valley is named, is now the site of mellow Alexander Valley Vineyards. The place is known for its Chardonnays, Cabernet Sauvignons, and trio of Zinfandel wines, including the widely distributed Sin Zin. The standard tasting is free, but consider opting for the reserve tasting ($10) to sample the single-vineyard Cabernet Sauvignon, the Bordeaux blend called Cyrus, and other award-winning wines. From April to August, a $25 wine-and-cheese pairing is offered. A tour takes in the winery and wine caves dug deep into a nearby hillside; there's a lovely picnic area nearby. ■TIP→ Check on the winery's website for a printable coupon good for free reserve tastings. ✉ *8644 Hwy. 128, at Sonnikson Rd.* ☎ *707/433–7209* ⊕ *www.avvwine.com* 🖃 *Tastings free–$25, tour free* ⊗ *Daily 10–5; tour at 11 and 2.*

Dry Creek Peach & Produce. If you happen by this farm stand in the summer, don't pass up the chance to sample the tree-ripened white and yellow peaches, some of which may have been harvested moments before you arrived. You can buy peaches in small quantities, as well as organic peach jam. How good are these peaches? The customers include the famed Chez Panisse Restaurant in Berkeley. ✉ *2179 Yoakim Bridge Rd., near Dry Creek Rd.* ☎ *707/433–8121* ⊕ *www. drycreekpeach.com* ⊗ *July–mid-Sept., Fri.–Sun. noon–5.*

Foppiano Vineyards. Here's the rare Russian River Valley winery where Chardonnay and Pinot Noir don't reign supreme: the flagship wine at family-owned Foppiano is a Petite Sirah from grapes grown in a nearby warmer-than-average sliver of the AVA. Foppiano has operated continuously since 1896—the clan weathered Prohibition in part by selling home wine-making kits to do-it-yourself vintners. The current winemaker, Natalie West, the daughter of longtime Dry Creek Valley grape growers, has revived Foppiano's Chardonnay line, and the citrusy initial vintages show promise. Her Pinot Noir manages to be light yet fruit forward, vaguely floral yet sufficiently bold. ■TIP➔ If you've had enough of too-precious tasting rooms, you'll find that the one at Foppiano is refreshingly old school. ✉ *12707 Old Redwood Hwy., off U.S. 101* ☎ *707/433–7272* ⊕ *www.foppiano.com* 🍷 *Tasting $5* ⊙ *Daily 10–4:30.*

Gary Farrell Winery. Pass through an impressive metal gate and wind your way up a steep hill to reach Gary Farrell, a spot with knockout views over the rolling hills and vineyards below. The winery has changed hands a few times since Farrell sold it in 2004, but it's managed to continue producing well-regarded bottles, these days by winemaker Theresa Heredia. Though its Zinfandels and Chardonnays often excel, the winery has built its reputation on its Pinot Noirs. ✉ *10701 Westside Rd.* ☎ *707/473–2909* ⊕ *www.garyfarrellwines.com* 🍷 *Tastings $15–$25, tour $35* ⊙ *Daily 10:30–4:30; tour by appointment.*

Healdsburg Museum and Historical Society. To take a short break from wine tasting, visit the Healdsburg Museum and its collection of local historical objects, including baskets and artifacts from native tribes. Other exhibits cover the Mexican Rancho period, the founding and growth of Healdsburg in the 1850s, and the history of local agriculture. ✉ *221 Matheson St., at Fitch St.* ☎ *707/431–3325* ⊕ *www.healdsburgmuseum.org* 🍷 *Free* ⊙ *Wed.–Sun. 11–4.*

Jordan Vineyard and Winery. A visit to this sprawling property north of Healdsburg revolves around an impressive estate built in the early 1970s to replicate a French château. Seated tastings of Cabernet Sauvignon and Chardonnay are held in the château itself, in a secluded room that once served as a private cellar. The hour-long Library Tasting includes food and cheese prepared by Executive Chef Todd Knoll. The Winery Tour and Tasting, which lasts 90 minutes, winds from the château past a garden and through vine-

CLOSE UP

Dry Creek Valley

If you drive north along Healdsburg Avenue and turn left onto Dry Creek Road, you'll soon feel like you've slipped back in time. Healdsburg looks totally urban in comparison with the pure, unspoiled countryside of Dry Creek Valley. Although the region has become renowned for its wines, it preserves a rural simplicity rarely found in California's Wine Country today. The valley's well-drained, gravelly floor is planted with Chardonnay grapes to the south, where an occasional sea fog creeping in from the Russian River cools the vineyards. Sauvignon Blanc is planted in the north, where the vineyards are warmer. The red decomposed soils of the benchlands bring out the best in Zinfandel—the grape for which Dry Creek has become famous—but they also produce great Cabernet Sauvignon. And these soils seem well suited to such Rhône varieties as Cinsault, Mourvèdre, and Marsanne, which need heat to ripen properly. Wineries within this AVA include Dry Creek, Ferrari-Carano, Preston, Quivira, and Ridge.

yards shaded by century-old oak trees. For an even more elaborate experience, consider the three-hour Estate Tour and Tasting. ⊠ *1474 Alexander Valley Rd., on Greco Rd.* ☎ *800/654–1213, 707/431–5250* ⊕ *www.jordanwinery. com* 🍷 *Library tasting $20, winery tour and tasting $30* ⊙ *Library tasting mid-Nov.–mid-Apr., Mon.–Sat. 10 and 2; mid-Apr.–mid.-Nov., Mon.–Sat. 10 and 2, Sun. 11, 1, and 3; winery tour mid-Nov.–mid-Apr., Mon.–Sat. at 11; mid-Apr.–mid-Nov., Mon.–Sat. at 11, Sun. at 11.*

La Crema. The tasteful decor of La Crema's tasting room perfectly suits the high-profile brand's well-composed Chardonnays and Pinot Noirs. A basic tasting provides a good overview of the offerings, but consider requesting a Pinot Noir appellation tasting, which allows you to sample wines whose grapes derive from several coastal AVAs. The extra heat that grapes from the Russian River Valley receive makes that area's wine the perkiest of the bunch, but each has its virtues. You can almost taste the sand and seashells in the more ascetic Sonoma Coast Shell Ridge Pinot Noir, and the Anderson Valley wine is soft, sweet, and mildly flowery. ■TIP→ For a slightly higher fee you can taste the more exclusive 9 Barrels vintages. ⊠ *235 Healdsburg Ave., near Matheson St.* ☎ *800/314–1762, 707/431–9400* ⊕ *www. lacrema.com* 🍷 *Daily 10:30–5:30* ⊙ *Tastings $10–$30.*

QUICK BITES. **Moustache Baked Goods.** This shop specialize sweets incorporating local, organic ingredients: cupcakes (try the one with locally sourced bacon), whoopie pies, and macaroons, to name a few. Wash everything down with Blue Bottle Coffee. ⊠ *381 Healdsburg Ave., at North St.* ☎ *707/395–4111* ⊕ *moustachebakedgoods.com* ⊗ *Daily 10–6.*   10:30

Papapietro Perry. Pinot Noir and Zinfandel (some of the region's best) are the mainstays of this small operation in the heart of the Dry Creek Valley, but lately the winery has also begun producing small lots of Chardonnay. Most of the grapes come from the Russian River Valley, though there's a Pinot from Sonoma Coast grapes and another from fruit grown in neighboring Mendocino County; one Zin is made from Dry Creek fruit. Standard tastings at the copper-topped bar include five pours, and it always pays to ask what else is open in the back (the 777 Clones Pinot is particularly delicious). ⊠ *4791 Dry Creek Rd., at Timber Crest Farms* ☎ *707/433–0422, 877/467–4668* ⊕ *www.papapietro-perry.com* ⊠ *Tasting $10* ⊗ *Daily 11–4:30.*

recommended

6

Rodney Strong Vineyards. The late Rodney Strong was among the first winemakers to plant Pinot Noir grapes in the Russian River Valley; his namesake winery still makes Pinot Noirs, but it's best known for Cabernet Sauvignon–based wines. The headliners include the Bordeaux-style blend Symmetry and three single-vineyard Alexander Valley Cabernets: Alexander's Crown, Rockaway, and Brothers Ridge. You can sample Cabs and Pinots—along with Sauvignon Blanc, Chardonnay, Malbec, Zinfandel, and other wines— in the attractive octagonal tasting room. A self-guided tour provides a good view of the fermentation tanks and other machinery, as do twice-daily guided tours. The winery hosts outdoor jazz and rock concerts during summer. ⊠ *11455 Old Redwood Hwy., north of Eastside Rd.* ☎ *707/431–1533, 800/678–4763* ⊕ *www.rodneystrong.com* ⊠ *Tastings free– $15, tour free* ⊗ *Daily 10–5; tour at 11 and 3.*

Seghesio Family Vineyards. If the Napa Valley's devotion to   ∦ Cabernet Sauvignon and Sonoma County's current Pinot Noir mania have left you feeling slighted, head to Seghesio, where the ancestors of the current winemaker, Ted Seghesio, planted some of the Alexander Valley's earliest Zinfandel vines. The grapes harvested here produce sophisticated wines, among them the potent Home Ranch Zinfandel. Seghesio crafts most of his wines—including Pinot Noir,

Sangiovese, and Omaggio, a super-Tuscan blend of Cabernet Sauvignon and Sangiovese—using estate-grown grapes from the Alexander, Dry Creek, and Russian River valleys. ■ TIP→ Consider the $50 Family Tables tasting, where limited-release wines are paired with food prepared by executive chef Peter Janiak. ✉ *700 Grove St., off W. Grant St.* ☎ *707/433–3579* 🌐 *www.seghesio.com* 🎟 *Tastings $15–$50* ⏲ *Daily 10–5.*

Thumbprint Cellars Tasting Lounge. With its exposed-brick walls, sleek leather chairs, silk curtains, and artwork on the walls, this stylish tasting room has the feel of a very hip friend's San Francisco loft. The provocatively named wines (including Arousal, Four Play, and Three Some) come primarily from Russian River and Dry Creek grapes. ✉ *102 Matheson St., at Healdsburg Ave.* ☎ *707/433–2393* 🌐 *www.thumbprintcellars.com* 🎟 *Tasting $5 and up* ⏲ *Daily 11–6.*

WHERE TO EAT

★ Fodor's Choice 🍴 **Barndiva.** *American.* This hip joint abandons the homey vibe of so many Wine Country spots for a younger, more urban feel. Electronic music plays quietly in the background while hipster servers ferry inventive seasonal cocktails. The food is as stylish as the well-dressed couples cozying up next to each other on the banquette seats. Make a light meal out of starters like "The Artisan," a bountiful plate of cheeses and charcuterie, or settle in for the evening with such dishes as pork tenderloin with potato purée or crispy young chicken served with roasted brussels sprouts, pancetta ricotta, and egg-yolk ravioli. During warm weather the open-air patio is the place to be. [$] *Average main: $31* ✉ *231 Center St., at Matheson St.* ☎ *707/431–0100* 🌐 *www.barndiva.com* ⏲ *Closed Mon. and Tues.*

$$$$

$$$ 🍴 **Bistro Ralph.** *French.* There was a time when Bistro Ralph was *the* good restaurant downtown, and long before the concept of "fresh, simple, local" became culinary gospel, that hallowed refrain coursed through the kitchen of this Healdsburg pioneer. The menu shifts seasonally. In spring, for example, you might find extraordinary grilled marinated asparagus; at other times look for grilled Columbia River sturgeon or Dungeness crab ravioli. Standbys include fried Szechuan-pepper calamari, chicken livers (locals love them), lamb burgers, and duck confit. This place does as spectacular a job with shoestring potatoes as it does with ahi tuna, and even the cocktails—martinis are a specialty—are executed with precision and flair. The wines are all from Healdsburg, but with dozens of wineries within city

The rolling hills of the Russian River Valley

limits, the selection is more than sufficiently varied. $ *Average main: $27* ✉ *109 Plaza St., near Healdsburg Ave.* ☎ *707/433–1380* ⊕ *www.bistroralph.com* ⊗ *No dinner Sun.*

$$$ ✕ **Café Lucia.** *Portuguese.* The flavors of Portugal dazzle diners at this handsome restaurant run by Healdsburg native Lucia Azevedo Fincher. You can go the tapas-only route—the fried Sonoma goat cheese and the crunchy pig's-ear-and-parsley salad are two standouts—or order a few small plates before moving on to a full entrée. A fine accompaniment either way is *caldo verde,* a potato-thickened beef consommé with thinly sliced collard greens and linguiça sausage. Among the noteworthy mains is *feijoada completa,* the Brazilian national dish, a thick mass of stewed beef, pork, smoked sausage, and black beans. The Portuguese variation on paella is also a winner. ■TIP→ The restaurant is in back of the building that houses La Crema's tasting room. $ *Average main: $25* ✉ *235 Healdsburg Ave., near Matheson St.* ☎ *707/431–1113* ⊕ *www.cafelucia.net* ⚄ *Reservations not accepted.*

$ ✕ **Costeaux.** *French.* This French-style bakery and café has won numerous awards for its bread, and the croissants are among Sonoma County's best. Breakfast, served all day, includes homemade quiche, the signature omelet (sun-dried tomatoes, applewood-smoked bacon, and Brie), and French toast made from thick slabs of cinnamon-walnut bread. Among the lunch items are two au courant variations on classic sandwiches: a French dip made from house-roasted rib eye and a Monte Cristo (turkey, ham, and Jarlsberg cheese) on that addictive cinnamon-walnut bread. ■ TIP→ Arrive early on weekends to grab a seat on the open-air patio. [$] *Average main: $13* ✉ *417 Healdsburg Ave., at North St.* ☎ *707/433–1913* 🌐 *www.costeaux.com* ⏲ *No dinner.*

★ Fodor's Choice ✕ **Downtown Bakery & Creamery.** *Bakery.* If you
$ want to catch the Healdsburg spirit, hit the plaza in the early morning to down a cup of coffee and a fragrant sticky bun or a too-darlin' *canelé,* a French-style pastry with a soft custard center surrounded by a dense caramel crust. Until 2 pm you can also go the full breakfast route: pancakes, granola, poached farm eggs on polenta, or perhaps the dandy bacon-and-egg pizza. For lunch there are sandwiches and focaccia. The bakery uses local fruit and dairy products in its breads, pastries, and ice creams. [$] *Average main: $8* ✉ *308A Center St., at North St.* ☎ *707/431–2719* 🌐 *www.downtownbakery.net* ⚠ *Reservations not accepted* ⏲ *No dinner.*

$$$$ ✕ **Dry Creek Kitchen.** *Modern American.* Chef Charlie Palmer's ultramodern destination restaurant enchants diners with clever combinations of flavors and textures in dishes based on seasonal, often local ingredients. A perennial favorite among the starters is the diver scallops in a pastry shell; tableside, the shell is slit open and a black truffle beurre rouge sauce is poured in. The shell remains flaky, and the truffles, butter, and wine float atop the rich flavors of the scallops. A similar level of complexity reveals itself in main courses that might include smoked duck breast with Pinot Noir–braised cabbage and pan-roasted Petaluma chicken. ■ TIP→ The restaurant waives the corkage fee on wines from Sonoma County, which can take the edge off your final tab. [$] *Average main: $33* ✉ *Hotel Healdsburg, 317 Healdsburg Ave., near Matheson St.* ☎ *707/431–0330* 🌐 *www.drycreekkitchen.com* ⏲ *No lunch Mon.–Thurs.*

$$ ✕ **Healdsburg Charcuterie.** *Eclectic.* This cozy restaurant with a slightly Provençal feel serves a hodgepodge of cuisines, from an all-American chicken-salad sandwich and an excellent house-cured pork tenderloin sandwich, both for lunch, to Italian favorites like fusilli and smoked chicken in a basil cream sauce for dinner. Some of the standout dishes are French through and through, such as the escargots in garlicky herb butter and a generous charcuterie plate that includes pork-pepper pâté, duck rillette, and garlic salami. The vibe is casual rather than refined, but the reasonable prices and ample portions make this one of Healdsburg's better values for a sit-down meal. ■ TIP→ If you're planning

The photogenic Honor Mansion

a picnic, the restaurant is happy to pack up some food to go. [$] *Average main: $21* ✉ *335 Healdsburg Ave., at North St.* ☎ *707/431–7213* 🌐 *www.charcuteriehealdsburg.com.*

★ **Fodor's Choice** 🍴 **Scopa.** *Italian.* At this tiny eatery, chef Ari
$$ Rosen cooks up such rustic Italian specialties as house-made ravioli stuffed with ricotta cheese, braised chicken with greens and polenta, and *sugo Calabrese* (tomato-braised beef and pork rib served with smoked mozzarella in a tomato sauce). Simple thin-crust pizzas are worth ordering, too. Locals love the restaurant for its lack of pretension: wine is served in juice glasses, and the friendly hostess makes the rounds to see that all are satisfied. You'll be packed in elbow-to-elbow with your fellow diners, but for a convivial evening over a bottle of Nebbiolo, there's no better choice. [$] *Average main: $20* ✉ *109A Plaza St., near Healdsburg Ave.* ☎ *707/433–5282* 🌐 *www.scopahealdsburg.com* ⊗ *No lunch.*

★ **Fodor's Choice** 🍴 **Spoonbar.** *Modern American.* Cantina doors
$$$ that open onto Healdsburg Avenue make this trendy eatery especially appealing in summer, when warm breeze wafts into the stylish space. Midcentury modern furnishings, concrete walls, and a long communal table fashioned from rough-hewn acacia wood create an urbane setting for chef Louis Maldonado's contemporary American fare. Divided into five sections, the menu lets you mix and match to create a memorable meal. The mains might include Cornish game hen roulade with artichokes or loin of beef in red wine jus,

served with quinoa and cider-braised root vegetables. The perpetually packed bar, known for inventive seasonal and historic cocktails, is the real draw for many locals. [$] *Average main: $23* ✉ *h2hotel, 219 Healdsburg Ave., at Vine St.* ☎ *707/433–7222* 🌐 *www.h2hotel.com/spoonbar* ⏲ *No lunch Mon.–Thurs. in winter.*

★ Fodor's Choice ✕ **Willi's Seafood & Raw Bar.** *Seafood.* The per-
$$$ petually packed Willi's draws a festive crowd that likes to enjoy specialty cocktails at the full bar before sitting down to a dinner of small, mostly seafood-oriented plates. A few dishes, such as the warm Maine lobster roll with garlic butter and fennel, conjure up a New England fish shack, and others, like the top-notch ceviches and the scallops served with a cilantro-and-pumpkin-seed pesto, have a Latin American accent. The desserts transport diners to France (wildly flavorful crème brûlée) and beyond. ■ TIP→ The same owners operate the Bravas Bar de Tapas at 420 Center Street, another good choice if this place is packed. [$] *Average main: $25* ✉ *403 Healdsburg Ave., at North St.* ☎ *707/433–9191* 🌐 *www.willisseafood.net* ✍ *Reservations not accepted.*

$$$ ✕ **Zin Restaurant and Wine Bar.** *American.* Concrete floors and large canvases on the walls lend the restaurant a casual, industrial, and slightly artsy feel. The American cuisine—such as the roasted pork belly with pickled apples or the free-range chicken braised in red wine—is hearty and highly seasoned. Portions are large, so consider sharing if you hope to save room for such desserts as the brownie sundae with house-made ice cream. As you might have guessed from the name, Zinfandel is the drink of choice here, though Sonoma County's other major varietals show up on the 100-bottle wine list. From Sunday through Thursday, blue-plate specials featuring homey fare (like pot roast and chicken and dumplings) make this place a bargain. [$] *Average main: $25* ✉ *344 Center St., at North St.* ☎ *707/473–0946* 🌐 *zinrestaurant.com* ⏲ *No lunch weekends.*

WHERE TO STAY

$ 🏨 **Best Western Plus Dry Creek Inn.** *Hotel.* The lackluster location of this Spanish Mission–style motel near U.S. 101 nevertheless means quick access to downtown Healdsburg and other Wine Country hot spots. **Pros:** free Wi-Fi and laundry facilities; frequent Internet discounts available. **Cons:** thin walls; basic furnishings in standard rooms. [$] *Rooms from: $145* ✉ *198 Dry Creek Rd.* ☎ *707/433–0300, 800/222–5784* 🌐 *www.drycreekinn.com* 🛏 *163 rooms* 🍴 *Breakfast.*

$$ 🏨 **Camellia Inn.** *B&B/Inn.* In a well-preserved Italianate Victorian constructed in 1869, this colorful B&B sits on a quiet residential street a block from the main square. **Pros:** reasonable rates; family-friendly atmosphere; within easy walking distance of restaurants. **Cons:** a few rooms have a shower but no bath; all rooms lack TVs. [$] *Rooms from: $215* ✉ *211 North St.* ☎ *707/433–8182, 800/727–8182* 🌐 *www.camelliainn.com* ⇨ *8 rooms, 1 suite* 🍴 *Breakfast.*

★ Fodor's Choice 🏨 **h2hotel.** *B&B/Inn.* Eco-friendly touches
$$ abound at this hotel, from the undulating plant-covered "green roof" to wooden decks made from salvaged lumber. **Pros:** stylish modern design; Healdsburg's most popular bar; king beds can be converted to two twins. **Cons:** least expensive rooms lack bathtubs; no fitness facilities, but bike rentals are free. [$] *Rooms from: $200* ✉ *219 Healdsburg Ave.* ☎ *707/922–5251* 🌐 *www.h2hotel.com* ⇨ *34 rooms, 2 suites* 🍴 *Breakfast.*

★ Fodor's Choice 🏨 **The Honor Mansion.** *B&B/Inn.* An 1883 Itali-
$$$ anate Victorian houses this photogenic hotel; rooms in the main house preserve a sense of the building's heritage, whereas the larger suites are comparatively understated. **Pros:** homemade sweets available at all hours; spa pavilions by pool available for massages in fair weather. **Cons:** almost a mile from Healdsburg's plaza; walls can seem thin. [$] *Rooms from: $305* ✉ *891 Grove St.* ☎ *707/433–4277, 800/554–4667* 🌐 *www.honormansion.com* ⇨ *5 rooms, 7 suites, 1 cottage* ⏲ *Closed 2 wks around Christmas* 🍴 *Breakfast.*

$$$ 🏨 **Hotel Healdsburg.** *Resort.* Across the street from the tidy town plaza, this spare, sophisticated hotel caters to travelers with an urban sensibility. **Pros:** several rooms overlook the town plaza; comfortable lobby with a small attached bar; extremely comfortable beds. **Cons:** exterior rooms get some street noise; rooms could use better lighting. [$] *Rooms from: $375* ✉ *25 Matheson St.* ☎ *707/431–2800, 800/889–7188* 🌐 *www.hotelhealdsburg.com* ⇨ *49 rooms, 6 suites* 🍴 *Breakfast.*

★ Fodor's Choice 🏨 **Hôtel Les Mars.** *Hotel.* This Relais & Châ-
$$$$ teaux property takes the prize for opulence with guest rooms spacious and elegant enough for French nobility, 18th- and 19th-century antiques and reproductions, canopy beds dressed in luxe linens, and gas-burning fireplaces. **Pros:** large rooms; just off Healdsburg's plaza; Bulgari bath products. **Cons:** very expensive. [$] *Rooms from: $500* ✉ *27 North St.* ☎ *707/433–4211* 🌐 *www.hotellesmars.com* ⇨ *16 rooms* 🍴 *Breakfast.*

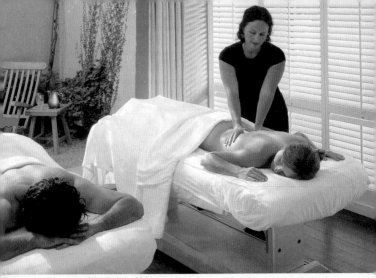

The spa at the Hotel Healdsburg

$$$ 🖼 **Madrona Manor.** *B&B/Inn.* This Victorian mansion dating from 1881 is surrounded by 8 acres of wooded and landscaped grounds; rooms in the three-story mansion, the carriage house, and the three separate cottages are gloriously ornate, with mirrors in gilt frames and paintings covering every wall. **Pros:** old-fashioned and romantic; pretty veranda perfect for a cocktail. **Cons:** pool heated May through October only; some might find decor too fussy. $ *Rooms from: $315* ⊠ *1001 Westside Rd.* ☎ *707/433–4231, 800/258–4003* ⊕ *www.madronamanor.com* ⇥ *18 rooms, 5 suites* ⊖*Breakfast.*

NIGHTLIFE AND THE ARTS

Bear Republic Brewing Company. Lovers of the brew make pilgrimages to Bear Republic to sample the flagship Racer 5 IPA, the Hop Rod Rye, the mighty Big Bear Black Stout, and many other offerings at this craft-brew pioneer. A recent menu upgrade has made the brewery's spacious pub a good stop for a casual lunch or dinner—all kinds of burgers (beef, salmon, veggie, and more), chili, pastas, and artisanal-cheese and charcuterie plates. ■TIP→ In warm weather there's often a wait for the seats outdoors, but there's usually room inside. $ *Average main: $1* ⊠ *345 Healdsburg Ave., at North St.* ☎ *707/433–2337* ⊕ *www.bearrepublic.com.*

★ **Fodor's Choice Bergamot Alley.** After a few minutes in this retro-hip but chill wine-and-beer bar, you might suddenly ask yourself, "Why is everyone here so good-looking? V really fit in?" Of course you will, because the welcoming vibe of the largely under-30 crowd is exceeded only by that of the hosts. Congeniality aside, the other draws here include the craft brews on tap, the change-of-pace selection of international wines (nothing from California), and the live-music, movie, and other event nights. ✉ *328 Healdsburg Ave., at North St.* ☎ *707/433–8720* ⊕ *bergamotalley.com.*

Raven Performing Arts Theater. The Philharmonia Healdsburg orchestra and the Raven Players theater group are this venue's resident companies. Charlie Musselwhite, Elvin Bishop, and other visiting talents have also taken the stage. Healdsburg Jazz Festival events take place here every year. ✉ *115 North St., at Center St.* ☎ *707/433–6335* ⊕ *www.raventheater.org.*

SHOPPING

Healdsburg is Sonoma County's most pleasant spot for an afternoon of window-shopping, with dozens of art galleries, boutiques, and high-end design shops clustered on or around Healdsburg Plaza. The town's food fetish extends to the specialty grocers and markets, but there are plenty of stores selling nonedibles, too. Should you weary of shopping, there are countless cafés and tasting rooms where you can revive yourself.

Christopher Hill Gallery. In a town with many worthy galleries, Christopher Hill's brick-walled space stands out for both the quality of the art and his willingness to exhibit edgier styles and subject matter than most of his counterparts. ✉ *326 Healdsburg Ave., at Plaza St.* ☎ *707/395–4646* ⊕ *www. chgallery.com* ☽ *Wed.–Mon. 10–5:30, Tues. by appointment.*

Copperfield's Books. In addition to magazines and best-selling books, this store, part of a local indie chain, stocks a wide selection of discounted and remaindered titles, including many cookbooks. ✉ *106 Matheson St., at Healdsburg Ave.* ☎ *707/433–9270* ⊕ *copperfieldsbooks.com/stores/healdsburg.*

Dry Creek General Store. The Dry Creek Valley is so picture-perfect, it would be a shame to pass up the opportunity to picnic at one of the wineries. For breakfasts, sandwiches, bread, cheeses, and picnic supplies, stop by the general store, established in 1881 and still a popular spot for locals to hang out on the porch or in the bar. ✉ *3495 Dry Creek Rd., at Lambert Bridge Rd.* ☎ *707/433–4171* ⊕ *www.dry-creekgeneralstore1881.com.*

Healdsburg Center for the Arts. A block off the plaza, this center displays work by local artists. In addition to larger-scale paintings and photography, look for suitcase-friendly jewelry and fine crafts. ✉ *130 Plaza St., at Center St.* ☎ *707/431–1970* ⊕ *www.healdsburgcenterforthearts.com.*

★ **Fodor's Choice Healdsburg Farmers' Market.** The long-running market, held from late spring into the fall, showcases locally produced cheeses, breads, herbs, meats, and oils, in addition to the usual (ultratasty) fruits and vegetables. The flavors and smells arouse the senses, and the passion of the participating artisans warms the heart. The main market takes place in the municipal parking lot west of Healdsburg Plaza from May through November on Saturday from 9 am to noon. June to October, a smaller edition unfolds on the plaza on Wednesday between 4 and 6:30. ✉ *North and Vine Sts., 1 block west of Healdsburg Plaza* ☎ *707/431–1956* ⊕ *www.healdsburgfarmersmarket.org.*

Jimtown Store. The Alexander Valley's best picnic-packing stop has great espresso and a good selection of deli items, including the signature Brie-and-chopped-olive sandwich. While you're here, take a few minutes to browse through the gifts, which include both housewares and old-fashioned toys like sock monkeys. ✉ *6706 Hwy. 128, near W. Sausal La.* ☎ *707/433–1212* ⊕ *www.jimtown.com* ☉ *Mon., Wed., and Thurs. 7:30–4; Fri.–Sun. 7:30–5.*

Lime Stone. Owned by Dry Creek Kitchen chef Charlie Palmer and his wife, Lisa, this shop carries wine-related items, kitchen accoutrements, and household accessories. The hip and tasteful Lisa does all the buying. ✉ *Hotel Healdsburg, 318 Healdsburg Ave., near Matheson St.* ☎ *707/433–3080* ⊕ *www.limestonehealdsburg.com.*

M Clothing. A high-end women's-clothing boutique, M carries dresses, skirts, sweaters, and accessories from Diane von Furstenberg, Nanette Lepore, and other top designers. ✉ *333 Healdsburg Ave., at Plaza St.* ☎ *707/431–8738* ⊕ *www.martymclothing.com.*

Oakville Grocery. The Healdsburg branch of this Napa-based store is filled with wine, condiments, and deli items, and sells sandwiches and other picnic fixings. A terrace with ample seating makes a good place for an impromptu meal, but you might want to lunch early or late to avoid the crowds. ✉ *124 Matheson St., at Center St.* ☎ *707/433–3200* ⊕ *www.oakvillegrocery.com.*

WORD OF MOUTH. "A ride through the Alexander Vall
Creek Valley wouldn't disappoint with wineries along
Visit the Oakville Grocery store for gourmet picnic g|
lunch."—nancytwo

One World Fair Trade. Independent artisans in developing countries create the clothing, household items, jewelry, gifts, and toys sold in this bright, well-designed shop whose owner has a shrewd eye for fine craftsmanship. ✉ *106 B Matheson St., at Healdsburg Ave.* ☎ *707/473–0880* ⊕ *www. oneworldfairtrade.net.*

Plaza Gourmet. You'll find not only wine-related gadgets but also a wide selection of kitchenware and serving pieces at this appealing shop. ✉ *108 Matheson St., at Healdsburg Ave.* ☎ *707/433–7116.*

Saint Dizier Home. This shop is a reminder of why the universe provides us with decorators and designers—they really do know best. With this selection of exquisitely crafted furniture and contemporary items like hand-painted silk pillows, designer Jacques Saint Dizier and buyer Cathy Hopkins prove the point. ✉ *259 Center St., at Matheson St.* ☎ *707/473–0980* ⊕ *www.saintdhome.com.*

6

SPAS

★ **Fodor's Choice Spa Dolce.** Owner Ines von Majthenyi Scherrer has a good local rep, having run a popular nearby spa before opening this stylish facility just off Healdsburg Plaza. Spa Dolce specializes in skin and body care for men and women, and makeup, waxing, and nail care for women. Curved white walls and fresh-cut floral arrangements set a subdued tone for such treatments as the exfoliating Hauschka body scrub, which combines organic brown sugar with scented oil. There's a romantic room for couples to enjoy massages for two. Many guests come just for the facials, which range from a straightforward cleansing to an anti-aging peel. ✉ *250 Center St., at Matheson St.* ☎ *707/433–0177* ⊕ *www.spadolce.com* ▱ *Treatments $20–$210* ☉ *Tues.–Sun. 10–7.*

The Spa Hotel Healdsburg. Taking a page from its restaurant's farm-to-table approach, the Hotel Healdsburg's spa also sources many of its treatments' ingredients from area farms. The plush Frette robes for patrons, an outdoor Jacuzzi, and soothing minimalist decor make this a tranquil choice for massages, body wraps, facials, and hand and foot treatments. The most popular ones include the Meyer lemon body polishes, herbal wraps, and massages and the lavender-and-peppermint restorative massage, all of which leave the skin tingling and rejuvenated. The hotel's signature Swedish-style massage involves aromatic oils, hot stones, and, as necessary, acupressure. ✉ *327 Healdsburg Ave., at Matheson St.* ☎ *707/433–4747* ⊕ *www.hotelhealdsburg. com/spa* ✑ *Treatments $45–$240* ☉ *Daily 9–8.*

SPORTS AND THE OUTDOORS

BICYCLING

A mostly gentle 20-mile loop starting and ending in Healdsburg Plaza will take you past several good wineries—and infinitely beautiful scenery that includes vineyard-covered hills, the rolling Russian River, and a gently rusting trestle bridge. Start by heading south from the plaza on Healdsburg Avenue. Turn west onto Mill Street, whose name changes to Westside Road after you cross under U.S. 101. Follow Westside for almost 10 miles, stopping at wineries (among them Rochioli) as time permits. Unless you're heading to Gary Farrell Winery, which is a little farther south, turn east on Wohler Road and then north on Eastside Road. Copain is among the wineries along this view-filled portion of the ride. Head north again at Old Redwood Highway—J Vineyards and Rodney Strong are at this intersection. The name of the road changes to Healdsburg Avenue after you cross under U.S. 101; the avenue leads back to the plaza.

Wine Country Bikes. This shop in downtown Healdsburg is perfectly located for single or multiday treks into the Dry Creek and Russian River valleys. Bikes, including tandems, rent for $35 to $125 a day. One-day tours start at $139. ✉ *61 Front St., at Hudson St.* ☎ *707/473–0610, 866/922–4537* ⊕ *www.winecountrybikes.com.*

BOATING

Russian River Adventures. This outfit rents inflatable canoes for half- and full-day trips down the Russian River; the fee includes a shuttle back to the starting point at the end of the journey. You can also hire a guide for the day to explain the terrain and show you the best places to swim and swing on a rope. Guides will also take kids out on the river while you hit the wineries. ✉ *20 Healdsburg Ave., at S. University St.* ☎ *707/433–5599, 800/280–7627* ⊕ *www. russianriveradventures.com* ✑ *$42.50 per person half day, $50 full day.*

GEYSERVILLE

8 miles north of Healdsburg.

Several of the Alexander Valley AVA's high-profile wineries, including the splashiest of them all, the Francis Ford Coppola Winery, can be found in the town of Geyserville. Not long ago Geyserville was a dusty farm town with little to offer travelers besides a grocery store. Downtown retains its dusty character, but the restaurants, shops, and tasting rooms along the short main drag make it worth a stroll.

GETTING HERE AND AROUND

From Healdsburg, the quickest route to downtown Geyserville is north on U.S. 101. For a more scenic drive, head north from Healdsburg Plaza along Healdsburg Avenue. About 3 miles north the road forks north and east. The north fork, signed as Lytton Springs Road, leads to Ridge Vineyards. From Lytton Springs, head north on Geyserville Avenue to reach Geyserville. The east fork, Alexander Valley Road, heads into the Alexander Valley. Just after the road merges with Highway 128, you'll find the Jimtown Store, and beyond that Stryker Sonoma.

EXPLORING

TOP ATTRACTIONS

David Coffaro Estate Vineyard. David Coffaro himself tends to every aspect of the wine-making process at his namesake winery, where his beloved Oakland Raiders memorabilia lines the wall behind the bar. (On game days, you might find staffers watching the action on a large screen tucked between the barrels.) Despite the relaxed attitude, Coffaro is serious about wines. He makes a handful of single-varietal wines but specializes in crafting unique blends—mixing up, for example, Cabernet Sauvignon, Petite Sirah, Petite Verdot, and Tannat, a varietal that's popular in Europe's Basque region but rarely grown in the United States. ■TIP→ If you're interested in learning more about the other unusual varietals that grow here, ask for a taste straight from the barrels. ⊠ *7485 Dry Creek Rd.* ☎ *707/433–9715* ⊕ *www.coffaro.com* ☜ *Tasting $5, tour free* ☉ *Daily 11–4; tour Fri. at 11 and 1 by appointment.*

★ **Fodor'sChoice Francis Ford Coppola Winery.** The famous film
FAMILY director's over-the-top fantasyland is the sort of place the midlevel Mafiosi in his *The Godfather* saga might declare had "real class"; the "everyday wines" poured here are pretty much beside the point, but still, it's an entertain-

A Great Drive in Northern Sonoma County

CLOSE UP

Dabble in three AVAs in one day on a scenic drive that begins in downtown Healdsburg. Break your fast at Flying Goat Coffee or Downtown Bakery & Creamery, then grab everything you need for a picnic at nearby Oakville Grocery. Thus prepared, hop in the car and head south on Healdsburg Avenue and west on Mill Street.

Shortly after Mill Street becomes Westside Road, the tree-lined landscape and weathered farm buildings will already have you feeling transported to a more pastoral age. Continue south to **Rochioli Vineyards and Winery**—if it's Tuesday or Wednesday, when the winery is closed, continue on a few miles to **Gary Farrell Winery.** After your winery visit, backtrack north on Westside Road for about 5 miles from Rochioli.

Turn northwest at the intersection of Westside and West Dry Creek roads—**Madrona Manor,** known for its well-tended estate garden, borders them both—and continue on West Dry Creek for about 9 miles to **Preston of Dry Creek.** Sample some wines and perhaps purchase one—the peppy Sauvignon Blanc is a natural on a hot summer day—to

enjoy while picnicking on the property.

Let your mood determine your stop in the Alexander Valley. To get here from Preston, head southeast on West Dry Creek Road and east on Yoakim Bridge Road. If it's summer and the Dry Creek Peach Produce stand is open, stop to savor the season's bounty; otherwise continue directly to Dry Creek Road and turn south, heading east after about ¼ mile onto Canyon Road. After 2 miles, just after you pass under U.S. 101, turn south onto Highway 128 east, also signed as Geyserville Avenue. Taste flights of wines from small producers at the **Locals Tasting Room,** or for stunning architecture and hearty Cabs and Zins, continue east on Highway 128 to **Stryker Sonoma.** If Hollywood glitz is more your speed, head south on Geyserville Avenue to U.S. 101, hop on the freeway for 1 mile, and take the Independence Lane exit. Follow signs west from the exit to **Francis Ford Coppola Winery.**

After your Alexander Valley stop, either enjoy dinner at Diavola Pizzeria & Salumeria in Geyserville or head back to Healdsburg on U.S. 101.

ing scene. The fun is all in the excess, and you may find it hard to resist having your photo snapped standing next to Don Corleone's desk from *The Godfather,* at the re-created bandstand from its famous wedding scene, or beside memorabilia from other Coppola films, including some directed by his daughter, Sofia. The bandstand is the centerpiece of a large, popular pool area where you can rent a *cabine* (changing room), complete with shower, and spend the afternoon lounging under striped umbrellas, perhaps ordering food from the poolside café. The winery's more elaborate restaurant, Rustic, overlooks the vineyards. ⊠ *300 Via Archimedes, off U.S. 101* ☎ *707/857–1400* ⊕ *www.franciscoppolawinery.com* ⊠ *Tastings free–$15, tours $20–$55, pool pass $20* ⊙ *Tasting room daily 11–6, restaurant daily 11–9; pool hrs vary seasonally.*

★ **Fodor's Choice Locals Tasting Room.** Downtown Geyserville remains little more than a crossroads with a few shops and a good restaurant, but this storefront is worth a stop for serious wine tasters. Area winemakers and visitors come to taste wines produced by about a dozen small wineries without tasting rooms of their own. There's no fee for tasting—rather a bargain for wines of this quality—and the extremely knowledgeable staff is happy to pour you a flight of several wines so you can compare, say, different Cabernet Sauvignons. ⊠ *21023A Geyserville Ave., at Hwy. 128* ☎ *707/857–4900* ⊕ *www.tastelocalwines.com* ⊠ *Free* ⊙ *Daily 11–6.*

Stryker Sonoma. The tasting room's vaulted ceilings and walls of windows onto the vineyards suggest nothing less than a cathedral to viniculture, and the wines are nearly as impressive as the architecture. Most of them are single varietals, such as Chardonnay, Merlot, Zinfandel, Cabernet Sauvignon, and the lush, highly tannic Tannat, whose grapes come from the Basque area of France and Spain. The exceptions are a few Bordeaux-style blends, including the powerful E1K, which, unfortunately, is not usually poured in the tasting room. Call ahead to book a spot on a tour that concludes on the observation deck overlooking the vineyards. ■TIP→ In summer the picnic area is a marvelous place to bask in the warmth and quiet of the Alexander Valley countryside. ⊠ *5110 Hwy. 128, at Beleson Cemetery Rd.* ☎ *707/433–1944, 800/433–1944* ⊕ *www.strykersonoma. com* ⊠ *Tasting $10, tour $15* ⊙ *Daily 10:30–5.*

6

WORTH NOTING

Trentadue Winery. When Leo and Evelyn Trentadue decided to move to a rural location in 1959, they found their new home in a neglected Alexander Valley prune and pear orchard. True to their Tuscan heritage, the couple planted classic Italian grape varietals at Trentadue Winery. They still produce wines that are 100% Sangiovese—these remain among the best wines produced here—and Carignane, something of a rarity in the area, but the diverse lineup includes everything from a sparkler made from Chardonnay grapes to wines made from Viognier, Merlot, Tempranillo, Cabernet Sauvignon, Petite Sirah, and Zinfandel. ■TIP→ When visiting this ivy-covered villa, be sure to sample the most celebrated wine, La Storia Meritage, a blend of Bordeaux varietals. ✉ *19170 Geyserville Ave., off U.S. 101* ☎ *707/433–3104* ⊕ *www.trentadue.com* ⌸ *Tastings $5–$25, tour $20* ☉ *Daily 10–5; tours by appointment.*

WHERE TO EAT

★ Fodor'sChoice ✕ **Diavola Pizzeria & Salumeria.** *Italian.* A cozy
$$ dining room with hardwood floors, a pressed-tin ceiling, and exposed-brick walls seems a fitting setting for the rustic cuisine at this Geyserville charmer. Chef Dino Bugica studied with several artisans in Italy before opening this spot, which specializes in pizzas pulled from a wood-burning oven and several types of house-cured meats. A small selection of salads and meaty main courses round out the menu. If you're impressed by the antipasto plate, stop by the deli case on your way out and pick up some smoked pork belly, pancetta, or spicy Calabrese sausage to take home. Ⓢ *Average main: $19* ✉ *21021 Geyserville Ave., at Hwy. 128* ☎ *707/814–0111* ⊕ *www.diavolapizzeria.com* ⌸ *Reservations not accepted.*

FORESTVILLE

13 miles southwest of Healdsburg; 14 miles northwest of Santa Rosa.

To experience the Russian River AVA's climate and rusticity, follow the river's westward course to the town of Forestville, home to a highly regarded restaurant and inn and a secluded winery that looms large in the hearts of Pinot Noir aficionados.

The tasting room at Stryker Sonoma

GETTING HERE AND AROUND

To reach Forestville from U.S. 101, drive west from the River Road exit north of Santa Rosa. From Healdsburg, follow Westside Road west to River Road and then continue west.

EXPLORING

★ **Fodor's Choice Hartford Family Winery.** Pinot Noir lovers appreciate the subtle differences in the wines Hartford's Jeff Stewart crafts from grapes grown in Sonoma County's three top AVAs for the varietal—Los Carneros, Russian River Valley, and the Sonoma Coast—along with one from the Anderson Valley, just north in Mendocino County. The Pinot Noirs win consistent praise from major wine critics, and Stewart also makes highly rated Chardonnays and old-vine Zinfandels. A reserve tasting ($15) includes a flight of six wines; a tour of the winery is part of the seated private library tasting ($35). ■TIP→ If the weather's good and you've made a reservation, your reserve tasting can take place on the patio outside the opulent main winery building. ⊠ *8075 Martinelli Rd., off Hwy. 116 or River Rd.* ☎*707/887–8011, 800/588–0234* ⊕*www.hartfordwines.com* ⊠*Tastings $15–$35* ⊙ *Daily 10–4:30; tours by appointment.*

CLOSE UP

Alexander Valley AVA

The lovely Alexander Valley, one of Sonoma's least-visited regions, extends northeast of Healdsburg through Geyserville all the way to Mendocino County. Driving through the rolling hills along Highway 128, you're more likely to have to slow down for tandem bicyclists than for other drivers. And you might find you're the only visitor in the tasting room at some of the small, family-owned wineries.

The Alexander Valley AVA got a boost in 2006, when director and winemaker Francis Ford Coppola bought the old Chateau Souverain winery and opened a tasting room, but some combination of distance from San Francisco (a drive here takes about 2½ hours on a good day) and hairpin switchback roads seems to have preserved the unpretentious, rustic nature of this region. Restaurants and B&Bs are relatively few and far between, and this remains a spot to enjoy life in the slow lane.

As recently as the 1980s the Alexander Valley was mostly planted in walnuts, pears, prunes, and bulk grapes, so one might argue that experimentation here has hardly begun. So far, Chardonnay, Sauvignon Blanc, Zinfandel, and Cabernet Sauvignon seem to do well in places. Italian grapes such as Sangiovese or the Rhône varieties, which do so well in the Dry Creek Valley, are also beginning to make great wines in the valley's warmer sections.

WHERE TO EAT AND STAY

★ $$$$ **Fodor'sChoice** 🍴 **The Farmhouse Inn.** *French.* From the personable sommelier who assists you with wine choices to the servers who describe the provenance of the black truffles shaved over the intricate pasta dishes, the staff matches the quality of this restaurant's outstanding French-inspired cuisine. The signature dish called "Rabbit Rabbit Rabbit," a rich trio of confit of leg, rabbit loin wrapped in applewood-smoked bacon, and roasted rack of rabbit with a whole-grain mustard sauce, is typical of preparations that are both rustic and refined. ■ **TIP**→ The inn is a favorite of wine-industry foodies, so reserve well in advance; if it's full, you might be able to dine in the small lounge. [$] *Average main: $52* ✉ *7871 River Rd., at Wohler Rd.* ☎ *707/887–3300, 800/464–6642* 🌐 *www.farmhouseinn.com* ✍ *Reservations essential* ⏲ *Closed Tues. and Wed. No lunch.*

Dessert at the Farmhouse Inn and Restaurant

★ Fodor's Choice 🏨 **The Farmhouse Inn.** *B&B/Inn.* With a rustic-farmhouse-meets-modern-loft aesthetic, the spacious rooms in this pale yellow farmhouse dating from 1873 are filled with king-size four-poster beds, whirlpool tubs, and terraces overlooking the hillside. **Pros:** home of one of Sonoma's best restaurants; luxury bath products; full-service spa uses many local ingredients. **Cons:** rooms closest to the street get a bit of road noise. [$] *Rooms from: $350* ✉ *7871 River Rd.* ☎ *707/887–3300, 800/464–6642* 🌐 *www.farmhouseinn.com* 🛏 *12 rooms, 6 suites* 🍴 *Breakfast.*

$$$

SPORTS AND THE OUTDOORS

Burke's Canoe Trips. You get a real feel for the Russian River's flora and fauna on a leisurely 10-mile paddle from Burke's downstream to Guerneville. A shuttle bus returns you to your car at the end of the journey, which is best taken from late May through mid-October. The cost is $60 per canoe. ✉ *8600 River Rd., at Mirabel Rd.* ☎ *707/887–1222* 🌐 *www.burkescanoetrips.com.*

CLOSE UP

Russian River Valley AVA

As the Russian River winds its way from Mendocino to the Pacific Ocean, it carves out a valley that's a near-perfect environment for growing certain grape varietals. Because of its low elevation, sea fog pushes far inland to cool the soil, yet in summer it burns off, giving the grapes enough sun to ripen properly. Fog-loving Pinot Noir and Chardonnay grapes are king and queen in the Russian River Valley AVA, which extends from Healdsburg west to the town Guerneville. The namesake river does its part by slowly carving its way downward through many layers of rock, depositing a deep layer of gravel that in parts of the valley measures 60 or 70 feet. This gravel forces the roots of grapevines to go deep in search of water and nutrients. In the process, the plants absorb trace minerals that add complexity to the flavor of the grapes.

GUERNEVILLE

7 miles northwest of Forestville; 15 miles southwest of Healdsburg.

Although most visitors to the Russian River Valley stay in Healdsburg, there's a lot to be said for peaceful Guerneville, a popular destination for gay and lesbian travelers who stay in the rustic resorts and sunbathe on the bank of the river. The town's most famous winery is Korbel Champagne Cellars, established here nearly a century and a half ago. Even older are the stands of redwoods that except on the coldest of winter days make Armstrong Woods State Natural Reserve such a perfect respite from wine tasting.

GETTING HERE AND AROUND

To get to Guerneville from Healdsburg, follow Westside Road south to River Road and turn west. From Forestville, head west on Highway 116; alternatively, you can head north on Mirabel Road to River Road and then head west.

EXPLORING

Armstrong Woods State Natural Reserve. Here's your best opportunity in the western Wine Country to wander amid *sequoia sempervirens*, also known as coast redwood trees. The oldest example in this 805-acre state park, the Colonel Armstrong Tree, is thought to be more than 1,400 years old. A half mile from the parking lot, the tree is easily accessible, and you can hike a long way into the forest before things get too hilly. ■TIP→ During hot summer days, Armstrong Woods's tall trees help the park keep its cool. ✉ *17000 Armstrong Woods Rd., off River Rd.* ☎ *707/869–2958 visitor center, 707/869–2015 park headquarters* ⊕ *www.parks.ca.gov* 🎫 *$8 per vehicle, free to pedestrians and bicyclists* ☉ *Park daily 8–one hr after dusk, visitor center daily 11–3.*

Korbel Champagne Cellars. The three brothers Korbel (Joseph, Francis, and Anton) planted Pinot Noir grapes in the Russian River Valley in the 1870s, pioneering efforts that are duly noted on 50-minute tours of the well-known brand's Guerneville facility. Tours include a clear explanation of the *méthode champenoise* used to make the company's sparkling wines, a walk through ivy-covered 19th-century buildings, and tastings of Korbel's reasonably priced bubblies and still wines. You can also taste without touring. ■TIP→ If you have the time, take a spin through the rose garden, home to more than 250 varieties. ✉ *13250 River Rd., west of Rio Nido* ☎ *707/824–7000* ⊕ *www.korbel.com* 🎫 *Tasting and tour free* ☉ *Winery daily 10–4:30, tours daily 11–3; garden tour mid-Apr.–mid-Oct., Tues.–Sun. 1 and 3.*

WHERE TO STAY

$ 🏨 **Applewood Inn & Restaurant.** *B&B/Inn.* On a knoll sheltered by towering redwoods, this romantic inn a short drive from Guerneville's village center has two distinct types of accommodations in an older building and two newer ones. **Pros:** secluded location; great breakfasts; outdoor pool and large whirlpool. **Cons:** may feel too remote to some; sounds can carry in the Belden House. 🅢 *Rooms from: $195* ✉ *13555 Rte. 116* ☎ *707/869–9093, 800/555–8509* ⊕ *www.applewoodinn.com* 🛏 *19 rooms* ❄️ *Breakfast.*

ENROUTE. Between Guerneville and Freestone you'll pass through Occidental, where the Bohemian Highway is briefly called Main Street. Formerly a major hippie hangout, Occidental is worth a stop to poke around several artist-run shops like Verdigris, at 72 Main Street, which sells stylish lamps made out of everything from old samovars and fire extinguishers to antique movie projectors. The organically inclined Howard Station Cafe, at 3611 Main Street, is the town's go-to spot for breakfast or lunch.

Crush Camp in Sonoma County

The harvest in late summer and early fall is a prime time to connect with the beauty of sprawling Sonoma County, the rhythms of agricultural life, and the passionate professionalism of its grape farmers and winemakers. To go behind the scenes and meet the people who make the wine, consider attending a "crush camp" like the **Sonoma County Grape Camp,** two and a half days of immersion in grape harvesting, wine blending, and food-and-wine pairing. You'll see the inner workings of the wineries and even blend your own bottle. And yes, you'll taste wine: several dozen Pinot Noirs, Chardonnays, Zinfandels, Cabernets, Sauvignon Blancs, and other vintages.

A friendly blending competition was a highlight of a recent crush camp, as teams of four crafted a wine by blending a French Burgundy and two California Pinot Noirs. In a nod to marketing—wine making is about farming, science, and the subtleties of taste, but it's also a business—the teams named their blends and created labels. The winners won a bottle of Pinot Noir from a top winery.

THE BOTTOM LINE

There's a premium fee for this curated access to wine professionals and outstanding food: $2,000 per person, which includes accommodations, food and wine, and transportation during the trip. As for your fellow attendees, expect wine lovers enthusiastic about learning, not wine snobs.

After this unique communal experience—celebrated on the final day at a lavish dinner—you'll never drink a glass of wine the same way. For information contact the Sonoma County Winegrape Commission (☏ 707/522-5864 ⊕ www.sonomagrapecamp.com).

FREESTONE

6 miles west of Sebastopol; 18 miles south of Guerneville.

A few decades ago, calling tiny Freestone (population 92) a sleepy village was overstating the case. Not so any more, and the rebranding of the local tasting room as the Joseph Phelps Freestone Vineyards Guest Center in late 2012 has instantly conferred all-star status on a wine-making operation that was already attracting a steady stream of Pinot-loving pilgrims. Oh yes, and bread lovers. The marvelous Wild Flour Bread has adherents nearly as fervent as the wine lovers. The guest center is open daily, but in keeping with Freestone's laid-back traditions, the bakery is open only four days a week.

GETTING HERE AND AROUND

To get to Freestone from Santa Rosa, drive west on Highway 12 through Sebastopol, following signs toward Bodega Bay. Turn north at the Bohemian Highway, and you've arrived. From Guerneville, head west on Highway 116 for 4 miles to the town of Monte Rio, then turn south on Church Street and travel past the old Rio Theater and over the bridge spanning the Russian River. At this point the road is signed as the Bohemian Highway, which takes you into town.

EXPLORING

★ Fodor'sChoice **Joseph Phelps Freestone Vineyards Guest Center.** The renowned Napa Valley winery's western Sonoma outpost is a good place to learn about biodynamic growing techniques while tasting crisp Chardonnays and earthy Pinot Noirs. Phelps wines have always garnered praise for their expression of *terroir* (the land), and the ones made here have a composed, ascetic quality that perfectly mirrors the rugged Sonoma Coast. You can almost taste the vines sending out long roots to find nutrients in the rocky, mineral-laden soil. If prompted, your pourer may regale you with descriptions of biodynamic strategies that involve timing vineyard activities to the waxing or waning moon and compost preparations that incorporate yarrow, stinging nettle, and other herbs. Sonoma Coast wines predominate on the tasting list—the estate-grown Pinot Noir is a standout—but there's nearly always a Napa Valley selection also. ⊠ *12747 El Camino Bodega, at Bohemian Hwy.* ☎ *707/874–1010* ⊕ *www.josephphelps.com* 🍷 *Tastings $10–$15* ⊙ *Daily 11–5.*

QUICK BITES. **Wild Flour Bread.** The sticky buns at Wild Flour are legendary in western Sonoma, as are the mouthwatering rye breads and sock-it-to-me scones in such flavors as double chocolate, espresso, and hazelnut. There's a long table inside, but most patrons enjoy their baked goods on the benches outside. ■TIP➜ Get here early: on weekend afternoons the most popular items start running out. ⊠ **140 Bohemian Hwy., off El Camino Bodega** ☎ 707/874–2135 ⊕ www.wildflourbread.com ⊙ **Fri.–Mon. 8:30–6:30** ⊙ **Closed Tues.–Thurs.**

Iron Horse produces sparklers that make history.

SHOPPING

★ **Fodor's Choice Enduring Comforts.** This shop showcases what it calls "antiques and other delights," and owner Thea Doty has an eye for the unusual. Among the antiques are small items—lamps, vintage jewelry, stained glass—that might fit in your luggage. You might also consider scented candles, fragrant French soaps, and contemporary handbags, jewelry, and men's and women's hats. ⊠ *142 Bohemian Hwy., off El Camino Bodega* ☎ *707/874–1111* ⊗ *Closed Tues.–Thurs.*

SEBASTOPOL

6 miles east of Freestone; 7 miles southwest of Santa Rosa.

A stroll through downtown Sebastopol, a town formerly known for its Gravenstein apples but these days a burgeoning grape-growing hub, reveals glimpses of the distant and recent past and perhaps the future, too. Before entering the district of browsable, if mostly modest, shops, you may notice a sign declaring Sebastopol a "Nuclear Free Zone." Many hippies settled here in the 1960s and 1970s and, as the old Crosby, Stills, Nash & Young song goes, they taught their children well—the town remains steadfastly, if not entirely, countercultural.

Another strain of nostalgia runs even deeper, though, as evidenced by the popularity of the remarkably well-preserved Foster's Freeze stand (banana split, anyone?). Those hankering for a 1960s flashback can truck on over to the Grateful Bagel, complete with Grateful Dead logo.

Sebastopol has always had really good, if somewhat low-profile, wineries, among them Iron Horse, Lynmar Estate, and Merry Edwards. With the opening of a cluster of artisanal food and wine vendors, the town may be poised for a Healdsburg-style transformation. Then again, maybe not. Stay tuned.

GETTING HERE AND AROUND
Sebastopol can be reached by driving east on El Camino Bodega from Freestone or west on Highway 12 from Santa Rosa. From Forestville, head south for 7 miles on Highway 116.

EXPLORING

TOP ATTRACTIONS

★ Fodor'sChoice **Iron Horse Vineyards.** A meandering one-lane road leads to this winery known for its sparkling wines—from the bright and austere to the rich and toasty—as well as estate Chardonnays and Pinot Noirs. The sparklers have made history: Ronald Reagan served them at his summit meetings with Mikhail Gorbachev, George Herbert Walker Bush took some along to Moscow for treaty talks, and Barack Obama has included them at official state dinners. Despite the winery's frequent brushes with fame, a casual rusticity prevails at Iron Horse's outdoor tasting area (large heaters keep things comfortable on chilly days), which gazes out on acres of rolling, vine-covered hills. Tours, by appointment only, take place on weekdays at 10 am. Winemaker David Munksgard leads the Friday tour. ⊠ *9786 Ross Station Rd., off Hwy. 116* ☎ *707/887–1507* ⊕ *www. ironhorsevineyards.com* 🖃 *Tasting $15, tour $20* ☉ *Daily 10–4:30; tour weekdays at 10 by appointment.*

★ Fodor'sChoice **Merry Edwards Winery.** Winemaker Merry Edwards describes the Russian River Valley as "the epicenter of great Pinot Noir," and her namesake winery produces wines that express the unique characteristics of the soils, climates, and Pinot Noir clones from which they derive. (Edwards's research into Pinot Noir clones is so extensive that there's even one named after her.) The valley's advantage, says Edwards, are the warmer-than-average daytime temperatures that yield more intense fruit; the famous evening fogs mitigate the potential negative effects of the extra heat. Group tastings of the well-composed single-vineyard and blended Pinots are offered several times a day—no waltzing up to the wine bar here. Edwards also makes a fine Sauvignon Blanc that's lightly aged in old oak. Tastings end, rather than begin, with this lively white wine so as not to distract guests' palates from the Pinot Noirs. ⊠ *2959 Gravenstein Hwy. N/Hwy. 16, near Oak Grove Ave.* ☎ *707/823–7466, 888/388–9050* ⊕ *www.merryedwards. com* ⌕ *Tasting free* ⊙ *Daily 9:30–4:30; call for appointment or drop in and join next available tasting.*

WORTH NOTING

The Barlow. On the site of a former apple cannery, this cluster of buildings celebrates Sonoma County's "maker" culture with an inspired combination production space and market-place. The complex, which opened in 2013, contains brew-eries and wine-making facilities, along with areas where people create or sell crafts, large-scale artworks, and arti-sanal food, herbs, and beverages. Only club members can visit the anchor wine tenant, Kosta Browne, but La Follette (earthy but smooth Pinot Noirs and velvety Chardonnays) and other small producers have tasting rooms that are open to the public. Warped Brewing Company and Woodfour Brewing Company make and sell ales on-site, and you can have a nip of gin at Spirit Works Distillery. The owners of the popular Zazu restaurant bestowed instant culinary cred on this place when they announced plans to close their Santa Rosa location and reopen here. ⊠ *6770 McKinley St., at Morris St., north off Hwy. 12* ☎ *707/824–5600* ⊕ *www. thebarlow.net* ⊙ *Hrs vary.*

Lynmar Estate. *Elegant* and *balanced* describe Lynmar's landscaping and contemporary architecture, but the terms also apply to the wine-making philosophy. Expect gen-teel, handcrafted Chardonnays and Pinot Noirs with long, luxurious finishes, especially on those Pinots. The atten-tion to refinement and detail extends to the tasting room, where well-informed pourers serve patrons enjoying gar-den and vineyard views through two-story-tall windows. The consistent winner here is the Quail Hill Pinot Noir, a blend of some or all of the 14 Pinot Noir clones grown in the vineyard outside, but the Russian River Pinot Noir and the Hill Pinot Noir are also exceptional. Many of the wines, including a rich, deep Syrah, can be bought only online or at the winery. ✉ *3909 Frei Rd., off Hwy. 116* ☎ *707/829–3374* 🌐 *www.lynmarestate.com* 🎫 *Tastings $15–$70* 🕒 *Daily 10–4:30.*

WHERE TO EAT

$ 🍴 **Hole in the Wall.** *American.* In a region where bios usually tally up culinary degrees and stints at famous restaurants, this strip-mall spot's description of its chef is refreshingly modest: "Starting at age 15, Adam Beers began his first culinary job stirring gumbo." Good for him, and good for you, because as with the gumbo he serves now, the food here is down-home tasty with unexpected delights. Locals love the breakfasts, especially the challah French toast and the short ribs and hash. Burger options include the usual beef and turkey, but also portobello mushroom and black-bean editions for the crunchola crowd. The prize, though, goes to the duck burger for the accompanying pomegranate-and-mint aioli. Other menu favorites include the savory and dessert crepes. [$] *Average main: $8* ✉ *972 Gravenstein Hwy. S, at Fellers La.* ☎ *707/861–3777* 🌐 *www.holeinthewallsebastopol.com* ✍ *Reservations not accepted* 🕒 *No dinner Mon. and Tues.*

★ Fodor'sChoice 🍴 **Underwood Bar & Bistro.** *Modern American.*
$$$ Mere steps from Sebastopol, the hands-down best restaurant in the tiny hamlet of Graton admittedly doesn't have much competition, but it's so good, it would hold its own in San Francisco. Run by the same people who operate the Willow Wood Market Cafe across the street, the Underwood has a dual menu based on tapas-style small dishes from Spain, Portugal, Italy, France, and even Asia, along with larger plates like osso bucco and mushroom-leek ravioli. Perhaps most important, though, Underwood is the rare place in western Sonoma County where you can get a French onion soup and a glass of wine late on a Friday or Saturday night. ■ **TIP→** A bar menu is served between lunch and dinner most days, when many other restaurants close. [$] *Average main: $25* ✉ *9113 Graton Rd., about ½ mile west of Hwy. 116, Graton* ☎ *707/823–7023* 🌐 *www.underwoodgraton.com* 🕒 *Closed Mon. No lunch Sun.*

★ Fodor'sChoice 🍴 **Willow Wood Market Cafe.** *Modern American.*
$$ This small-town café across the street from the Underwood Bar & Bistro serves simple, tasty soups, salads, and sandwiches. The brunches are amazing, but even daily breakfast—the specialties include hot, creamy polenta and house-made granola—are modern-American down-home

solid. Dinner brings hearty entrées like vegetable ragout and pork tenderloin ragout. Two dishes that don't include polenta are the roasted half chicken with a tarragon-lemon rub and the grilled rib-eye steak, both accompanied by the creamiest of garlic mashed potatoes. ■TIP→ Take a few minutes to poke around the quirky general store while you're waiting for your food. [$] *Average main: $18* ✉ *9020 Graton Rd., about ½ mile west of Hwy. 116, Graton* ☎ *707/823–0233* 🌐 *willowwoodgraton.com* ✍ *Reservations not accepted* ⏲ *No dinner Sun.*

WHERE TO STAY

$ 🏨 **Sebastopol Inn.** *Hotel.* The simple but cheerful rooms at FAMILY this reasonably priced inn, freshly painted a sunny yellow and hung with blue-and-white-striped curtains, have a spare California country style. **Pros:** friendly staff; just steps from a café, wine bar, and spa. **Cons:** nice, but no frills; some will find the beds too firm. [$] *Rooms from: $135* ✉ *6751 Sebastopol Ave.* ☎ *707/829–2500* 🌐 *www.sebastopolinn.com* 🛏 *29 rooms, 2 suites.*

TRAVEL SMART
NAPA AND
SONOMA

GETTING HERE AND AROUND

Most travelers to the Wine Country start their trip in San Francisco. Getting to southern Napa or Sonoma takes less than an hour in normal traffic. Using public transportation isn't practical; the best options are driving or taking a tour, especially if you want to visit wineries that are far apart from each other. That said, if you prefer not to drive, it's possible to base yourself in towns like St. Helena or Yountville in the Napa Valley, or Sonoma or Healdsburg in Sonoma County, and then visit downtown tasting rooms or nearby wineries on foot.

▌ AIR TRAVEL

Nonstop flights from New York to San Francisco take about 5½ hours, and with the three-hour time change, it's possible to leave JFK by 8 am and be in San Francisco by 10:30 am. Some flights require changing planes midway, making the total excursion between 8 and 9½ hours.

More than three dozen airlines serve San Francisco's airport, and a few of the same airlines also serve the airports in Oakland and Sacramento. Fares to San Francisco are often the cheapest, but the two smaller airports can sometimes be more convenient, especially if your destination is southern Napa. Alaska, American, Delta, jetBlue, Southwest, and United serve all three airports.

Frontier and Virgin America serve San Francisco. Alaska's subsidiary, Horizon Air, serves Sacramento and the regional Charles M. Schulz–Sonoma County Airport, in Santa Rosa.

Airline Contacts Alaska Airlines ☎ 800/252–7522 ⊕ www.alaskaair.com. **American Airlines** ☎ 800/433–7300 ⊕ www.aa.com. **Delta Airlines** ☎ 800/221–1212 ⊕ www.delta.com. **Frontier Airlines** ☎ 800/432–1359 ⊕ www.frontierairlines.com. **jetBlue** ☎ 800/538–2583 ⊕ www.jetblue.com. **Southwest Airlines** ☎ 800/435–9792 ⊕ www.southwest.com. **United Airlines** ☎ 800/864–8331 ⊕ www.united.com. **Virgin America** ☎ 877/359–8474 ⊕ www.virginamerica.com.

AIRPORTS

The major gateway to the Wine Country is San Francisco International Airport (SFO), 60 miles from the city of Napa. Oakland International Airport (OAK), almost directly across San Francisco Bay, is actually closer to Napa, which is just 50 miles away. Most visitors choose SFO because it has more daily flights. If you're headed to Sonoma, check out flights into Charles M. Schulz-Sonoma County Airport (STS) in Santa Rosa. The airport is only 15 miles from Healdsburg. Yet another option is to fly into Sacramento International Airport (SMF), about 68 miles from Napa and 76 miles from Sonoma.

Airport Information Charles M. Schulz-Sonoma County Airport (STS). ☎ 707/565-7243 ⊕ www.sonomacountyairport.org. **Oakland International Airport (OAK).** ☎ 510/563-3300 ⊕ www.flyoakland.com. **Sacramento International Airport (SMF).** ☎ 916/929-5411 ⊕ www.sacramento.aero/smf. **San Francisco International Airport (SFO).** ☎ 800/435-9736, 650/821-8211 ⊕ www.flysfo.com.

GROUND TRANSPORTATION

To the Wine Country Two shuttle services serve Napa and Sonoma from both San Francisco International Airport and Oakland International Airport. Evans Airport Service, affiliated with California Wine Tours, is an option for travelers without cars staying in the communities of Napa or Yountville. The service, which costs $45 per person, drops you off at any hotel. If you're heading elsewhere in the area, the company will arrange for taxi service from its drop-off point. The Sonoma County Airport Express shuttles passengers between the airports and the cities of Santa Rosa, Rohnert Park, and Petaluma for $34. Ask the driver to call ahead so that a taxi is waiting for you when you arrive.

Private limousine service is more expensive—up to $300, depending on your destination. The dependable SF Limo Express charges $149 to take up to four people to the town of Sonoma, $189 to Calistoga, and $270 to Healdsburg.

Charles M. Schulz–Sonoma County Airport is just off U.S. 101

in Santa Rosa. Healdsburg is north of the airport via U.S. 101. For the town of Sonoma, drive south to Highway 12 and head east.

To San Francisco If you're headed to downtown San Francisco, a taxi ride from San Francisco International Airport costs $50 to $55. More economical are GO Lorrie's Airport Shuttle and SuperShuttle, both of which take you anywhere within the city limits for $17 per person. Both can be found on the airport's lower level near baggage claim. On the other end of the scale is SF Limo Express, which charges $75.

Bay Area Rapid Transit commuter trains take you directly to downtown San Francisco. The trip takes about 30 minutes and costs $8.25. BART trains depart from the international terminal every 15 minutes or 20 minutes, depending on the time of day. Another inexpensive option are two SamTrans buses: the 292 (55 minutes, $2) and the KX (35 minutes, $5; only one small carry-on bag permitted). Board SamTrans buses on the lower level.

A taxi from Oakland International Airport to downtown San Francisco costs from $40 to $45. By airport regulations, you must make reservations for shuttle service. BayPorter Express provides private service only ($90 for up to seven passengers). With SuperShuttle ($27 for the first passenger, $15 for each additional passenger), other travelers may join the ride.

The best public-transit option is BART. Take the AIR BART bus

($3) to the Coliseum/Oakland International Airport BART station; from there, the BART train to downtown San Francisco costs $3.85.

Limos and Shuttles BayPorter Express ☎ 415/467–1800 ⊕ www.bayporter.com. **Evans Airport Service** ☎ 707/255–1559 ⊕ www.evanstransportation.com. **GO Lorrie's Airport Shuttle** ☎ 415/334–9000 ⊕ www.gosfovan.com. **SF Limo Express** ☎ 415/990–6364 ⊕ www.sflimoexpress.net. **Sonoma County Airport Express** ☎ 707/837–8700, 800/327–2024 ⊕ www.airportexpressinc.com. **SuperShuttle** ☎ 800/258–3826 ⊕ www.supershuttle.com.

Public Transit Bay Area Rapid Transit (BART) ☎ 415/989–2278 ⊕ www.bart.gov. **SamTrans** ☎ 800/660–4287 ⊕ www.samtrans.com.

∎ BUS TRAVEL

The bus is an inconvenient way to explore the Wine Country. Service is infrequent and buses from San Francisco can get you only to Petaluma or Santa Rosa, hardly in the thick of the vineyard action. Sonoma County Transit offers daily bus service from those cities to points all over the county. VINE (Valley Intracity Neighborhood Express) provides bus service within the city of Napa and between other Napa Valley towns. **511 SF Bay Area** (☎ 511 ⊕ www.511.org) provides route information and online trip-planning.

∎ CAR TRAVEL

A car is the most logical and convenient way to navigate Napa and Sonoma. Although some thoroughfares can be congested, especially during rush hour and on summer weekends, there are plenty of less trafficked routes. Parking is generally not a problem.

To drive to the Wine Country from San Francisco International, follow signs north out of the airport to Interstate 380, which leads to Interstate 280. As you approach San Francisco, follow signs for the Golden Gate Bridge. By the time you begin crossing the bridge, you're on U.S. 101. Head north for northern Sonoma County. For southern Sonoma County and the Napa Valley, head east on Highway 37 at the town of Novato, then follow Highway 121 into southern Sonoma. At Highway 12, turn north to reach the town of Sonoma. For the Napa Valley, continue east on Highway 121 to Highway 29 and head north.

From Oakland International, the best way to get to Sonoma County is via Interstate 880 north. Follow signs for Interstate 80 East/Interstate 580 West, which takes you across the Richmond–San Rafael Bridge. After you cross the bridge, follow the signs to U.S. 101 North. From here, continue north for northern Sonoma County or head east of Highway 37 for southern Sonoma County and the Napa Valley. A quicker option if you're heading to the Napa Valley is to stay on Interstate 80 to Highway 37 in Vallejo. Head west on Highway 37 and north on Highway 29, following the signs for Napa.

If you fly into Sacramento International, take Interstate 5 South to Interstate 80 West. Exit onto Highway 12 and continue west to Highway 29 north for the city of Napa. For the town of Sonoma continue west on Highway 121 and north on Highway 12.

CAR RENTALS

If you're flying into the area, it's almost always easiest to pick up a car at the airport. You'll also find car-rental companies in the major towns around the Wine Country. The winding roads and beautiful landscapes make it a popular place for renting specialty vehicles, especially convertibles. Many agencies have a few on hand, but you have a better chance of finding one at Exotic Car Collection by Enterprise or the locally based City Rent-a-Car. ■TIP→ When renting a specialty car, ask about mileage limits. Some companies stick you with per-mile charges if you exceed 100 miles a day.

Most rental companies require you to be at least 20 years old to rent a car, but some agencies won't rent to those under 25; check when you book. Super Cheap Car Rentals, near San Francisco International, has competitive prices and, unlike many agencies, rents to drivers between 21 and 24 for no extra charge.

Car-rental costs in the area vary seasonally, but in San Francisco generally begin at $50 a day and $275 a week for an economy car with unlimited mileage. Rates can be slightly higher in Oakland and

substantially higher in Sacramento, often offsetting any airfare savings. This doesn't include tax on car rentals (8% in Sacramento, 8.5% in San Francisco, and 9% in Oakland) and other surcharges and fees.

Rates are sometimes—but not always—better if you book in advance or reserve through a rental agency's website. Rental agencies in California aren't required to include liability insurance in the price of the rental. If you cause an accident, you may be liable. When in doubt about your own policy's coverage, take the liability coverage that the agency offers. If you plan to take the car out of California, ask in advance about the company's policies.

Automobile Associations American Automobile Association (AAA) ☎ 415/565-2141 ⊕ www.aaa.com. **National Automobile Club** ☎ 800/622-2136 ⊕ www.thenac.com.

Local Agencies City Rent-a-Car ✉ 1433 Bush St., near Van Ness Ave., Van Ness/Polk ☎ 415/359-1331, 866/359-1331 ⊕ www.cityrentacar.com. **Super Cheap Car Rental** ✉ 10 Rollins Rd., at Millbrae Ave., Millbrae ☎ 650/777-9993 ⊕ www.supercheapcar.com.

Major Agencies Alamo ☎ 800/462-5266 ⊕ www.alamo.com. **Avis** ☎ 800/331-1212 ⊕ www.avis.com. **Budget** ☎ 800/527-0700 ⊕ www.budget.com. **Exotic Car Collection by Enterprise** ☎ 650/238-5338 ⊕ exoticcars.enterprise.com/sanfrancisco. **Hertz** ☎ 800/654-3131 ⊕ www.hertz.com. **National Car Rental** ☎ 800/227-7368 ⊕ www.nationalcar.com.

GASOLINE

Gas is readily available on all but the most remote back roads. Be prepared for sticker shock, however, since gas prices in California are among the highest in the country. Expect to pay from 10% to 20% more than you would back home.

PARKING

Finding a place to leave your wheels is rarely a problem in the Wine Country, as wineries and hotels have ample free parking. A few towns—notably St. Helena, Sonoma, and Healdsburg—can get a bit congested during the day, but you can always find a spot a block or two off the main drag. In some communities, street parking is limited to two hours during the day. There are often reasonably priced municipal lots downtown; signs will generally point you in the right direction.

ROAD CONDITIONS

Whether they are four-lane highways or winding country lanes, the roads in the Wine Country are generally well maintained. Traffic jams do occur, though the biggest tie-ups you'll experience will likely be in and around San Francisco. Trying to negotiate morning and afternoon rush hours will add considerable time to your trip. Sunday evenings you'll encounter lots of traffic as you head back to San Francisco, but it's nothing compared with the crush of cars trying to leave San Francisco on a Friday afternoon. Traffic can be equally bad heading north from Oakland to Napa along Interstate 80, espe-

cially during the afternoon rush hour. For up-to-the-minute traffic info, visit ⊕ *www.traffic.511.org* or tune your radio to **740 AM and 106.9 FM,** which broadcast traffic news every 10 minutes.

Once you've reached the Wine Country, the roads become less crowded and more scenic. Expect heavier traffic during rush hours, generally between 7 and 9 am and 4 and 6 pm. Things can also get congested on Friday and Sunday afternoons, when weekenders add to the mix. Highway 29, which runs the length of Napa Valley, can be slow going in summer, especially on weekends, and it can slow to a crawl around the town of St. Helena.

ROADSIDE EMERGENCIES

Dial 911 to report accidents on the road and to reach police, the highway patrol, or the fire department. The American Automobile Association and the National Automobile Club provide roadside assistance to members.

RULES OF THE ROAD

To encourage carpooling during rush hour, some freeways have special lanes for so-called high-occupancy vehicles (HOVs)—cars carrying more than one or two passengers. Look for the white diamond in the middle of the lane. Signs next to or above the lane indicate the hours that carpooling is in effect. If you get stopped for not having enough passengers, expect a fine of nearly $500.

Don't overindulge when you go wine tasting, and don't drive if you've enjoyed more than a couple of sips. Local cops keep an eye out for drivers who've had one too many, especially on summer weekends. If you can, bring a designated driver. State law bans drivers from using handheld mobile telephones while operating a vehicle, and the use of seat belts in both front and back seats is required. Children must ride in a properly secured child passenger safety restraint in the backseat until they are eight years old or 4 feet 9 inches tall. The speed limit on city streets is 25 mph unless otherwise posted. A right turn after stopping at a red light is legal unless posted otherwise.

▌ TAXI TRAVEL

Taxis aren't a common sight in the Wine Country—most visitors are driving a rental car, or perhaps riding in a chauffeured limo. Still, you might want to take a cab to and from dinner, especially if you want to indulge in a cocktail or a few glasses of vino. Some hotels and inns operate scheduled shuttle service to the nearest town; even if yours doesn't, you may be offered a lift if a staff person is available.

All cabs are metered: expect to pay from $2.50 to $3 upon pickup and another $2.50 to $3 per mile thereafter, depending on the city you're in. Taxi drivers usually expect a 15%–20% tip for good service. Cabs must be called rather than hailed.

The very fine A to Z Cab, based in St. Helena, serves the entire Napa Valley. Napa Valley Cab, based in the city of Napa, is another option. A-C Taxi of Santa Rosa, Healdsburg Taxi Cab Company, and Vern's Taxi serve all of Sonoma County. Yellow Cab serves Santa Rosa and Kenwood.

Taxi Companies A-C Taxi of Santa Rosa ✉ *Santa Rosa* ☎ *707/777-7777* ⊕ *www.a-ctaxi.com.* **A to Z Cab** ✉ *St. Helena* ☎ *707/666-1555* ⊕ *www.atozcab.com.* **Healdsburg Taxi Cab Company** ✉ *Healdsburg* ☎ *707/433-7088.* **Napa Valley Cab** ✉ *Napa* ☎ *707/257-6444.* **Vern's Taxi** ☎ *707/938-8885* ⊕ *www.taxicabsonoma.com.* **Yellow Cab** ☎ *707/544-4444* ⊕ *www.yellowtaxirides.com.*

ESSENTIALS

▌ ACCOMMODATIONS

Wine Country lodgings range from low-key to utterly luxurious, and generally maintain high standards. Newer hotels tend to have a modern, streamlined aesthetic. Most of the bed-and-breakfasts are in historic Victorian and Spanish buildings, and the breakfast part of the equation often involves fresh local produce. Many hotels and B&Bs have excellent restaurants on their grounds, and those that don't are a short drive away from gastronomic bliss.

RESERVATIONS

Reservations are a good idea, especially from late spring through the fall harvest season and on many weekends. Two- or even three-night minimum stays are commonly required, especially at smaller lodgings. If you'd prefer to stay a single night, innkeepers are more flexible in winter. Some lodgings aren't suitable for kids, so ask before you make a reservation.

The official Visit Napa Valley and Visit Sonoma Wine Country websites have comprehensive lists of places to stay. BedandBreakfast. com has details about member inns in the area.

Information and Reservations
BedandBreakfast.com
⊕ www.bedandbreakfast.com.
Visit Napa Valley ⊕ www.visitnapa valley.com. **Visit Sonoma**
⊕ www.sonomacounty.com.

FACILITIES

When pricing accommodations, always ask what's included. Some small inns may not have air-conditioning, so be sure to ask if you're visiting in July or August, when temperatures can reach 90°F. Many hotels now have Wi-Fi, although it's not always free. Most large properties have pools and fitness rooms; those without usually have arrangements at nearby gyms, sometimes for a fee.

PRICES

Wine Country lodging prices, which on average exceed those even in high-end San Francisco, may come as an unpleasant surprise. Even the humblest accommodations start at nearly $200 a night in high season. If you're having difficulty finding something in your price range, remember that Napa and Santa Rosa have the widest selection of moderately priced rooms. Rates vary widely; call the property directly, but also check its website and online booking agencies.

Our local writers vet every hotel to recommend the best overnights in each price category, from budget to expensive. Unless otherwise specified, you can expect private bath, phone, and TV in your room. *Prices in the reviews are the lowest cost of a standard double room in high season.* For expanded reviews, facilities, and current deals, visit Fodors.com.

▮ COMMUNICATIONS

INTERNET

Given the California Wine Country's proximity to Silicon Valley and San Francisco, it's no surprise that it's easy to get connected almost everywhere you go. Most cafés in the Wine Country also offer Wi-Fi service, often for free if you order something.

Contacts OpenWiFiSpots
⊕ www.openwifispots.com.

▮ EATING OUT

There is perhaps no place in the United States where you'll find food that's as consistently excellent as it is in California's Wine Country. In part you can thank the vintners and other folks in the wine industry, who spend years developing their palates—they bring a keen, appreciative attitude to the table. These winemakers know that there is no better way to show off their wines than with creative cooking, so they've encouraged a lively, top-notch food scene.

But we can't give the wine industry all the credit for those organic frisée salads and galettes made with perfectly ripe peaches. California's unique climate nurtures a rich variety of produce year-round, so Wine Country chefs are able to take advantage of ripe, local fruits and vegetables and artisanal products that simply aren't available elsewhere.

The Wine Country's top restaurants tend to serve what is often called "California cuisine," which incorporates elements of French and Italian cooking and emphasizes the use of fresh, local products. If the restaurant scene here has a weakness, it's the absence of a greater variety of cuisines. However, the number of immigrants from Latin America ensures that in almost any town you'll find good, inexpensive spots selling tacos, fajitas, and similar fare.

Vegetarians shouldn't have any trouble finding excellent choices on Wine Country menus. The region's bounty of fresh produce and California's general friendliness toward vegetarians mean that restaurants are usually willing to go out of their way to accommodate you.

The Wine Country's restaurants, though excellent, can really dent your wallet. One way to avoid sticker shock is to try restaurants at lunch, when prices are marginally lower. It also doesn't hurt to ask about a restaurant's corkage policy: some restaurants eliminate their corkage fee one night a week, or even every night, hoping to attract locals in the wine industry who would rather drink bottles from their own cellar than the restaurant's. The sheer number of restaurants means you can always find an empty table somewhere, but it pays to call ahead for a reservation, even if only a day or two before you visit. For the big-name restaurants such as Press, Terra, Goose & Gander, and Farmhouse Inn, calling a few weeks in advance is advised, though you can often get in on short notice if you're willing to eat early or late. (For the famed French Laundry, you must call two months ahead to the day.)

Prices in the reviews are the average cost of a main course at dinner or, if dinner is not served, at lunch.

MEALS AND MEALTIMES

Lunch is typically served from 11:30 to 3, and dinner service in most restaurants starts at 5 or 5:30 and ends around 9 or 10. The Wine Country is short on late-night dining, so don't put off eating until any later than 10, or you might end up raiding your room's minibar. Most hotels and inns offer breakfast service—anything from a basic continental breakfast to a lavish buffet to an individually prepared feast—but if yours doesn't, you'll find a good bakery in just about every Wine Country town.

Some restaurants close for a day or two a week, most often on Tuesday or Wednesday, when the number of visitors is fewest, so be sure to check in advance if you're planning on dining midweek. Unless otherwise noted, the restaurants listed here are open daily for lunch and dinner.

PAYING

Almost all restaurants in the Wine Country accept credit cards. On occasion, you might find a bakery or a casual café that takes cash only. *For guidelines on tipping see ⇨ Tipping, below.*

RESERVATIONS AND DRESS

Restaurants throughout the Wine Country tend to be fairly casual, especially in Sonoma. This is less true in the Napa Valley, where you're unlikely to see jeans or shorts at dinner except at casual restaurants. Jackets, however, are very rarely required for men. At French Laundry, though, they're necessary for both lunch and dinner. At top-tier restaurants like the Restaurant at Meadowood and the Farmhouse Inn, they would certainly be appropriate.

Regardless of where you are, it's a good idea to make reservations if you can. We mention them specifically only when essential (there's no other way you'll ever get a table) or when they are not accepted. For popular restaurants, book as far ahead as you can (often 30 days), and reconfirm as soon as you arrive. (Large parties should always call ahead to check the reservations policy.) We mention dress only when men are required to wear a jacket or a jacket and tie.

Online reservation services make it easy to book a table before you even leave home. Tables at many Wine Country restaurants are available at the OpenTable and Urbanspoon sites.

Contacts Open Table ⊕ *www.opentable.com.* **Urbanspoon** ⊕ *www.urbanspoon.com.*

WINES, BEER, AND SPIRITS

Nowhere in the United States are you more likely to see someone enjoying a glass or two of wine not only with dinner, but with lunch as well. Only the smallest dives and most casual cafés lack a wine menu; lists here are usually strongest in local bottles, with other West Coast wines and perhaps some French and Italian wines as well. Upscale restaurants generally have full bars. Though it's legal to serve alcohol as late as 2 am in California, most restaurants close down by 10 pm or so.

▮ HOURS OF OPERATION

Winery tasting rooms are generally open from 10 or 11 am to 4:30 or 5 pm. Larger wineries are usually open every day, but some of the smaller ones may open only on weekends or for three or four days. Tuesday and Wednesday are the quietest days of the week for wine touring. If you have a particular winery in mind, check its hours before you visit, and keep in mind that many wineries are open by appointment only.

▮ MONEY

The sweet life costs a pretty penny in most Wine Country areas, where even a basic hotel tends to cost around $200 a night. That said, it is possible to stick to a lower budget if you're willing to stay in a fairly basic motel, eat at some of the less expensive restaurants, and take advantage of the many picnicking opportunities.

ITEM	AVERAGE COST
Cup of Coffee (Not a Latte!)	$2
Glass of Wine	$11
Glass of Beer	$7
Sandwich	$9
One-Mile Taxi Ride	$6
Museum Admission	$5

Prices here are given for adults. Substantially reduced fees are almost always available for children, students, and senior citizens.

▮ SAFETY

The Wine Country is generally a safe place for travelers who observe all normal precautions. Most visitors will feel safe walking at night in all the smaller towns and in the downtown area of towns like Sonoma. Still, the largest towns, such as Napa and Santa Rosa, have a few rougher areas (typically far from the tourist spots), so you should check with a local before you go wandering in unknown neighborhoods. Car break-ins are not particularly common here, although it's always best to remove valuables from your car, or at least keep them out of sight.

The main danger you face in the Wine Country is the threat of drunk drivers. Keep an eye out for drivers who may have had one too many glasses of wine, as well as for bikers who might be hidden around the next bend in the road.

▮ SHIPPING

Because alcoholic beverages are regulated by individual states, shipping wine back home can be easy or complicated, depending on where you live. Some states, among them Alabama, Pennsylvania, and Utah, prohibit all direct shipments from wineries. Others allow the shipment of limited quantities—a certain number of gallons or cases per year—if a winery has purchased a permit to do so. The penalties for noncompliance can be steep—it's a felony, for instance, to ship wines to Kentucky or Utah (this includes shipping the wines yourself). Since selling wine is their business, wineries are well versed in the regulations.

If you decide to send wines back home, keep in mind that most states require that someone 21 or older sign for the delivery. The Wine Institute, which represents California wineries, has up-to-date information about shipping within the United States and abroad.

Information Wine Institute
⊕ www.wineinstitute.org/initiatives/stateshippinglaws.

▌SPECIAL-INTEREST TOURS

BICYCLING TOURS

Biking tours of the Wine Country range from one-day excursions to weeklong vacations with lavish picnic lunches, leisurely dinners, and stays at some of the region's fanciest inns. You might pay less than $100 for a half- or full-day trip; multiday excursions can cost $250 to $500 per day, including accommodations.

Some companies, such as Backroads, provide guides and lay out extravagant picnics, whereas others will set you up with everything you need and transfer your luggage, but otherwise leave you alone. Napa & Sonoma Valley Bike Tours offers afternoon and all-day tours of wineries, vineyards, and other sights. One tour starts with an early-morning balloon ride. Wine Country Bikes, based in Healdsburg, specializes in Sonoma trips.

Tours Backroads ☏ 800/462–2848 ⊕ www.backroads.com.
Napa & Sonoma Valley Bike Tours ☏ 707/251–8687 for Napa trips, 707/996–2453 for Sonoma trips ⊕ www.napavalleybiketours.com.
Wine Country Bikes ☏ 707/473–0610, 800/922–4537 ⊕ www.winecountrybikes.com.

CULINARY TOURS

Tours usually include one or more of the following: cooking classes, festive dinners at fine restaurants, excursions to local markets, and the opportunity to meet some of the area's top chefs. Tours can last from a few days to a week and start at around $500 per day, accommodations included. Epiculinary's tours have a strong emphasis on cooking workshops. Food & Wine Trails develops customized tours for its clients.

Tours Epiculinary ☏ 707/815–1415 ⊕ www.epiculinary.com. **Food and Wine Trails** ☏ 800/367–5348 ⊕ www.foodandwinetrails.com.

WINERY TOURS

With several million visitors to the Wine Country every year, dozens of tour companies have sprung up to provide tours. Many of these companies are well organized and will chauffeur you to places you might not otherwise find on your own. Whether you're content to tour the Wine Country in a full-size bus with dozens of other passengers or you want to spring for your own private limo to take you to your favorite wineries, there are plenty of operators who can accommodate you. If you know the wineries, regions, or even the grape varietals that interest you, these operators can help you develop a satisfying itinerary. All visit both Napa and Sonoma wineries.

Most companies offer a range of tours, usually lasting five to seven hours and stopping at four or five wineries. Rates vary widely, from $80 per person for a day of touring to $250 or more, depending on the type of vehicle and whether the tour includes other guests. You can also book a car and driver by the hour for shorter trips. Rates for limos generally run from $50 to $85 per hour, and there's usually a two- or three-hour minimum. A typical California Wine Tours outing takes in small and large wineries and includes a tour of the wine-making facilities at one of the stops. The rates include some tasting fees but not lunch. Local concierges wholeheartedly recommend the first-class Perata Luxury Tours & Car Services, whose staffers ask clients about their preferences, then create customized tours that nearly always earn raves. Rates don't include tasting fees or lunch. The owners of Platypus Wine Tours pride themselves on delivering a "fun" experience at off-the-beaten-path wineries. The fee includes lunch but not tasting fees.

You can tour the region "at your own pace" at Valley Wine Tours, which specializes in historic, family-owned wineries. Rates include tasting fees and a vineyard gourmet picnic lunch—on china with cloth napkins, no less. If you want to meet a guy who loves his work, book a tour with the personable Woody Guderian, owner of Woody's Wine Tours. You'll have a blast, mostly at small wineries, and learn a lot. Woody also conducts tours of craft-beer breweries. Tasting fees and lunch are not included in the rates.

Tours California Wine Tours ☎ *800/294–6386* ⊕ *www.californiawinetours.com.* **Perata Luxury Tours & Car Services** ☎ *707/227–8271* ⊕ *www.perataluxurycarservices.com.* **Platypus Wine Tours** ☎ *707/253–2723* ⊕ *www.platypustours.com.* **Valley Wine Tours** ☎ *707/975–6462* ⊕ *www.valleywinetours.com.* **Woody's Wine Tours** ☎ *707/396–8235* ⊕ *www.woodyswinetours.com.*

▌ TAXES

Sales tax is 8% in Napa County and 8.25% in Sonoma County (slightly more in a few cities). Nonprepared foods bought in grocery stores are exempt. The tax on hotel rooms adds from 9% to 14% to your bill in Sonoma County and from 12% to 14% in Napa County.

▌ TIME

California is on Pacific Time. Chicago is two hours ahead of the West Coast, and New York is three hours ahead. Depending on whether daylight saving time is in effect, London is either 8 or 9 hours ahead and Sydney is 17 or 18 hours ahead.

▮ TIPPING

TIPPING GUIDELINES FOR NAPA AND SONOMA	
Bartender	About 15%, starting at $1 a drink at casual places
Bellhop	$1 to $5 per bag, depending on the level of the hotel
Hotel concierge	$5 or more, if he or she performs a service for you
Hotel doorman, room service, or valet	$2–$3
Hotel maid	$3–$4 a day (either daily or at the end of your stay, in cash)
Taxi Driver	15%–20%, but round up the fare to the next dollar amount
Tour Guide	10% of the cost of the tour
Waiter	15%–20%, with 20% being the norm at high-end restaurants; nothing additional if a service charge is added to the bill

▮ VISITOR INFORMATION

To begin your pretrip planning, visit the websites of the Wine Country's official tourism bureaus, Visit Napa Valley and Visit Sonoma. Three visitor centers are worth checking out while you're in the Wine Country: the California Welcome Center in Santa Rosa, the Napa Valley Welcome Center in downtown Napa, and the Sonoma Valley Visitors Center in Sonoma Plaza.

The Discover California Wines website, run by the California-based Wine Institute, has information about many Napa and Sonoma wineries in its North Coast section. Other websites with useful winery information include those of the Alexander Valley Winegrowers, the Carneros Wine Alliance, the Heart of Sonoma Valley Winery Association, the Napa Valley Vintners Association, the Russian River Wine Road, Sonoma County Vintners, the Sonoma Valley Vintners & Growers Alliance, the West Sonoma Coast Vintners, and the Winegrowers of Dry Creek Valley.

Many wineries require reservations for tours, seminars, and even tastings, which is why Vino-Visit has become so popular. You can book these through this website, as well as plan your entire itinerary. Wine Country and Winery Finder, two good mobile apps available through iTunes, Google Play, and other vendors, give you discounts on tasting fees and provide information about restaurants.

Visitor Centers California Welcome Center ⊠ *9 4th St., at Wilson St., Santa Rosa* ☎ *800/404–7673* ⊕ *www.visitcalifornia.com/ california-welcome-centers/santa-rosa.* **Napa Valley Welcome Center** ⊠ *600 Main St., at 5th St., Napa* ☎ *707/251–5895* ⊕ *www. visitnapavalley.com/welcome_* centers.htm. **Sonoma Valley Visitors Center** ✉ *453 1st St. E, in Sonoma Plaza, Sonoma* ☎ *707/996–1090, 866/996–1090* ⊕ *www.sonomacounty.com/sonoma-listings/visitor-centers.*

Visitor Information Visit Napa Valley ☎ *707/251–5895* ⊕ *www.visitnapavalley.com.* **Visit Sonoma** ☎ *707/522–5800, 800/576–6662* ⊕ *www.sonomacounty.com.*

Websites and Apps VinoVisit ✉ *Sonoma* ☎ *888/252–8990* ⊕ *www.vinovisit.com.* **Wine Country** ⊕ *www.winecountry.com.* **Winery Finder** ⊕ *www.econcierges.com.*

Wines and Wineries
Alexander Valley Winegrowers ☎ *888/289–4637* ⊕ *www.alexandervalley.org.* **Carneros Wine Alliance** ☎ *707/996–4140* ⊕ *www.carneros.com.* **Discover California Wines** ☎ *415/512–0151* ⊕ *www.discovercaliforniawines.com/north-coast.*

Heart of Sonoma Valley Winery Association ☎ *707/431–1137, 866/794–9463* ⊕ *www.heartofsonomavalley.com.* **Napa Valley Vintners Association** ☎ *707/963–3388* ⊕ *www.napavintners.com.* **Russian River Wine Road** ☎ *707/433–4335, 800/723–6336* ⊕ *www.wineroad.com.* **Sonoma County Vintners** ☎ *707/522–5840* ⊕ *www.sonomawine.com.* **Sonoma Valley Vintners & Growers Alliance** ☎ *707/935–0803* ⊕ *www.sonomavalleywine.com.* **West Sonoma Coast Vintners** ⊕ *www.westsonomacoast.com.* **Winegrowers of Dry Creek Valley** ☎ *707/433–3031* ⊕ *www.wdcv.com.*

INDEX

PHOTO CREDITS

Front cover: Gerald French/CORBIS [Description: Sonoma]. Spine: Fairmont Hotels & Resorts. 1, Ljupco Smokovski/Shutterstock. 2, Terry Joanis/Frog's Leap. 3 (top), Fairmont Hotels & Resorts. 3 (bottom), French Laundry. 4 (top left), Round Pond Estate. 4 (top right), Oxbow Public Market. 4 (bottom), Meadowood Napa Valley. 5 (top), ZUMA Wire Service / Alamy. 5 (bottom), Meadowood Napa Valley. 6 (top), Keith Ferris/The Culinary Institute of America. 6 (bottom), di Rosa. 7, Hoberman / age fotostock. 8 (top left), RENAULT Philippe / age fotostock. 8 (top right), Farmhouse Inn. 8 (bottom), Napa Valley Bike Tours. 10, Robert Holmes. Chapter 1: Experience Napa and Sonoma: 12-13, Robert Holmes. 14, sddbb, Fodors.com member. 14 (left), Robert Holmes. 14 (right),Vincent Thompson, Fodors.com member. 18 (left), The Hess Collection. 18 (top right), Tori Wilder. 18 (bottom right), Far Niente+Dolce+Nickel & Nickel. 19 (top left), Artesa Vineyards and Winery. 19 (bottom left), Rocco Ceselin. 19 (top right), M. J. Wickham. 19 (bottom right), Eric Risberg/Schramsberg Vineyards. 20 (left), Rocco Ceselin/Ram's Gate Winery 20 (top right), M. J. Wickham/Benziger Family Winery 20 (bottom right), Copain Wines 21 (top left), Laurence G. Sterling/Iron Horse Vineyards, 21 (bottom left), Matanzas Creek 21 (top right), Robert Holmes, 21 (bottom right), Merry Edwards Winery. 22, Robert Holmes. 23, di Rosa. 24, Sonoma County Tourism. 25 (left) Robert Holmes. 25 (right), Meadowood Napa Valley. 26, michale/Flickr. 27, Mustards Grill. Chapter 2: Visiting the Wineries: 29-48, Robert Holmes. 54, Warren H. White. 56, Beltane Ranch. 59, Benziger Family Winery. 66, Robert Holmes. Chapter 3: Napa Valley: 69, 3Neus/Flickr. 71, Robert Holmes. 73, Opus One. 79, Robert Holmes. 88, © Teodora George | Dreamstime.com. 92, Robert Holmes Photography. 97, star5112/Flickr. 98, Robert Holmes. 102, Robert Holmes Photography. 105, Far Niente+Dolce+Nickel & Nickel.106, hirohama/Flickr. 111, Olaf Beckman. 115, The Culinary Institute of America. 116, John McJunkin. 119, Avis Mandel. 120, Scott Chebagia. 125, Meadowood Napa Valley. 131, © Smcfeeters | Dreamstime.com. 132, Chuck Honek/Schramsberg Vineyard. 137, Calistoga Ranch. 140-41, Robert Holmes. Chapter 4: The Carneros District: 143, Robert Holmes. 149, Rocco Ceselin/Ram's Gate Winery. 150, di Rosa. 153, Avis Mandel. 155, Robert Holmes. 156, Robert Holmes. Chapter 5: Sonoma Valley: 159, REBECCA GOSSELIN PHOTOGRAPHY. 164, Robert Holmes. 167, Public domain. 169, Nigel Wilson/Flickr. 172, Leo Gong. 177, Fairmont Hotels & Resorts. 178, Robert Holmes. 184, The Fig Cafe. 185, Robert Holmes. 186, REBECCA GOSSELIN PHOTOGRAPHY. 188-89, Beltane Ranch. 191, jumpy-jodes/Flickr. Chapter 6: Northern Sonoma County: 195, M. J. Wickham. 200, Jeffrey M. Frank/Shutterstock. 203, Warren H. White. 204, Joe Shlabotnik/Flickr. 206, Martinelli Winery. 212, Maggie Preston. 214, Jamey Thomas/Ridge Vineyards. 219, Warren H. White. 221, The Honor Mansion. 224, Cesar Rubio. 233, star5112/Flickr. 235, The Farmhouse Inn and Restaurant. 240, Laurence G. Sterling/Iron Horse Vineyards.

NOTES

Fodor's InFocus NAPA & SONOMA

Publisher: Amanda D'Acierno, *Senior Vice President*

Editorial: Arabella Bowen, *Executive Editorial Director*; Linda Cabasin, *Editorial Director*

Design: Fabrizio La Rocca, *Vice President, Creative Director*; Tina Malaney, *Associate Art Director*; Chie Ushio, *Senior Designer*; Ann McBride, *Production Designer*

Photography: Melanie Marin, *Associate Director of Photography*; Jessica Parkhill and Jennifer Romains, *Researchers*

Maps: Rebecca Baer, *Map Editor*; Mark Stroud, Moon Street Cartography, *Cartographer*

Production: Linda Schmidt, *Managing Editor*; Evangelos Vasilakis, *Associate Managing Editor*; Angela L. McLean, *Senior Production Manager*

Sales: Jacqueline Lebow, *Sales Director*

Marketing & Publicity: Heather Dalton, *Marketing Director*; Katherine Fleming, *Senior Publicist*

Business & Operations: Susan Livingston, *Vice President, Strategic Business Planning*; Sue Daulton, *Vice President, Operations*

Fodors.com: Megan Bell, *Executive Director, Revenue & Business Development*; Yasmin Marinaro, *Senior Director, Marketing & Partnerships*

Copyright © 2014 by Fodor's Travel, a division of Random House, Inc.

Writer: Daniel Mangin

Editors: Linda Cabasin, Mark Sullivan

Production Editor: Carrie Parker

Fodor's is a registered trademark of Random House, Inc. Published in the United States by Fodor's Travel, a division of Random House, Inc., and in Canada by Random House of Canada, Limited, Toronto. Distributed by Random House, Inc., New York. All rights reserved. No maps, illustrations, or other portions of this book may be reproduced in any form without written permission from the publisher.

2nd Edition

ISBN 978-0-7704-3218-8

All details in this book are based on information supplied to us at press time. Always confirm information when it matters, especially if you're making a detour to visit a specific place. Fodor's expressly disclaims any liability, loss, or risk, personal or otherwise, that is incurred as a consequence of the use of any of the contents of this book.

SPECIAL SALES

This book is available at special discounts for bulk purchases for sales promotions or premiums. For more information, e-mail specialmarkets@randomhouse.com

PRINTED IN CHINA

10 9 8 7 6 5 4 3 2 1

ABOUT OUR WRITER

Daniel Mangin returned to California, where he's maintained a home for three decades, after two stints at the Fodor's editorial offices in New York City, the second one as the Editorial Director of Fodors.com and the Compass American Guides. While at Compass he was the series editor for the *California Wine Country* guide and commissioned the *Oregon Wine Country* and *Washington Wine Country* guides. A wine lover whose earliest visits to Napa and Sonoma predate the Wine Country lifestyle, Daniel is delighted by the evolution in wines, wine making, and hospitality. With several dozen wineries less than a half-hour's drive from home, he often finds himself transported as if by magic to a tasting room bar, communing with a sophisticated Cabernet or savoring the finish of a smooth Pinot Noir.